Collins

Social Studies for Jamaica

GRADE

8

for Jamaica

T0312331

Series Editor: **Farah Christian**

Collins

William Collins' dream of knowledge for all began with the publication of his first book in 1819. A self-educated mill worker, he not only enriched millions of lives, but also founded a flourishing publishing house. Today, staying true to this spirit, Collins books are packed with inspiration, innovation and practical expertise. They place you at the centre of a world of possibility and give you exactly what you need to explore it.

Collins. Freedom to teach.

Published by Collins
An imprint of HarperCollins*Publishers*
The News Building
1 London Bridge Street
London
SE1 9GF
UK

HarperCollins*Publishers*
Macken House,
39/40 Mayor Street Upper,
Dublin 1,
D01 C9W8,
Ireland

Browse the complete Collins Caribbean catalogue at
collins.co.uk/caribbeanschools

© HarperCollins*Publishers* Limited 2024

10 9 8 7 6 5 4 3

ISBN 978-0-00-841397-2

All rights reserved. No part of this publication may be reproduced, stored in a retrieval system, or transmitted in any form by any means, electronic, mechanical, photocopying, recording or otherwise, without the prior written permission of the Publisher or a licence permitting restricted copying in the United Kingdom issued by The Copyright Licensing Agency Ltd, 5th Floor, Shackleton House, 4 Battle Bridge Lane, London, SE1 2HX.

British Library Cataloguing in Publication Data
A catalogue record for this publication is available from the British Library.

The publishers gratefully acknowledge the permission granted to reproduce the copyright material in this book. Every effort has been made to trace copyright holders and to obtain their permission for the use of copyright material. The publishers will gladly receive any information enabling them to rectify any error or omission at the first opportunity. See page 300 for acknowledgements.

Series editor: Farah Christian
Author: Laura Pountney
Reviewers: Monique Campbell and Kayon Williams
Editorial consultancy: Oriel Square Limited
Publisher: Dr Elaine Higgleton
Product developer: Saaleh Patel
Development editors: Megan La Barre, Bruce Nicholson and Helen Cunningham
Copy editor: Lucy Hyde
Typesetters: Siliconchips Services Ltd UK and Jouve India Pvt. Ltd.
Mapping: Gordon MacGilp
Cover design: Kevin Robbins and Gordon MacGilp
Cover photo: Eric Laudonien/SS
Production controller: Lyndsey Rogers
Printed and bound in Great Britain by Bell and Bain Ltd, Glasgow

Contents

How to use this book

This page gives a summary of the exciting new ideas you will be learning about in the unit.

This is the topic covered in the unit, which links to the syllabus.

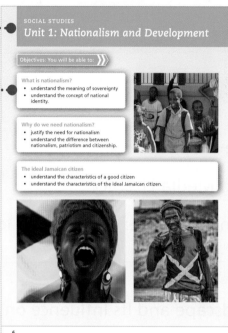

SOCIAL STUDIES
Unit 1: Nationalism and Development

Objectives: You will be able to:

What is nationalism?
- understand the meaning of sovereignty
- understand the concept of national identity.

Why do we need nationalism?
- justify the need for nationalism
- understand the difference between nationalism, patriotism and citizenship.

The ideal Jamaican citizen
- understand the characteristics of a good citizen
- understand the characteristics of the ideal Jamaican citizen.

6

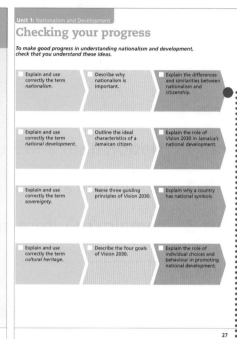

Unit 1: Nationalism and Development
Checking your progress

To make good progress in understanding nationalism and development, check that you understand these ideas.

Explain and use correctly the term *nationalism*.	Describe why nationalism is important.	Explain the differences and similarities between nationalism and citizenship.
Explain and use correctly the term *national development*.	Outline the ideal characteristics of a Jamaican citizen.	Explain the role of Vision 2030 in Jamaica's national development.
Explain and use correctly the term *sovereignty*.	Name three guiding principles of Vision 2030.	Explain why a country has national symbols.
Explain and use correctly the term *cultural heritage*.	Describe the four goals of Vision 2030.	Explain the role of individual choices and behaviour in promoting national development.

27

These lists at the end of a unit act as a checklist of the key ideas of the unit.

Unit 3: Jamaica's Culture and Heritage: Our Cultural Icons
Cultural identity

We are learning to:
- define the relevant terms and concepts: national and Jamaican identity.

National identity

Identity can be defined as the characteristics, style or manner that define a person and how that person is recognised. Identity can be influenced by personal choice but also by society through existing social and cultural situations.

National identity is the idea of what it means to belong to a particular country, state or a nation. Unlike identity, our national identity is not something we are born with, but instead is a common set of experiences or characteristics that people share.

Often, national identity is carried in shared characteristics such as language, national colours and symbols, the history of the nation, family connections, culture, cuisine, music and heritage. Most countries have:

- a flag, an anthem and a national emblem
- a shared history and culture
- a currency (the money used in that country)
- national holidays, customs and traditions.

We discussed in Grade 7 that a cultural background includes things that a group of people shares, such as their religion, language, music, traditions, customs, art and history.

Our cultural heritage consists of the cultural traditions that we have inherited from past generations. Together our cultural background and cultural heritage help to create our national identity.

Research

Research either the national flag, anthem or emblem of Jamaica. Find out its history and collect pictures using newspapers, magazines and the internet.

Lignum Vitae is the national flower of Jamaica.

Exercise

1. Write your own definition of national identity. Add this to your portfolio.
2. Name three ways in which national identity can be shown by a country.
3. What are some examples of national identity of people in Jamaica?

62   Social Studies for Jamaica: Cultural identity

These learning objectives tell you what you will be learning about in the lesson.

Try these questions to check your understanding of each topic. Green questions test recall; yellow questions require critical thinking and application of facts; and orange questions require higher order thinking, analysis and/or extended learning activities.

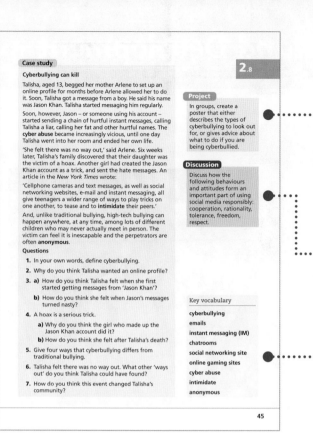

Case study

Cyberbullying can kill

Talisha, aged 13, begged her mother Arlene to set up an online profile for months before Arlene allowed her to do it. Soon, Talisha got a message from a boy. He said his name was Jason Khan. Talisha started messaging him regularly.

Soon, however, Jason – or someone using his account – started sending a chain of hurtful instant messages, calling Talisha a liar, calling her fat and other hurtful names. The **cyber abuse** became increasingly vicious, until one day Talisha went into her room and ended her own life.

'She felt there was no way out,' said Arlene. Six weeks later, Talisha's family discovered that their daughter was the victim of a hoax. Another girl had created the Jason Khan account as a trick, and sent the hate messages. An article in the *New York Times* wrote:

'Cellphone cameras and text messages, as well as social networking websites, e-mail and instant messaging, all give teenagers a wider range of ways to play tricks on one another, to tease and to **intimidate** their peers.'

And, unlike traditional bullying, high-tech bullying can happen anywhere, at any time, among lots of different children who may never actually meet in person. The victim can feel it is inescapable and the perpetrators are often **anonymous**.

Questions

1. In your own words, define cyberbullying.

2. Why do you think Talisha wanted an online profile?

3. **a)** How do you think Talisha felt when she first started getting messages from 'Jason Khan'?

   b) How do you think she felt when Jason's messages turned nasty?

4. A hoax is a serious trick.

   a) Why do you think the girl who made up the Jason Khan account did it?

   b) How do you think she felt after Talisha's death?

5. Give four ways that cyberbullying differs from traditional bullying.

6. Talisha felt there was no way out. What other 'ways out' do you think Talisha could have found?

7. How do you think this event changed Talisha's community?

2.8

Project
In groups, create a poster that either describes the types of cyberbullying to look out for, or gives advice about what to do if you are being cyberbullied.

Discussion
Discuss how the following behaviours and attitudes form an important part of using social media responsibly: cooperation, rationality, tolerance, freedom, respect.

Key vocabulary

cyberbullying

emails

instant messaging (IM)

chatrooms

social networking site

online gaming sites

cyber abuse

intimidate

anonymous

45

Project and Research features allow you to work on your own or in groups to explore the topic further and present your findings to your class or your teacher. Along with the Activity features, and higher order thinking questions, the Project and Research features reflect the STEM/STEAM principles embedded within the curriculum.

Discussion features allow you to work in pairs, in a group or as a class to explore the topic further.

These are the most important new social studies words in the topic. Check their meanings in the Glossary at the end of the book.

These end-of-unit questions allow you and your teacher to check that you have understood the ideas in the unit by applying the skills and knowledge you have gained.

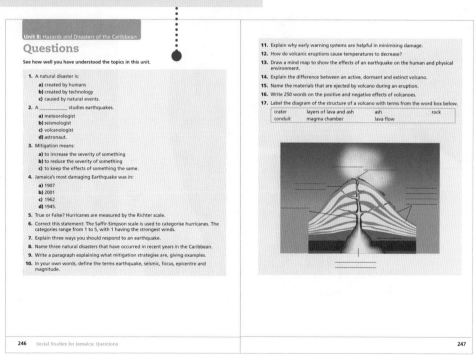

Unit 8: Hazards and Disasters of the Caribbean

Questions

See how well you have understood the topics in this unit.

1. A natural disaster is:
   a) created by humans
   b) created by technology
   c) caused by natural events.

2. A _____ studies earthquakes.
   a) meteorologist
   b) seismologist
   c) volcanologist
   d) astronaut.

3. Mitigation means:
   a) to increase the severity of something
   b) to reduce the severity of something
   c) to keep the effects of something the same.

4. Jamaica's most damaging Earthquake was in:
   a) 1907
   b) 2001
   c) 1962
   d) 1945.

5. True or False? Hurricanes are measured by the Richter scale.

6. Correct this statement: The Saffir-Simpson scale is used to categorise hurricanes. The categories range from 1 to 5, with 1 having the strongest winds.

7. Explain three ways you should respond to an earthquake.

8. Name three natural disasters that have occurred in recent years in the Caribbean.

9. Write a paragraph explaining what mitigation strategies are, giving examples.

10. In your own words, define the terms earthquake, seismic, focus, epicentre and magnitude.

11. Explain why early warning systems are helpful in minimising damage.

12. How do volcanic eruptions cause temperatures to decrease?

13. Draw a mind map to show the effects of an earthquake on the human and physical environment.

14. Explain the difference between an active, dormant and extinct volcano.

15. Name the materials that are ejected by volcano during an eruption.

16. Write 250 words on the positive and negative effects of volcanoes.

17. Label the diagram of the structure of a volcano with terms from the word box below.

| crater | layers of lava and ash | ash | rock |
| conduit | magma chamber | lava flow | |

Unit 1: Nationalism and Development

Objectives: You will be able to: ⟫

What is nationalism?

- understand the meaning of sovereignty
- understand the concept of national identity.

Why do we need nationalism?

- justify the need for nationalism
- understand the difference between nationalism, patriotism and citizenship.

The ideal Jamaican citizen

- understand the characteristics of a good citizen
- understand the characteristics of the ideal Jamaican citizen.

What is Vision 2030?

- explain Vision 2030
- understand the guiding principles of Vision 2030.

What are the four goals of Vision 2030?

- list the four goals of Vision 2030
- examine Goals 1–4 of the National Development Plan
- identify the challenges of achieving the goals of 2030.

What is national development?

- explain how individual behaviours and decision-making affect national development.

What is nationalism?

We are learning to:

- understand the meaning of sovereignty
- understand the concept of national identity.

A **nation** is a large group of people united by common descent, history, culture, or language, living in a particular country or territory.

A **state** is a territory, or area with its own political community and institutions. A nation-state is a cultural group (a nation) that is also a state (and may, in addition, be a sovereign state).

What is sovereignty?

Sovereignty is the full right and power of a governing body over itself, without any interference from outside sources or bodies. In other words, a country that has sovereignty has the power to control itself and to determine its actions without anyone interfering.

For example, no one should cross over into the land, water, or air where international law says a government is **sovereign**, unless they have authorisation from that sovereign government.

Jamaica became a sovereign state on 6 August, 1962, after it gained its independence from the British occupiers. Jamaica is a constitutional monarchy, which has King Charles III as the head of state, as well as being a parliamentary democracy. The monarch appoints the Governor-General on the advice of the Prime Minister of Jamaica and the cabinet (the cabinet are the ministers who help to run the country).

The King's Royal title is Charles the Third.

What does sovereignty mean for Jamaicans?

Sovereignty means several things for Jamaicans.

1. Complete control over its own laws, within Jamaica. For example, the right of Jamaicans to govern their own people.

2. Sovereignty can also be understood as national pride. For example, people within a sovereign state usually feel a sense of pride knowing that they are a free independent state with no other state having control over them.

3. Sovereignty is also used as a legal term, when describing Jamaica's actions and relationships with other countries. For example, Jamaica will or will not accept fishing boats from other countries in our waters. It is a way of showing our control over our own territory.

Sovereignty is the full right and power of a governing body over itself.

Discussion

Discuss why sovereignty is important for Jamaicans. Give examples of laws that have been created in Jamaica for Jamaican people.

Exercise

1 What is meant by sovereignty?

2 What role does King Charles III have in Jamaica?

3 Give an example of how sovereignty can be used as a legal term.

4 Create a timeline to show how many Governor Generals Jamaica has had since 1962.

National identity ⟫⟫

Identity can be defined as the way people see us and how we see ourselves. Identity can be influenced by personal choice but also by society through existing social and cultural situations.

National identity is the idea of what it means to belong to a particular country, state or nation. National identity is not something that we are born with, rather it is a common set of experiences or characteristics that people share.

Often, national identity is carried in shared characteristics such as language, national colours and symbols, the history of the nation, family connections, culture, cuisine, music and heritage. Most countries have:

- a flag, an anthem and a national emblem
- a currency (the money that is used in that country)
- national holidays, customs and traditions.

Cultural background includes the things that a group of people share, such as their religion, language, music, traditions, customs, art and history.

Our **cultural heritage** consists of the cultural traditions that we have inherited from past generations. Together they help shape our national identity.

Jamaica's history and natural wealth are symbolised in each part of the Coat of Arms. The two figures on either side of the shield represent the first inhabitants of Jamaica, the **Taino** tribe. The **crocodile** on top of the royal helmet of the British monarchy and the **pineapples** on the shield represent the indigenous animals and fruits of the island. The motto, **"Out of Many, One People"**, is a tribute to the unity of the multicultural nation.

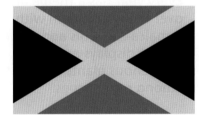

The colours of the national flag symbolise different aspects of the island. **Gold** represents the country's wealth and sunshine, **green** reflects the island's rich vegetation and **black** stands for the creativity and strength of the people.

Research

Carry out research into Jamaica's national song. Underline all words and phrases in the song that represent nationalism. Discuss the meaning of these with your class.

Exercise

5 Write your own definition of national identity.

6 Name three ways that national identity can be shown by citizens of a country.

7 Identify three shared characteristics associated with national identity.

Key vocabulary

nation

state

sovereignty

sovereign

identity

national identity

cultural background

cultural heritage

Why do we need nationalism?

We are learning to:

- justify the need for nationalism
- understand the difference between nationalism, patriotism and citizenship.

Nationalism is where people identify with their own nation and support its interests. Nationalism, therefore, seeks to preserve and foster a nation's traditional culture. It also encourages pride in national achievements, and is closely linked to patriotism.

Case study

Jamaica Day

Jamaica Day is designed to contribute to citizen education, enhance the appreciation for Jamaica's rich heritage and culture, and build a positive identity in young people.

Jamaicans celebrate the good and positive things about the country. It is an opportunity to showcase aspects of Jamaica's culture through the performing arts, visits to historical sites, sporting activities and recognition of outstanding citizens.

Every year has a theme and all themes for Jamaica Day over the years begin with two words – 'Celebrating Jamaica'. Schools and students are encouraged to mount displays and have conversations about food, arts, indigenous plants and protection of the environment, among other issues.

Jamaica Day is designed to contribute to a positive identity in young people.

Discussion

As a class, discuss and make a list of ten persons you would consider to be patriots. In groups of five, select one person listed and role-play a major aspect of that person's life.

Patriotism »

Patriotism means showing a deep love for, and devotion to, your country. It means taking pride in what your country has achieved and it also means looking after your country and being tolerant and caring of other people who live there.

Patriotism can be demonstrated by showing respect for the environment and our national emblems, conservation and preservation of our resources and participation in national events.

Nationalism and the conservation and preservation of natural and cultural heritage »»

In Grade 7 we found out about the cultural heritage of Jamaica. We discovered the importance of conserving our heritage and resources, so that future generations will understand what it means to be Jamaican and be part of the Caribbean. We learned that to preserve something

Activity

Create a cartoon strip showing two different ways that students can show patriotism while attending a national function.

(preservation) means to keep it in its original state and to conserve something (conservation) means that we keep it from being damaged.

Our cultural heritage is the cultural traditions that we have inherited from past generations. They can be artefacts, such as paintings, drawings or sculptures; or buildings and historical monuments; or natural features, such as the Blue Mountains. They can also be things which we cannot touch such as stories, the performing arts and customs.

Several sites of historical and natural importance have been identified as areas of significant historical and natural importance in Jamaica. The aim is to ensure the preservation of these sites as they are part of the heritage of Jamaica. Examples include:

- Blue and John Crow Mountains National Park (World Heritage Site)
- Cockpit Country
- Dunn's River Falls
- Pedro Bank
- Two Sisters Cave.

Blue and John Crow Mountains National Park.

Heritage plays a key role in building nationalism among the people within a country as heritage contributes to the pride that individuals feel towards their country. Heritage helps to create a sense of identity and unity among a people. This in turn pushes individuals more to conserve and preserve the resources and heritage of a nation.

What is the difference between nationalism and citizenship?

Citizenship is the legal status that a person holds in a nation or country. This includes both a set of rights that the citizen possesses, and a set of duties that they owe to that nation and their fellow citizens in return.

Nationalism includes the feelings, ideas and attitudes individuals have towards their country. It is seen when people want to support their nation and feel part of it, whereas citizenship is a legal status that combines duties and responsibilities of the citizen. Nationalism is usually displayed by and seen among the citizens of a country.

Research

With your teacher, plan a field trip to one of Jamaica's heritage sites. During the visit, make notes on its history and why the place was selected as a heritage site.

A passport will state your citizenship.

Exercise

1. Using your own words, explain the difference between nationalism and citizenship.

2. Think about how nationalism is encouraged in your school. What activities in your school help you develop patriotism? Give examples.

Key vocabulary

nationalism

patriotism

citizenship

11

The ideal Jamaican citizen

We are learning to:

- understand the characteristics of a good citizen
- understand the characteristics of the ideal Jamaican citizen.

A **citizen** is someone who belongs to a nation, or country. If you are a citizen of a country, you will have particular rights, freedoms and responsibilities in your country.

Characteristics of a good citizen

In Grade 7, we looked at the characteristics which make a good citizen. These include:

- respecting the rights and freedoms of others
- knowing and accepting our responsibilities to our community and country
- knowing the national anthem and standing when it is playing
- loving our country Jamaica
- understanding and knowing the history of Jamaica
- obeying the law
- voting in elections
- helping in the community, for example to pick up litter.

The ideal Jamaican citizen

So what qualities does someone need to have to be the **ideal** Jamaican citizen? Ideally, a Jamaican citizen should want to protect and promote their country. Some ideal characteristics of a Jamaican citizen are:

- wanting to help Jamaica be a better place
- helping in the community, such as doing **voluntary** work
- helping to protect the environment
- being law abiding
- fulfilling your duty to vote
- participating in local and national events
- helping to promote the preservation and conservation of Jamaica's cultural heritage
- helping to educate others about the importance of Jamaica's cultural heritage.

Activity

Write a description of someone you know who you consider to be an ideal Jamaican citizen, giving examples of what activities they do. What can you do to become a better citizen? Make a list of three goals to improve your own citizenship.

Research

Search for 'history' on the Governor-General web site (ggpe.org.jm) to research the history of the Governor-General's Achievement Award and the reasons why it was set it up.

Exercise

1. In your own words, define the term citizen and the characteristics of a good citizen.

2. Why do you think a Jamaican citizen should be law abiding?

3. What aspect of Jamaica's cultural heritage do you feel is important to preserve?

Case study

A life of service

Astley Smith, a resident of the May Day community in Manchester, Jamaica, was today honoured for a life time of service to education, by having the May Day Basic School named in his honour. Everyone present at the ceremony sang the praises of this unsung hero.

If it were left to the residents of the May Day community, their blessing in the form of Astley Smith would be revered with the entire area being named in his honour.

Smith's life epitomises selfless service for nation building. Stanford Davis, principal of May Day High School said, "His love for young people, education and community development cannot be overemphasised. He has made his contribution solely out of love for others".

For 40 years, Smith has dedicated his life to the development of the basic school, among other institutions in the parish. He is said to have sponsored a student each year to attend the University of the West Indies and he has been the vice-president of the citizens' association and neighbourhood watch for the past 16 years.

"In 2010, he was given the Governor General's Achievement Award. His dream is to witness the certified basic school become an infant school" said justice of the peace and former principal of May Day High, Stanley Skeene.

In his response, Smith acknowledged that it is his God-given duty here on Earth to help all those he is able to.

Questions

1. In what ways has Astley Smith helped his community?

2. What qualities has Astley Smith shown to be the ideal Jamaican citizen?

3. Why do you think Astley Smith has dedicated his life to helping the community?

Source: adapted from Jamaica Gleaner

Activity

Create a spidergram which includes the positive elements of patriotism, nationalism and citizenship. How are these similar? Explain how they overlap.

Activity

Make a list of the documents that can be used to prove that a person is a citizen of Jamaica. From the list, select one and create your own version of this document.

Key vocabulary

citizen

ideal

voluntary

What is Vision 2030?

We are learning to:

- explain Vision 2030
- understand the guiding principles of Vision 2030.

According to the Vision 2030 website, Vision 2030 was developed in the midst of a global financial and economic crisis that is the most serious since the Great Depression of 1929. It is a **national development** plan which attempts to try to resolve short and long term problems and to encourage growth and development.

It was not only financial problems that were affecting Jamaica. Other issues included:

- poor economic growth
- high levels of national debt
- unacceptable levels of unemployment and poverty
- high levels of crime and violence
- low levels of skill, weak business and industry
- very rapid urbanisation, migration and globalisation which had a negative impact on the structure and stability of the Jamaican family.

Where other plans before Vision 2030 failed to be effective, this plan involves both the public and the private sector as well as charities and other organisations, to make sure that the vision is shared.

> **Did you know...?**
>
> Vision 2030 was launched in 2009 and has four National Goals.

Explaining the Vision

Vision 2030 Jamaica is our country's first long-term National Development Plan which aims to put Jamaica in a position to achieve developed country status by 2030. It is based on a comprehensive vision:

> "Jamaica, the place of choice to live, work, raise families, and do business".
>
> Source: Vision 2030 Jamaica website

Vision 2030 Jamaica logo.

This vision means a major transformation from a middle income developing country to one which provides its citizens with a high quality of life and world-class standards in areas including education, health care, nutrition, basic amenities, access to environmental goods and services, civility and social order.

These different areas are essential to make sure the country makes progress towards a more sustainable society which integrates and balances the economic, social, environmental, and governance areas of national development.

To make sure that Vision 2030 is a success, it is guided by a range of important values which should ensure that it is implemented effectively. These include:

- *Social cohesion:* ensuring that different groups and individuals are in agreement
- *Equity:* making sure that society is equal and fair
- *Transformational leadership:* having leaders who can make significant changes in society
- *Sustainability (economic, social, environmental):* conserving natural resources to ensure that they are protected long term and there is balance between the environment and the economy
- *Sustainable urban and rural development:* ensuring communities and businesses grow in ways which do not negatively affect the environment
- *Partnership:* working with different groups in society to meet the goals
- *Transparency and accountability:* being clear and open about what is taking place, and taking responsibility for what has already happened.

Source: Vision 2030 Jamaica website

Research

Carry out some research into Vision 2030; find out when it was established and by whom.

Andrew Holness is Jamaica's current leader.

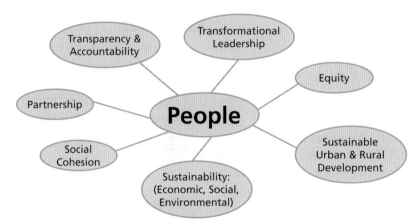

Exercise

1. What is meant by a 'national development plan'?

2. What is a more sustainable society?

3. Describe the problems Jamaica faced when Vision 2030 was set up, using your own words.

4. Why is it a good thing that Vision 2030 involves a range of organisations?

Key vocabulary

national development

What are the four goals of Vision 2030?

We are learning to:

- list the four goals of Vision 2030
- examine Goals 1 and 2 of the National Development Plan.

The National Development Plan for Jamaica, or Vision2030, has four goals (see diagram). Each National Goal has a number of National Outcomes and these are detailed below.

Goal 1: Jamaicans are empowered to achieve their fullest potential

There are four National Outcomes for Goal 1:

1. *A healthy and stable population* – that everyone in society is healthy and has free healthcare

2. *World-class education and training* – that education is high quality

3. *Effective social protection* – to care and protect the vulnerable and those who have disabilities

4. *Authentic and transformational culture* – that important heritage sites are protected and valued.

How is Goal 1 being implemented?

Some of the measures put in place in recent years to help achieve Goal 1 include:

- free healthcare in public hospitals, free measles vaccinations for children aged 1–6, increased access to the flu vaccine to Jamaicans, and improvements in facilities
- the training of teachers to help deliver the new National Standards Curriculum (NSC) for Grades 7–9; new infant, primary and secondary schools
- more opportunities of scholarships and grants for students, and training and employment opportunities for those in work
- in 2014, the National Disabilities Act was passed to help include people with disabilities in society
- in 2015, the Blue and John Crow Mountains were designated a **World Heritage Site**. This status helps to protect them
- The Creative Production and Training Centre (CPTC) was re-launched to record, archive and promote Jamaican culture, via its cable channel JamVision, within the Caribbean and globally.

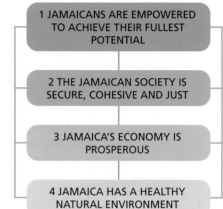

1 JAMAICANS ARE EMPOWERED TO ACHIEVE THEIR FULLEST POTENTIAL

2 THE JAMAICAN SOCIETY IS SECURE, COHESIVE AND JUST

3 JAMAICA'S ECONOMY IS PROSPEROUS

4 JAMAICA HAS A HEALTHY NATURAL ENVIRONMENT

The four goals for the National Development Plan.

Research

Carry out research into the PATH programme and explore what the organisation does, giving examples. How will this programme support Goal 1?

World Heritage Site.

Did you know...?

Saudi Arabia also has a Vision 2030 programme.

Goal 2: The Jamaican society is secure, cohesive and just

There are two National Outcomes for Goal 2:

1. *Security and Safety* – to make sure that people feel safe and secure from crimes and bad behaviour

2. *Effective Governance* – to make sure that Jamaica is run properly and fairly by the government.

How is Goal 2 being implemented?

Some of the measures put in place in recent years to help achieve Goal 2 include:

- installation of closed-circuit television (CCTV) cameras in major towns; launching of the Stay Alert mobile application which enables persons to send information to the police

- having more mobile stations to increase community access to the police, and more motor vehicles, body cameras to help the police carry out their duty

- new laws passed to make sure all Jamaican people are legally represented

- an awareness campaign to let Jamaicans know and understand their right to access government documents

- improvements in tackling human trafficking and meeting international **trafficking** laws and standards.

Discussion

In small groups, discuss why it is important to have free medical care in society. How should this be paid for?

CCTV helps to provide security and hold criminals to account.

The Stay Alert app helps people to send information to the police.

Exercise

1. How many goals does the National Development Plan for Jamaica have?

2. What measures has Jamaica put in place to ensure the island has a healthy and stable population?

3. Which National Outcome was the National Disabilities Act passed for in 2014? Give reasons.

4. Explain why it is important to have a healthy population.

Key vocabulary

World Heritage Site

governance

trafficking

What are the four goals of Vision 2030?

We are learning to:

- examine Goal 3 of the National Development Plan
- examine Goal 4 of the National Development Plan.

Every country in the world needs to have a strong, stable **economy** to help look after its citizens and to make the country prosperous. One of the goals of Vision 2030 is to make a stronger economy.

The central business district in Kingston.

Goal 3: Jamaica's economy is prosperous 》

There are six National Outcomes for this National Goal:

1. *A stable macro economy (large scale)* – to reduce debt, do tax reform and ensure prices are stable

2. *An enabling business environment* – to create an economy where business can thrive

3. *Strong economic infrastructure* – making sure that businesses are secure and not likely to fail

4. *Energy security and efficiency* – making sure that there is a good supply of gas and electricity at all times and that there is little waste

5. *A technology-enabled society* – good access to the internet and forms of technology

6. *Internationally competitive industry structures* – making sure that businesses are able to compete with those in other countries.

JPS is the sole provider of electricity in Jamaica and is state-owned.

Wind farms help to create renewable energy.

How is Goal 3 being implemented? 》》

Some of the measures put in place in recent years to help achieve Goal 3 include:

- in 2016, the government launched the Economic Growth Council which advises the government on ways to support economic growth
- in 2010, it was agreed that the Wigton Windfarm would be extended to help generate renewable energy
- in 2016, the government extended its Tablet in Schools project to all colleges after an initial pilot project to a small number of schools
- in 2014, the government launched Start-Up Jamaica a programme designed to help young technology entrepreneurs by providing them with the skills, to help grow their ideas into marketable products.

Key vocabulary

economy

Exercise

1. Explain what is meant by the term economy.

2. Which National Outcome was the Start-Up Jamaica programme created for in 2014? Give reasons.

3. Why is access to the internet important for economic growth in Jamaica?

In a competitive global market, the natural environment plays a role in the success of any country's economy.

Goal 4: Jamaica has a healthy natural environment

There are three National Outcomes for this National Goal.

1. *Sustainable management and use of environmental and natural resources* – to make sure that the natural resources of Jamaica are protected and conserved

2. *Hazard risk reduction and adaptation to climate change* – to make sure that plans are in place to help protect people, such as against natural disasters

3. *Sustainable urban and rural development* – to make sure that building is carefully planned and checked to ensure that the environment is protected.

The annual Coastal Clean-up Day takes place on the 3rd Saturday of September.

The National Clean-Up Campaign was launched in 2016.

How is Goal 4 being implemented?

Some of the measures put in place in recent years to help achieve Goal 4 include:

- on the third Saturday of each September, the annual International Coastal Clean-up Day takes place, run in Jamaica by the National Environment and Planning Agency (NEPA)

- in 2016, the government launched the National Clean-up Campaign to encourage the correct disposal of garbage on the island and the destruction of mosquito breeding sites, which can be a source of dengue. The government also strengthened anti-litter laws on the island

- renewable energy plants set-up – these include the Wigton III and BMR Jamaica wind farms

- the government gave further support to farmers to help boost economic growth in the agriculture sector, and also introduced training for farmers in climate-smart agricultural practices

- repairs to major roadways in Kingston, and to water systems across the island.

Activity

Organise a clean-up day in and around your school grounds. Produce posters explaining how it supports Vision 2030, and take pictures.

Exercise

4. Identify two hazards to the environment in Jamaica.

5. Which National Outcome was the National Clean-up Campaign created for in 2016? Give reasons.

6. Why do you think it is important to repair major roadways?

7. Write a paragraph about the advantages of wind farms.

What are the four goals of Vision 2030?

We are learning to:

- identify the challenges of achieving the goals of 2030.

What are the challenges of achieving the goals of Vision 2030? »

The goals of Vision 2030 are ambitious and involve a lot of careful planning and hard work. There are 12 Thematic Working Groups that meet regularly to monitor the progress Vision 2030 is making in reaching its goals. There are several reasons why achieving the goals of Vision 2030 are difficult, or challenging.

- *Cost* – the goals require a lot of investment from the government.
- *Commitment* – people from different groups need to be dedicated to reaching these goals.
- *Changing people's beliefs and attitudes* – it takes time to encourage people to think differently and believe in the values of Vision 2030.
- *Educational performance of boys* – currently lower than girls, meaning they are less likely to make progress and meet their goals.
- *Parenting skills* – making sure that parents are raising their children with positive parenting and to believe in themselves.
- Positive values such as honesty are not always present.

Norman Manley International Airport: The National Development Plan includes the cost of infrastructure.

Some of the challenges outlined at local level in the National Development Plan include:

- *Healthcare:* under-resourced facilities and aging infrastructure; growth in chronic and lifestyle diseases; overburdening of secondary health care institutions; shortage of health personnel; unhealthy environments spreading disease
- *Education:* under-resourced schools; performance of children; poor school attendance; violence in schools
- *Employment:* untrained workforce; funding not available for training; culture of entrepreneurship not encouraged
- *Social provision:* under resourced services; legislation that does not work; issues with pension scheme; lack of resources in rural areas
- *Culture:* inadequate preservation and conservation of heritage sites; under resourced sport facilities; little family support
- *Crime:* high levels of violence; distrust of police
- *Governance:* inefficient justice system; perception of corruption; human rights infringement; gender inequality
- *Economic:* high public wage bill; tax reform; changes to banking system; government debt
- *Trade:* too dependent on primary exports; issues with regional integration

- *Infrastructure:* cost of maintaining rail, road, air facilities
- *Climate change:* vulnerability of Jamaica's location and disaster preparedness.

(Source: Vision 2030: Jamaica National Development Plan, "Planning for a Secure & Prosperous Future", © 2009 by the Planning Institute of Jamaica)

There have been and remain some global challenges that present difficulties in achieving Vision 2030 such as Coronavirus which led to a review of Vision 2030 goals. Other challenges include global recessions, which have affected credit markets allowing governments to raise funds, and the economies of developed and developing countries. The impact on Jamaica includes:

- reduced direct investment
- greater difficulty in sourcing financing from global capital markets
- reduction in demand for Jamaica's exports
- a downturn in tourism earnings, also caused by the coronavirus pandemic.

Progress with Vision 2030 》》》

- The most success has been made towards Goal 1: "Jamaicans are Empowered to Achieve their Fullest Potential"; for example, increased life expectancy, a reduced child mortality rate and improved grade 4 literacy and numeracy rates.
- Goal 3: "Jamaica's Economy is Prosperous" has shown signs of progress. However there are increasing levels of poverty and disease, and the global pandemic has had an impact on the national economy.
- The area of greatest concern for the country is Goal 2 "The Jamaican Society is Secure, Cohesive and Just" with very little progress in 2015. Despite this, corruption is reducing and government is becoming more effective.
- Under Goal 3 "Jamaica's Economy is Prosperous", 46% of the targets were either met for 2016/17 and the economy was moving towards meeting the target.
- Goal 4 – there is some progress with secure housing, but this still needs improvement.

Activity

Select two aspects of Vision 2030 in which little progress has been made. Write a letter to the Planning Institute of Jamaica in which you express concern about the progress of Vision 2030 and list five plans of action to increase awareness and advance the areas identified.

Exercise

1 Explain why cost is a major issue to achieve Vision 2030.

2 Why do you think it would be difficult to persuade people about Vision 2030?

3 Write a paragraph about some of the global challenges to overcome.

Project

Working in groups, your teacher will assign you one of the Vision 2030 goals. Work together to review the implementation of the plan and identify ways in which you and your community can contribute towards the accomplishment of the goal.

Use the information to write a blog, record a podcast or make a vlog to share your ideas.

What is national development?

We are learning to:

- explain how individual behaviours and decision-making affect national development.

National development refers to the development in a nation/society as a whole and includes improvements in the social welfare of the people, the economy and governance of the country.

Examples for Jamaica include:

- providing social **amenities** like quality education
- ensuring that everyone has access to drinkable water
- a transportation system that is efficient and affordable
- medical care for all
- education for all.

Exercise

1. Using examples, explain how Vision 2030 is a good plan for achieving national development.

2. Identify two potential obstacles to national development.

3. Write a short report on the benefits of national development in Jamaica for your life.

Project

Working in groups, outline a national educational campaign which aims to increase awareness and encourage participation in national development among young adults.

Share your campaign with the rest of the class, including photographs and music.

How does individual behaviour affect national development?

In order for national development programmes to be effective, individuals and organisations need to be fully **committed** to the goals of the programme. Individual people have choices to make about their behaviour such as:

- choosing to buy sustainable goods, for example buying recycled paper, fairtrade goods
- using renewable energy sources, such as windfarm electricity, rather than non-renewable energy sources such as coal
- getting involved with community activities such as cleanup days
- recycling goods
- using public transport, cycling or walking rather than driving
- improving attitudes, for example parenting skills, or being willing to learn to change these practices
- volunteering, or getting involved with organisations that help people in need or who help protect the environment.

National Outcomes Goal 1 is that everyone in society is healthy and has free healthcare.

The role of the individual ⟫⟫

Although there are many central government agencies involved in implementing the National Development Plan, it is important that we all play an individual role in helping to successfully implement Vision 2030. The National Development Plan, published in 2009, stresses the need for everyone to be involved.

'For us to be successful in realizing our Vision, we must all become excited about this challenging opportunity, and transform our hearts and minds towards positive action through a shared vision that is realistic and relevant to us as individuals, to our families and the society.'

(Source: Vision 2030: Jamaica National Development Plan, "Planning for a Secure & Prosperous Future", © 2009 by the Planning Institute of Jamaica, page 1)

How does decision making affect national development? ⟫⟫⟫

Exercise

4 As we have seen, individual decision making can have a real impact on national development. Consider the following decisions below and write an appropriate response to each, imagining you want to positively affect national development.

   a) You are a parent and you need to bring your children up with a set of values and morals, plus set an example for them.

   b) You are looking for an energy supplier, for your electricity.

   c) You have some free time and you want to use it wisely. What sorts of activities could you choose?

   d) Your local area has become dirty and there is a lot of litter.

   e) You are looking for a job. What affects your decision about the kind of employer you want to have?

   f) You want to buy a new house, what sorts of things are important to consider?

5 For each of the decisions above, explain which national goal within Vision 2030 they relate to.

6 Write a short essay explaining the importance of individual behaviour and decision-making on national development.

7 Write a list of all the kinds of behaviours and decision-making that are possible in your school, to ensure that national development takes place. Produce a wall display highlighting the key points in your school.

8 Consider what obstacles or challenges you might face in implementing each decision you make. Create a list of these, along with ideas about how you might overcome these challenges.

Activity

Think about the choices you and your family make which may contribute to national development. Make a list of these choices and decide if you are working towards national development as much as you can be. Choose three goals/areas of improvement you would like to work on.

Eco-friendly housing is a positive national development.

Key vocabulary

amenities

committed

23

Questions

See how well you have understood the topics in this unit.

1. Explain the term national identity.

2. A _____ is a person who belongs to a nation, or a country.
   a) individual
   b) citizen
   c) alien
   d) member of the public

3. _____ is where people feel a strong sense of pride in their country, similar to patriotism.
   a) Migration
   b) Nationalism
   c) Bravery
   d) Heroism

4. Name four characteristics of a good citizen.

5. In your own words, explain what Vision 2030 aims to achieve.

6. True or False? 'Vision 2030 has 7 goals'.

7. Correct this statement: National development refers to wanting to strengthen the economy only.

8. Explain three characteristics of an ideal Jamaican citizen.

9. Write a short definition of the following terms:
   sovereign
   state
   nation
   cultural heritage.

10. Match the goals to their objectives.
   1) Goal 1: Jamaicans are empowered
   2) Goal 2: The Jamaican society is secure
   3) Goal 3: Jamaica's economy
   4) Goal 4: Jamaica has a healthy

   a) is prosperous
   b) natural environment
   c) to achieve their fullest potential
   d) cohesive and just.

11. Give two examples of ways Goal 1, 'Jamaicans are empowered to achieve their fullest potential', is being implemented.

12. Give two examples of ways Goal 2, 'The Jamaican society is secure, cohesive and just' is being implemented.

13. Give two examples of ways Goal 3, 'Jamaica's economy is prosperous' is being implemented.

14. Give two examples of ways Goal 4, 'Jamaica has a healthy natural environment' is being implemented.

15. Give two reasons why Jamaica needed a national development plan, using examples.

16. Imagine that you work for an organisation that works towards one of the goals of Vision 2030 in Jamaica. Write an essay of about 200 words describing how you will reach the goal.

17. Outline some of the challenges at local level identified in the National Development Plan.

18. Outline some of the global challenges to implementing the National Development Plan.

Grade 8 Unit 1 Summary

Nationalism

In this chapter, you have learned about:

- What is meant by nation and state
- What it means for a country to have sovereignty
- The meaning of sovereignty for Jamaicans
- The concepts of national identity, cultural background and cultural heritage
- The connection between nationalism and patriotism
- The role of nationalism in the preservation of natural and cultural heritage
- How nationalism differs from citizenship.

Citizenship

In this chapter, you have learned about:

- What is meant by citizen and citizenship
- What it means to be a good citizen
- The characteristics of the ideal Jamaican.

Vision 2030 and national development

In this chapter, you have learned about:

- Jamaica's national development plan, Vision 2030
- The explanation behind Vision 2030
- What the guiding principles behind Vision 2030 mean
- The four goals of Vision 2030 and how they are being implemented
- The challenges of achieving the goals of Vision 2030
- The level of progress experienced in implementing Vision 2030
- What national development means
- The role of the individual and the effect of individual behaviour on national development
- How individual decision making affects national development.

Checking your progress

To make good progress in understanding nationalism and development, check that you understand these ideas.

Explain and use correctly the term *nationalism*.

Describe why nationalism is important.

Explain the differences and similarities between nationalism and citizenship.

Explain and use correctly the term *national development*.

Outline the ideal characteristics of a Jamaican citizen.

Explain the role of Vision 2030 in Jamaica's national development.

Explain and use correctly the term *sovereignty*.

Name three guiding principles of Vision 2030.

Explain why a country has national symbols.

Explain and use correctly the term *cultural heritage*.

Describe the four goals of Vision 2030.

Explain the role of individual choices and behaviour in promoting national development.

Unit 2: Communication and Media Literacy

Objectives: You will be able to:

Communication
- classify the forms of communication.

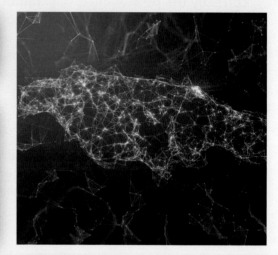

What is the mass media?
- assess the influence of the mass media on social life and values
- analyse the impact of access to information on social and economic life in Jamaica.

The difference between fact, opinion and propaganda
- distinguish between fact, opinion and propaganda.

What messages are being transmitted through the media?
- discuss the social impact of prejudice and stereotyping on society: news media and social media.

What is social media?
- evaluate the role of social media in society
- discuss the role of mass media in decision-making.

Negative effects of modern communication technology
- understand the negative effects of modern communication technology: cyberbullying.

Responsible use of social media
- demonstrate responsible use of social media.

Communication

We are learning to:

• classify the forms of communication.

Communication refers to the way people share information with each other. Communication can come in many forms; spoken, known as **verbal** communication, or **non-verbal**, which involves forms such as writing, texting or messaging. Communication can take place in many different ways, with either one-to-one communication or many people communicating at the same time. The **medium** or method through which communication occurs is known as the **media**.

A common way people communicate in today's world is by using the internet.

In recent years, due to advances in technology, the internet and mobile phones and other devices have enabled many new ways to communicate.

Communication is the transfer of information between a **sender** and **receiver**. We communicate with people all the time in many different ways. We can talk, nod or shake our heads, wave, listen, write a note or letter, use a telephone, send an email, or use the internet to have a video call.

Good, fast communication is an essential part of any business, especially a global one. Businesses need computer networks, up-to-date software and reliable internet connections, as well as skilled employees to ensure efficient communication. Investment in the latest communication technology will allow both employees and customers to access information quickly and customers can benefit from a more efficient service.

In communicating, the following terms are important:

• sender – a person who has written a message or produced an image and has sent it to another individual or group

• receiver – a person or group who gets the message or image

• **feedback** – this refers to the response of the receiver as to the message sent to him/her by the sender

• medium – this is the method through which communication takes place, for example sending a text message on a smartphone

• message – the information sent in written form, vocal or image-based

• transparency – where communication is clear and open, or explicit in its message

• media literacy – this is the extent to which people have the skills to use the various forms of media to communicate.

Activity

Your teacher will put you in groups and give each group a message to communicate to the rest of the class (but they won't know what it is). Your task is to share your message using a non-verbal form of communication. You may use art forms such as pictures, mime and dramatisation.

Did you know...?

Development started on the internet in the 1960s, but it didn't begin officially until January 1983. The World Wide Web was developed by Tim Berners-Lee in 1990.

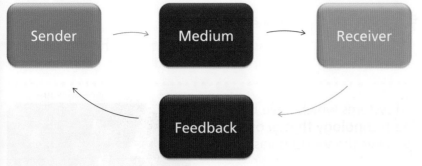

The communication process.

Discussion

Do you think you are media literate? Why? How did you learn to become media literate? Why might people not be media literate?

Symbols

Symbols are images which can be used to represent an idea or a message. These are important today in communicating messages on and offline. Think about the symbols you see in everyday life. Often symbols are used to represent a company or a product. A tick sign for example, represents Nike™ products. Symbols often represent values or feelings, to encourage you to think in a particular way. Look at the Jamaican flag and think about what values and ideas it represents.

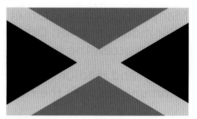

The national flag is an important symbol.

Exercise

1 Explain the different components in the communication process in the diagram above: sender, medium, receiver, feedback.

2 Make a list of different types of communication used in the past, including verbal and non-verbal.

3 Write a paragraph explaining some of the disadvantages of communicating through new forms of technology.

4 Create a two-column table with 'Now' as the heading of the left column and 'Then' as the heading of the right column. List four types of communication that are used now and four types that were used more than 50 years ago.

Key vocabulary

communication

verbal

non-verbal

medium

media

sender

receiver

feedback

Technology

We are learning to:

* assess the influence of the mass media on social life and values.

Technology consists of devices and systems which have been created for practical purposes. The technology that allows us to communicate with people all over the world is vast and complex. Satellites orbit the globe to relay weather reports and televised images to all parts of the world and the internet connects people with friends and family as well as with business partners.

In 2020, it was estimated that more than 59% of the world's population use the internet to communicate and to do research. The increase in access and usage over the last 20 years is quite staggering. In 1994 only 0.4% of the world's population used the internet.

Many people have internet access in their homes or through their mobile phones. Others make use of public **internet cafés** to access the internet.

All big- and medium-sized enterprises rely on the internet to communicate with their customers and suppliers.

Satellites orbiting the Earth provide information to all parts of the world everyday.

Businesses rely on the internet on a daily basis.

Communication technology 》》

Communication technology is all the equipment and programs used to process and communicate information between a sender and receiver. Another name for communication technology is information technology.

Smartphones, **tablets** and laptop computers are examples of communication technology devices we use for communication and entertainment. Cell phones, computers, MP3 players, game consoles, tablets and **ebooks** have changed the way we communicate, work and play.

The internet ▶▶▶

Whether you need to know today's weather or news, the starting time for a sports match or a detailed history of Jamaica, you can find the information on the internet. The internet has changed the way people find information and has been a positive development in many ways.

- You can find a wide range of information and entertainment easily – for example, sport through subscription boxes.
- Online shopping is readily available, offering cheap, fast delivery of goods and services.
- It can raise awareness of news and issues with a wider audience.

Negative consequences of the growth of the internet include:

- decline of publishing industry and use of libraries
- increase in piracy – ability to download copyrighted music and movies
- local culture and knowledge may be lost as global culture spreads
- it is time-consuming, leading to a more **sedentary** lifestyle
- **information overload**, resulting in anxiety and stress.

Research

Research the history of the internet and explain how it has evolved over time.

Activity

Write a reflective piece titled 'How do communication technologies influence my life?' Write about 150 words.

Exercise

1. Why do you think social media makes it easier to keep in touch with people in different parts of the world?

2. How many people in the world today have access to the internet?

3. In what ways can people today access the internet?

4. Why do you think businesses rely on the internet?

5. In your view does the internet bring more benefits or problems?

Key vocabulary

technology

internet café

communication technology

smartphones

tablets

ebooks

sedentary

information overload

What is the mass media?

We are learning to:

- analyse the impact of access to information on social and economic life in Jamaica.

The **mass media** refers to the various forms of communication technology used to share information with the public. There are many types of mass media including:

- *print media* – this is paper-based communication such as newspapers, magazines, leaflets
- *digital media/the internet* – this is communication that is based on computers, laptops and text messages
- *broadcast media* – this is generally verbal communication like television and radio; news is often communicated through television
- *social media* – this is communication that takes place on the internet on platforms such as Facebook and Instagram – it can be through texts, images or short videos.

Who has access to information?

Media literacy refers to the skills that a person has in using or accessing the media. However, not all Jamaicans have the same access to information. As of the beginning of 2023, it was estimated that just over 82% of the population were using the internet. Although this number has increased from 55% in 2017, it still means that over 17% of people are not able to access online media. There are several reasons why this number is not higher.

1. Lack of resources: some people may not be able to afford a smartphone, access to the internet or a computer or tablet.

2. The older generation and many others may not have the skills, knowledge or confidence to use modern forms of technology.

3. Not everyone can read and write. These groups may find it difficult to access or read technology-based information.

4. Some people with disabilities may be unable to access information using different forms of technology as a result of their disability.

In December 2020, the government declared that internet access should be a public good and launched the National Broadband Initiative which will seek to ensure every household has access to the internet by 2025.

Did you know...?

In October 2019, a total of 547 000 people in Jamaica used Facebook Messenger, a number that made up close to 19% of the country's population. Of these users, 52.7% were women. In the period between September 2018 and 2019, the number of monthly users of Facebook Messenger in Jamaica peaked in February 2019 with nearly 631 000 users, before significantly dropping to around 543 000 users a month later.

Discussion

What are the disadvantages of not having access to the internet? Discuss the effects this may have on people's lives. What are the advantages of being able to use the internet and other forms of technology?

The impact of media on social and economic life ⟩⟩⟩

What people read, see and hear in the media often has a significant impact on the way they behave. For example, it can influence the way people dress, where they live, the food they consume and the places they want to visit.

Exercise

1 Write about a recent example of how you have been influenced by the media. What did you read, see or hear and what did it encourage you to do, or not to do?

2 List two positive and two negative examples of how the media can influence people.

The news ⟩⟩⟩

News refers to public information that is shared through a range of media. It is generated by companies and organisations that choose what they consider to be 'newsworthy'. News is presented in terms of facts, opinions and sometimes, propaganda. News agencies want people to buy their products and/or click on their stories, so they think hard about how to make their content appealing.

What we call 'quality journalism' aspires to ethical standards. These standards include:

- *truthfulness/accuracy:* verifying all details that can be checked; using multiple original sources (individuals and documentation) wherever possible
- *independence:* putting the interests of the public above self-interest or special interests
- *balance:* giving a voice to multiple perspectives
- *fairness/avoidance of bias:* presenting facts and details in appropriate context, using neutral language
- *accountability:* acknowledging errors and correcting them promptly.

Discussion

Where do you get your news from? Do you think there are some news outlets that are more fact-based than opinion-based?

Activity

Choose a media item such as a song, movie or social media post and evaluate its influence on teenagers. Remember to explain what it was, what kind of impact it had, and whether the influence was positive or negative, or a mixture of the two.

Project

In groups, carry out a school survey to find out what types of media students use most. Ask them what they like and dislike about the media they use.

Brainstorm strategies to counter the negative influence of the media on teenagers and present your ideas to the rest of the class.

Newspapers provide news and opinions.

Key vocabulary

mass media

media literacy

What is the influence of the mass media on social life and values?

We are learning to:

- assess the influence of the mass media on social life and values.

Mass media ⟩⟩

Mass media is a term used to describe the different media technologies that are used to reach large numbers of people (the masses). These include print media like newspapers; broadcast media like radio, film and television; and electronic media, which is internet-based.

Some of the main functions of the mass media are:

- *to inform* – the mass media is essential for sharing news, current affairs and events
- *to educate* – people learn all the time through the mass media, about current events, history and much more
- *to entertain* – news, television, blogs, films and radio shows are all important aspects of day-to-day relaxation
- *to help create national identity* – the mass media is an important place where ideas about what it means to be Jamaican can be discussed and represented
- *to create cultural identity* – the mass media helps people express their own unique identity
- *to create employment* – there are now many jobs in the mass media, such as journalist, researcher and presenter.

Mass media includes newspapers, radio, film and television and electronic media.

Positive impact of mass media >>>

Mass media can have a positive impact. For example:

- it can offer personal development, by allowing people to share ideas, keep in touch and learn
- culturally, it can promote the way of life in Jamaica and the Caribbean region
- it encourages cultural creativity, for example through music and films
- it can help to promote good values, freedom of expression, national pride and identity
- it can help to promote social and economic programmes.

Negative impact of mass media >>>>

Mass media can also have a negative impact. For example:

- it can present images of violence, sexual activity, promiscuity and other risky behaviours (such as drug and alcohol abuse), which can influence younger members of society
- overseas media do not represent national or regional views, and these could get overshadowed by the global media.

There have been some concerns in recent years about the power of the mass media to shape the way that people think. This is because a small number of people own large sections of the mass media. It is argued that the views of the owners of the media are reflected in the information they share, perhaps overlooking other views.

Did you know...?

The newspaper *The Gleaner* was founded on September 13th, 1834 and was originally called *The Daily Gleaner*. Commercial radio was introduced in the 1940s.

A 1962 edition of the Jamaican Gleaner reporting on the independence celebrations.

Research

Using the internet, research how communication technology has an impact on the economy of Jamaica.

Exercise

1. Define the term mass media.

2. Give two examples of mass media and say how they are used.

3. Name two advantages of mass media to Jamaican society.

4. In groups of four or five, select any form of mass media shown on page 36. Use the form of media selected to explain the advantages and disadvantages of mass media to the rest of the class.

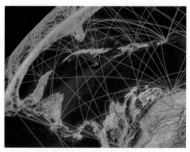

Jamaica and the digital networks.

Do you always know the intent?

We are learning to:

- explore and analyse the intention of authors in print, verbal, visual or multi-media
- distinguish between fact, opinion and propaganda.

All media is made for a reason and with an intention in mind. For example, this might be to inform people, to entertain them, or to persuade them to do something or behave in a certain way. Language, images and settings are used carefully in order to achieve this. So if a company wants to sell a vacation, they will show positive images of beautiful places and feature smiling families having fun.

What we see and read in the media is not necessarily a true reflection of reality. It is important to be aware that often, ideas and information are presented in ways that seek to shape the way we think about a particular issue. The media presents a mixture of facts, opinions and, sometimes, propaganda.

Facts ⟫

A **fact** is something that has become known as true. This means that a fact relies on some kind of provable evidence.

- Facts are definitely true.
- They can be backed up with evidence.
- An example is 'The Minister is giving a speech'.

Opinions ⟫⟫

Opinion is where a person or group presents a specific view on a topic or issue. It may use emotional appeals to persuade readers, viewers or listeners to consider the position it is arguing for (or against).

The message may include facts and evidence. This evidence may be open to some interpretation, but it is still clear and supported by reasoning. In addition, other views and positions may be presented for balance and contrast. To be a respected opinion, it should be supported by facts and clear arguments to explain why we should agree with the position.

- Your opinion is how you feel.
- Other people might think differently and they may have a different opinion.
- An example is 'Having a teenager as Prime Minister is a terrible idea'.

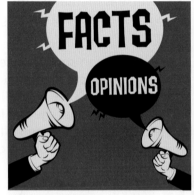

Some online news can make it difficult to work out what is fact and what is opinion.

Research

Identify a recent issue that has been in the news. Find as many different reports on it as you can. How are they similar and how are they different? Present your findings to the rest of the class.

Propaganda

Propaganda refers to views and ideas which express fears and worries; it distorts and manipulates facts and information, it often includes falsehoods and it is often one-sided. Propaganda most commonly uses emotional information in its efforts to persuade — especially attacks on opponents and strong emotional appeals, for example to stop people doing harmful things to themselves and others.

- Advertisements, while often honest, are used to promote a good or service. However, occasionally they may try to persuade a person to buy something by exaggerating, which may be considered propaganda.

- An example of where adverts may be considered propaganda are the 'before' and 'after' approach.

Activity

In groups of five, create a role-play that has three scenarios. The first scenario identifies fact, the second scenario identifies opinion, and the third scenario identifies propaganda.

Activity

Look at the images below. Identify which is fact, opinion or propaganda and explain why.

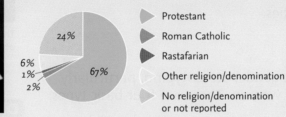

- Protestant
- Roman Catholic
- Rastafarian
- Other religion/denomination
- No religion/denomination or not reported

24% 67% 6% 1% 2%

Exercise

1 Explain the terms facts, opinions and propaganda in your own words.

2 Why might adverts contain propaganda?

3 What is a potential problem with using opinion instead of facts?

4 Write about the social issue of crime rates in Jamaica. Write a paragraph using facts, another using opinion and another using propaganda. When you write your opinion, remember to use language to convey how you feel and to try to persuade others to agree with you.

Discussion

When you have completed Exercise 4, swap with a partner and give each other feedback. Tell each other which paragraph you found the most effective and why.

Key vocabulary

fact

opinion

propaganda

What messages are being transmitted through the media?

We are learning to:

- discuss the social impact of prejudice and stereotyping on society: news media and social media.

Influence of news media and social media

One of the main places that children and adults learn **stereotypes** is from the mass media, which includes television, films, radio, adverts and social media (Facebook, X, Instagram). The media is full of racial and gender stereotypes. Examples include the representation of:

- ethnic groups
- gender: girls/women-**femininity**; and boys/men-**masculinity**
- sexual orientation
- people with disabilities.

This photo shows how the media can often show gender stereotyping.

Gender

The media often displays gender stereotyping, particularly negative stereotyping of women. There are four basic types:

- *Personality* – women are shown as submissive and passive; men are shown as aggressive and dominant
- *Behaviour at home* – women are portrayed as staying at home, cooking, doing the housework and child care; men earn the income
- *Occupations* – women are shown as having a traditionally female job such as a nurse, secretary or librarian; men have more physical jobs, such as construction, or higher-skilled jobs like doctors or lawyers
- *Appearance* – women are often shown as sexual objects and are defined by their perceived level of attractiveness; men are often shown as being **macho** (with a strong sense of masculinity).

Generally, women are portrayed as being weaker, less competitive and less adaptable than men.

Exercise

1. Name some of the racial and gender stereotypes represented by the media.
2. Draw a graphic organiser to show your understanding of the four gender stereotypes.

Discussion

As a class, discuss the following:

- are you able to identify the current trends in dancehall music?
- do you think these trends promote any kinds of stereotype or prejudices? Identify examples and state whether these were implicit or explicit in how they were conveyed.
- What impact could these trends and stereotypes have on the values of the Jamaican society?

Case studies

Stereotyping

1. Adverts that encourage gender stereotypes like women cleaning up after their family, or men failing to do housework, face being banned under strict new watchdog rules.

   Following a year-long inquiry the Advertising Standards Authority (ASA) in the UK has found there was evidence to support stronger rules, on the basis that harmful stereotypes 'can restrict the choices, aspirations and opportunities of children, young people and adults'.

   Controversial adverts by Gap, KFC and Protein World, all of which received a number of complaints last year, are examples which could be affected by the crackdown.

2. In 2005, Hurricane Katrina struck the Gulf Coast, killing more than 1000 people and leaving tens of thousands homeless.

   News media may have turned this natural disaster into a disaster for American race relations by repeatedly broadcasting images of black people who were often described as 'looting' in the catastrophic wake of the storm.

   According to a study these types of images lead some white people to endorse harsh treatment of black evacuees (by, for example, not allowing them to seek refuge in another state). Participants were not any less likely to help white evacuees, suggesting that racial stereotypes of black people as criminals may have played a role.

A stranded victim of Hurricane Katrina is taken ashore by rescue workers after being rescued from her home in high water on 5 September 2005 in New Orleans, Louisiana.

Research

Using the internet, create a brochure on the importance of using social media and information from the news media responsibly.

Questions

1. What stereotype does case study 1 highlight?

2. For what reason are some advertisements being banned by the ASA in case study 1?

3. What stereotype does case study 2 highlight? How do you think the media influenced this stereotype?

4. Write a newspaper article of about 200 words about the dangers of prejudice and stereotypes.

Key vocabulary

stereotypes

femininity

masculinity

What is social media?

We are learning to:

- evaluate the role of social media in society
- discuss the role of mass media in decision-making.

Social media ❯❯

Social media refers to communication technology programmes used for social networking. These include websites and applications which allows people to connect and create online communities through their computers, tablets and smart phones. Social media such as Facebook, X and Instagram are popular ways for people to stay in touch with their friends and family. Social media can have a positive impact.

- It can keep people connected when physically apart.
- Communities can gather support for issues.
- Businesses can build relationships with communities.
- People can become more engaged in topics that they are interested in, for example local or world issues.
- People can get in touch with each other faster.
- It can help businesses grow and can help students with their education, for example they can research their homework topic very quickly and easily.

There can be some disadvantages of social media.

- It can be addictive and distract people from their work and other activities.
- It can increase feelings of loneliness or depression.
- It can be used for cyberbullying, which can have serious consequences.

There are many issues with social media including:

- social media has the power to influence a person's **decision making** skills by connecting them to their peers
- people are able to be connected 24 hours a day to social media, allowing them constant exposure to carefully made profiles that show perfected images
- social media has been known to produce anxiety and low self-esteem problems in teenagers and adults. For example, there are millions of images of consumer goods that people may not be able to afford
- social media is full of advertisements and these can trigger stress and anxiety, as people feel like they want more and more expensive items that are made to seem so appealing on social media

Social media such as Facebook, X and Instagram help people to keep in touch.

Project

'Fake news' refers to information that is presented as true but, in reality, is not. Fake news is often found on the internet.

In groups, carry out research to find out more about some of the dangers of fake news, then work together to make a poster for Grade 7 students to make them aware of what you have found out.

Social media plays an important role in people's lives.

- social media sites may encourage risk taking behaviour which can cause accidents and harm to those who try to copy that behaviour
- there is also a danger that teenagers and children may become the target of strangers and predators online if their identity is revealed.

Social media and how we make decisions

Both social and mass media can have influence on the decisions we make about personal, social or political matters.

- A 2012 study carried out by Harvard University in the United States found that 54% of Americans consulted a social media website when making a buying decision about a product or service. This decision may be influenced by comments or reviews that people make about a product or service.
- Another study carried out in 2017 found that up to 40% of people consulted social media when making decisions about travel and up to 25% used social media to help make decisions about health care, financial services and retail services.
- Purchasing decisions are also influenced by the mass media by the way in which products or services are packaged and advertised to the public. Some tactics used include repetition and use of experts to speak about the product.
- Social media can influence what we think about a product or an issue. If we see a friend posting an item on social media, we often agree with what they have posted – whether it is a good purchase they have recently bought, or an opinion about an event in the news.
- People can be influenced by negative reviews of a product. For example, someone may be thinking of buying a new item for their house, but they read a negative online review about the product. They will then probably look at a different product.

Exercise

1. Name two different social media platforms that are influential on young peoples views and decision making in Jamaica.

2. How might images on social media lead to self-esteem issues among teenagers?

3. Imagine your friend spends too much time on social media, and you think that it is affecting their decision making in a negative way. Write a list of the advice you would give them.

4. Why do you think advertisements include experts talking about a product or service, or 'influencers' are used on social media?

Social media influencers draw in customers to their posts.

Discussion

Do you think that social media shapes the way you and your classmates see the world? How might social media affect your decisions, or shape what you buy or do?

Key vocabulary

social media

decision making

Negative effects of modern communication technology

We are learning to:

- understand the negative effects of modern communication technology: cyberbullying.

Cyberbullying ❯❯

Cyberbullying takes place when a person or a group of people use the internet, mobile phones, online games or any other type of digital technology to threaten, tease or humiliate someone.

Types of cyberbullying ❯❯❯

Online forums make it easy to bully or intimidate others:

- sending abusive or nasty **emails**, or sending emails to a group of people who join in the bullying
- using **instant messaging (IM)** and **chatrooms** to send threatening or abusive messages to someone; asking others to join in
- writing nasty or upsetting comments on someone's profile on a **social networking site**; making jokes or comments about others on your updates or tweets
- setting up a fake profile dedicated to bullying someone else
- abusing or harassing someone through a multi-player **online gaming site**
- sending abusive texts, video or photo messages via mobile phones.

What to do if you are being cyberbullied:

- talk to someone you trust, such as a parent, teacher or counsellor
- keep copies of any abusive messages or comments, and record the dates and times
- try not to reply to any messages you receive, as it can encourage bullies and upset you more
- report the bullying to the site you are using (for example, X, Facebook, Instagram); all social networking sites have help centres for people experiencing abuse.

Cyberbullying often takes place through mobile phones and the apps that people can get on them.

Activity

Write a short piece of about 100 words around the topic of responsible use of social media.

Discussion

With a partner, role-play a scenario. One of you is being cyberbullied and the other is giving advice. Take turns, then share your advice with the rest of the class.

Activity

In groups, role-play three effects that cyberbullying has on an individual and, by extension, on the family.

Case study

Cyberbullying can kill

Talisha, aged 13, begged her mother Arlene to set up an online profile for months before Arlene allowed her to do it. Soon, Talisha got a message from a boy. He said his name was Jason Khan. Talisha started messaging him regularly.

Soon, however, Jason – or someone using his account – started sending a chain of hurtful instant messages, calling Talisha a liar, calling her fat and other hurtful names. The **cyber abuse** became increasingly vicious, until one day Talisha went into her room and ended her own life.

'She felt there was no way out,' said Arlene. Six weeks later, Talisha's family discovered that their daughter was the victim of a hoax. Another girl had created the Jason Khan account as a trick, and sent the hate messages. An article in the *New York Times* wrote:

'Cellphone cameras and text messages, as well as social networking websites, e-mail and instant messaging, all give teenagers a wider range of ways to play tricks on one another, to tease and to **intimidate** their peers.'

And, unlike traditional bullying, high-tech bullying can happen anywhere, at any time, among lots of different children who may never actually meet in person. The victim can feel it is inescapable and the perpetrators are often **anonymous**.

Questions

1. In your own words, define cyberbullying.

2. Why do you think Talisha wanted an online profile?

3. **a)** How do you think Talisha felt when she first started getting messages from 'Jason Khan'?

   b) How do you think she felt when Jason's messages turned nasty?

4. A hoax is a serious trick.

   a) Why do you think the girl who made up the Jason Khan account did it?

   b) How do you think she felt after Talisha's death?

5. Give four ways that cyberbullying differs from traditional bullying.

6. Talisha felt there was no way out. What other 'ways out' do you think Talisha could have found?

7. How do you think this event changed Talisha's community?

Project

In groups, create a poster that either describes the types of cyberbullying to look out for, or gives advice about what to do if you are being cyberbullied.

Discussion

Discuss how the following behaviours and attitudes form an important part of using social media responsibly: cooperation, rationality, tolerance, freedom, respect.

Key vocabulary

cyberbullying

emails

instant messaging (IM)

chatrooms

social networking site

online gaming sites

cyber abuse

intimidate

anonymous

Responsible use of social media

We are learning to:

- demonstrate responsible use of social media.

Unplugging from social media for certain periods during the day may benefit brain development. Research has proven that rapid-paced television programming affects children's ability to focus and complete tasks. However, given the recent onslaught of social media, there is little data regarding social media's effects on brain development.

Parents and children need to recognise that updates and comments create a very intense and fast-paced environment that is similar to fast-paced television programming. A person could conclude that social media might produce similar results in brain function.

Online safety

Once children are old enough to use a computer, cell phones or tablets to access the internet, they must be made aware of the various dangers that exist online. Here are some safety tips.

1. Never share internet passwords with anyone other than parents, experts say.

2. If anyone is harassed or bullied through instant messaging features, or on social media, use the 'block' and 'report' features to prevent the bully from contacting them.

3. If anyone keeps getting harassing emails, delete that email account and set up a new one. Only give the new email address to family and a few trusted friends.

4. Set your accounts to the maximum privacy level. This allows you to choose who can view your profile.

5. Remember that strangers who approach people online aren't always who they say they are, so you should not engage with them at all.

6. Talk to your parents or another adult in charge if anything makes you feel uncomfortable online, while gaming or when using your cell phone.

7. Younger children should not join chat rooms or forums of any kind and must not share pictures and personal information (real name, age, address, phone number, email address) that could potentially be used to invite danger into the home.

Use the 'report' and 'block' buttons to prevent bullies making contact online.

Did you know...?

There was a law introduced in Jamaica in 2017 called the Cybercrimes Act to prevent and punish people committing crimes online.

8. Never, under any circumstance, arrange to physically meet someone you met online.

9. Remember that nothing really 'disappears' from the internet, even if it is deleted. Others may have already screenshotted embarrassing photos or posts and saved them, only for them to reappear later on forums and websites.

10. Do not to let anyone, even friends, take pictures or videos of them that could cause embarrassment or trouble online or offline.

Never share personal details online.

Responsible use of social media includes:

- regular breaks from social media

Taking breaks from social media is important for our mental health.

Activity

In small groups produce a wall display on 'online safety' for your school. Include all of the advice above, use images and text.

- making sure that social media is switched off after a particular time so that your mind can rest before sleeping
- making sure that you stay safe online, not giving away any information about your identity, for example, name, address, telephone or email address
- not speaking to strangers online
- making sure that your profile is not public or viewable.

Exercise

1 Name one benefit of turning social media off for a period of time during the day.

2 What can you do to prevent someone from contacting you on social media?

3 Write 100 words giving advice to young people about being safe online, using examples.

Questions

See how well you have understood the topics in this unit.

1. Define the following terms.

   a) Media literacy

   b) Mass media

   c) Social media

2. 'The World Wide Web was introduced in 1990' is a fact. That is:

   a) a statement based on opinions

   b) a statement made on the basis of observable evidence

   c) a politically motivated message, trying to persuade someone about something.

3. A/An _____ is a negative view of someone or something.

   a) role model

   b) responsibility

   c) stereotype

   d) image

4. Jamaica's Cybercrime Law was introduced in:

   a) 1967

   b) 1984

   c) 2001

   d) 2017.

5. True or False? Facebook is not popular as a social media platform in Jamaica.

6. Correct this statement: Everyone has access to the internet in Jamaica.

7. Explain the difference between fact, opinion and propaganda.

8. Make a list of four safety tips for using social media.

9. Which two of these are stereotypes that are often portrayed in the media?

   a) Being rich is important.

   b) Women are more powerful than men.

   c) How you look is more important than other things.

   d) How you look doesn't matter.

10. Give two examples of ways that new forms of technology can help children learn at school.

11. Name four ways that cyberbullying can take place.

12. What should you do if you are being cyberbullied?

13. Name three ways to use social media responsibly.

14. Find and read a blog or newspaper article and highlight parts of the article that are fact, opinion or propaganda.

15. Imagine that you work for an organisation that works for an online safety group in Jamaica. Write an essay of about 200 words describing your action.

Grade 8 Unit 2 Summary

Communication

In this chapter, you have learned about:

- What it means to communicate verbally and non-verbally
- The explanations for media and medium
- The four main components of the communication process
- The significance of symbols in communicating messages
- What technology and communication technology mean
- The role of the internet and the positive and negative consequences of it.

Mass media

In this chapter, you have learned about:

- What mass media means
- Who has access to information
- The importance of media literacy
- News and the standards associated with it
- The positive impact of mass media on individuals
- The negative impact of mass media on individuals.

Messages transmitted through the media and their impact

In this chapter, you have learned about:

- The differences between facts and opinions
- What propaganda is and its effects
- The influence of news media and social media on the values and attitudes of individuals in society
- The meaning of social media and its impact on individuals and social values
- Cyberbullying as a negative effect of modern communication technology
- The types of cyberbullying
- How to use social media responsibly
- Online safety.

Checking your progress

To make good progress in understanding communication and media literacy, check that you understand these ideas.

Explain and use correctly the term *communication*.

Describe how a person becomes media literate.

Explain the differences and similarities between fact, opinion and propaganda.

Explain and use correctly the terms *transparency* and *cyberbullying*.

Name the social advantages of social media.

Explain the role of social media in decision making.

Explain and use correctly the term *mass media*.

Name three economic advantages of using the internet.

Explain how to stay safe online.

Explain and use correctly the term *media literacy*.

Describe the importance of access to the internet.

Explain how the internet and social media reflect particular images of groups and individuals.

Unit 3: Jamaica's Culture and Heritage: Our Cultural Icons

Objectives: You will be able to: ⟫⟫

What is a cultural icon?
- construct meaning for the terms: cultural icon, cultural identity
- create a list of criteria for selection of cultural icons.

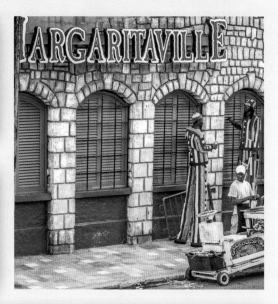

Cultural identity
- identify and describe the elements of culture
- define the relevant terms and concepts: national and Jamaican identity.

Significant historical events that have shaped Jamaican culture
- identify and outline the events in Jamaican history which have contributed to our culture.

Political icons in Jamaica

- outline the life and work of selected cultural icons in Jamaica.

Jamaican cultural icons and their contributions

- outline the life and work of selected cultural icons in Jamaica
- evaluate the contributions of selected persons to Jamaican culture in the areas of music, art, dance, sports and language
- justify how the contribution of these individuals help to create links with the rest of the world
- value the contributions of outstanding individuals locally and in the Caribbean region.

Remembering what is meant by culture, heritage and ancestors

We are learning to:

- define and use correctly the terms culture, heritage and ancestors.

Culture 〉〉

As we have discussed in Grade 7, **culture** is the customs, beliefs, arts and technology of a nation or people.

A culture usually includes:

- religious beliefs and traditions
- language, accent and style of speaking
- beliefs, morals and values
- customs and heritage.

Heritage is features that belong to the culture of a particular society which were created in the past and have a continuing historical importance to that society.

A country's heritage is made up of many different things. Examples from Jamaica include:

- traditions and festivals, such as the Jamaica Carnival
- cuisine, such as jerked chicken
- clothing, such as bandannas
- music and dance, such as reggae
- folklore and literature, such as Brother Anansi
- historical sites, such as The Blue and John Crow Mountains.

Dance styles can be part of a person's culture.

Exercise

1. In your own words define the terms culture and heritage, and gives examples of each.

2. Why do you think that a country's heritage is important?

Project

Create a digital scrapbook of images which represent the culture of Jamaica. These can be images of food you eat at home, buildings in the community, or people engaged in a specific activity or tradition.

Key vocabulary

culture

heritage

multicultural

ancestors

immigrants

cultural

Ancestors ▶▶▶

All countries in the Caribbean embrace many different cultures and people. Every country including Jamaica is a unique and **multicultural** country.

Our **ancestors** are the people from whom we are descended. They are members of our family who lived before us. The ancestors of people who live in your country today come from many different countries.

For example, in Jamaica some people are descended from the Amerindians who first lived on the islands. Others are descended from people who came to live here as **immigrants** later on.

These immigrants came from other Caribbean countries and from Africa, India, China and European countries such as Spain and Britain.

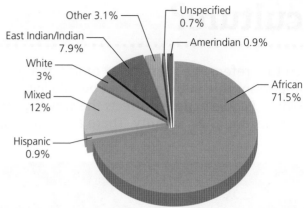

Most people in the Caribbean have East Indian or African cultural backgrounds.

Each of these immigrant groups added to the social, religious, ethnic, linguistic and **cultural** landscape of Jamaica.

The diverse cultural and religious backgrounds of these groups allow for many festivals and ceremonies throughout the cultural calendar year.

Exercise

3 Make a list of the cultural backgrounds in your community. Which cultural group does your family belong to?

4 Read the folk song lyrics on the right. Look up the song on the internet and think about what the words mean. How do they represent Jamaican culture?

5 Read the verse from the Mento style verse, a traditional folk music from Jamaica on the right. Where did this person's ancestors come from?

6 Name six countries from which our Jamaican ancestors came. Find these places on a map of the world.

Dis long time, gal, me never see yu,
Come mek me hol your han.
Dis long time, gal, me never see yu,
Come mek me hol your han.
Peel head John Crow sid upon tree-top
Pick off de blossom,
Mek me hold your han, gal, mek me hol
your han.
                    Folk Song

What are the elements of a culture?

We are learning to:

- identify and describe the elements of culture.

Culture refers to a shared way of life of a group of people. Each element of culture plays an important role in the way that people live, the choices they make and the way they see the world. People's culture affects the way they see themselves and the way that they see other people, and their **identity**. There are many aspects to culture, including the following.

Culture

1. Creative expressions and sports What are the traditions of dance, music, theatre and art in our society? What sports do we enjoy?	**2. What are some of the traditions of our system of education?** What level of education do I expect to reach over my lifetime? What is the level of my parents' education?	**3. Food** What types of food do we eat? How do we prepare the meals and dishes we eat? What meaning do we attach to specific foods?
4. Language What is the main language or languages spoken daily?	**5. Political/social organisation** How do we govern ourselves? What are the traditions carried out in our system of government, conduction of elections and civic duties?	**6. Relationships to family and others** What are the different family types? How do families relate, celebrate and socialise its members? What are some of our family rituals and traditions?
7. Religion How do we worship? What are some of the beliefs we have and rituals carried out when we worship? How does religion influence other aspects of our lives?	**8. Security/protection** How do we protect our communities and families? What are some of the values guiding how our security bodies operate and carry out their duties?	**9. Shelter** How do we design our homes? What factors influence how we design and decorate our homes?

Culture is not fixed, in fact it changes over time and varies from place to place. For example, the types of meals people ate in the past may now be prepared differently. People also create new dishes and modify old ones as they encounter other cultures.

We all belong to the general culture of the society we live in, but not everyone may have same cultural background based on their ethnicity. Once you are descended from a specific ethnic group, your cultural background is ascribed to you. This means you had no choice or control over these aspects of your background. For example, the language your family speaks and the religion they embrace.

As you get older, you may choose to continue embracing the aspects of your background or not. You may also develop new ideas, practices and values. All aspects of our culture are shaped by the people around us including:

- friends
- family
- media/social media
- religious groups
- political groups
- the police/law keepers
- teachers
- the arts, dance, theatre and sports
- the natural environment that you live in.

Project

Your teacher will share some online videos with you about Jamaican culture. Use these as inspiration to make a storyboard for your own video on Jamaican culture.

Project

In groups of ten, mount a class display highlighting at least ten practices carried out or items used by our ancestors. Practices should be clearly described and items labelled, and their uses outlined.

Activity

Describe your own cultural background, drawing on the categories above. Compare your description with the person next to you. Is your culture similar or different to theirs?

Exercise

1 Describe the aspects of your own cultural background, using the headings in the spidergram.

2 Write 100 words describing some of the ways in which culture has changed in Jamaica over the past 100 years, using examples.

Key vocabulary

identity

What is a cultural icon?

We are learning to:

- construct meaning for the terms: cultural icon, cultural identity
- create a list of criteria for selection of cultural icons.

A **cultural icon** can be a symbol, logo, picture, name, face, person, building, or other image. It is recognised easily and represents an object or idea with great cultural significance to a wide cultural group. Cultural icons have a special status in Jamaica as representing and being important to Jamaicans.

People who considered cultural icons are individuals, groups or community activists who are recognised for their significant contributions to our national heritage or the development of Jamaica. These persons would have dedicated their lives and talents in the fields of politics, science, culture (literature, music, dance, arts, and social works) and sports. Above all, they would have served with patriotism and love for their country.

Devon House is a cultural icon.

Cultural identity is the identity of belonging to a particular group of people who all share the same characteristics of that society, for example their ethnicity, history, geography and customs.

Research

Carry out research into cultural icons of Jamaica. Complete the following table:

Type of icon	Example	Explain why this is an icon	
Building			
Image			
Symbol			
Animal			
Plant			
Person			

Exercise

1. In your own words, explain the term cultural icon.

2. Why do you think cultural icons are important to a society?

3. Think about the term 'cultural icon'. Why do you think Usain Bolt is one of our greatest cultural icons?

Case study 1

The Hope Botanical Gardens

The Hope Botanical Gardens, also known as the Royal Botanical Gardens is a beautiful Jamaican landmark. These gardens include 200 acres of land in the Liguanea Plains area of St Andrew.

The gardens were established in 1873 on a section of land from the estate of Major Richard Hope. He was one of the original English colonisers who arrived with the invading force of Penn and Venables.

Today the gardens are the largest public green space in the Kingston metropolitan region. There are many rare and exotic species of plants and trees at Hope Botanical Gardens including the Hibiscus elatus (blue mahoe), the national tree of Jamaica.

Research

Carry out research to answer the following question: 'The Hope Botanical Garden is considered to be a part of our cultural identity. To what extent is this true?' Ask your teacher to take you on a field trip or conduct interviews in order to aid in your research.

Case study 2

Emancipation Park

The idea of emancipation is very important in Jamaica's historical background. Emancipation Day in Jamaica is celebrated on 1 August every year to mark the day when Africans in the British colonies of the Caribbean received their freedom in 1834.

To reflect on and celebrate emancipation, Emancipation Park was built and opened to the public in 2002. The park has now become an important landmark in the Kingston area, and is a popular venue for historical and cultural events. The park features three water fountains, beautiful gardens and a range of stonework and statues. At the entrance of the park, a male and female statue can be found, created to represent the freedom and strength of the Jamaican people.

The entrance to Emancipation Park, New Kingston.

Exercise

4 Explain what is meant by a cultural identity.

5 Explain why The Hope Botanical Gardens and Emancipation Park are a part of out cultural identity.

6 Describe a physical cultural icon that you have visited, explaining why it is seen as important.

7 Research a cultural symbol or animal of your choice and write about how and why it can be seen as a cultural icon of Jamaica.

Key vocabulary

cultural icon

cultural identity

What are the criteria for accepting persons as cultural icons?

We are learning to:

- create a list of criteria for selection of cultural icons.

A cultural icon is an object or person that has been identified by members of a culture as representative of that culture. It can be a natural feature of the landscape or a human-made object, such as a building. People can also be recognised as cultural icons.

For an individual to be recognised as a cultural icon in Jamaica that individual would have displayed **qualities** and carried out work that would have contributed in some way to the country's cultural and national development overall.

The achievements of such an individual would have enhanced Jamaica's standing on the world stage and would have generated great pride among the people of Jamaica. Such an individual would be considered a true symbol of who we are as Jamaicans.

Some examples of the actions of cultural icons in Jamaica include:

- exceptional contribution to knowledge, making a new discovery
- contributing to science, such as Dr Thomas Lecky, who was a pioneering cattle breeder who in the 1950s revolutionised how dairy farming was done in Jamaica
- displaying exceptional skills and talent in the sporting field and achieving in a specialised sporting field, locally and internationally, such as Usain Bolt
- some people, through their creative self-expression in areas such as drama, dance and music, have made an impact on their countries, such as Bob Marley in music

- achieving an important political goal such as helping a particular group to have rights, such as voting. An example is Michael Norman Manley who was an advocate of **universal suffrage** in the 1940s
- putting the needs of other people before your own
- expressing the ideas and wishes of Jamaican people
- initiating or taking part in activities that resulted in economic or social improvements in the country.

Usain Bolt represents a life of dedication to Jamaica, hard work and success.

Exercise

1 In your own words, define the term cultural icon.

2 In what areas of society can a cultural icon contribute to?

3 Would you agree that all countries need to have cultural icons? Why?

The characteristics of an icon

In order to be considered a Jamaican icon, some of the following characteristics or features will be present:

- easily recognisable
- represent the qualities and characteristics of the ideal Jamaican
- symbolise dedication to the country
- represent love for Jamaica and patriotism
- reflect particular parts of Jamaican culture that make it unique
- represent parts of Jamaica's history.

> **Did you know...?**
>
> Icon comes from the Greek word eikenai, meaning "to seem or to be like".

Activity

For each of these characteristics, research an icon (object, symbol or person) that represents Jamaican culture. For each, explain how it reflects Jamaican identity, culture or heritage.

Discussion

What characteristics do you think a cultural icon needs to have? Discuss these in your class and make a list.

Research

Carry out research on a cultural icon who lives outside Jamaica. Explain why this person is iconic and what they achieved in their lifetime. Present your findings back to your class.

Michael Norman Manley, a political icon of Jamaica.

Exercise

4 How does Jamaica recognise people who are icons?

5 Give three examples of cultural icons in Jamaica and explain how they demonstrate the characteristics of an icon.

Key vocabulary

qualities

universal suffrage

Cultural identity

We are learning to:

- define the relevant terms and concepts: national and Jamaican identity.

National identity

Identity can be defined as the characteristics, style or manner that define a person and how that person is recognised. Identity can be influenced by personal choice but also by society through existing social and cultural situations.

National identity is the idea of what it means to belong to a particular country, state or a nation. Unlike identity, our national identity is not something we are born with, but instead is a common set of experiences or characteristics that people share.

Often, national identity is carried in shared characteristics such as language, national colours and symbols, the history of the nation, family connections, culture, cuisine, music and heritage. Most countries have:

- a flag, an anthem and a national emblem
- a shared history and culture
- a currency (the money used in that country)
- national holidays, customs and traditions.

We discussed in Grade 7 that a cultural background includes things that a group of people shares, such as their religion, language, music, traditions, customs, art and history.

Our cultural heritage consists of the cultural traditions that we have inherited from past generations. Together our cultural background and cultural heritage help to create our national identity.

Research

Research either the national flag, anthem or emblem of Jamaica. Find out its history and collect pictures using newspapers, magazines and the internet.

Lignum Vitae is the national flower of Jamaica.

Exercise

1. Write your own definition of national identity. Add this to your portfolio.

2. Name three ways in which national identity can be shown by a country.

3. What are some examples of national identity of people in Jamaica?

Caribbean identity is the idea of what it means to belong to the Caribbean region. The characteristics of this include:

- *ethnicity* – people from shared racial and ethnic groups tend to have shared characteristics, which often cut across geographical borders
- *religion* – the religious groups people belong to give a strong basis for identity
- *history* – the shared history of the Caribbean, including enslavement indentureship and colonialism
- *politics* – people identify themselves based on political allegiances and these are often passed from one generation to the next
- *geography* – people identify themselves based on their place of birth
- *language* – the languages people speak, including creoles and dialects
- *customs* – social, religious, national holidays, etc.
- *arts* – the music, dance, stories, theatre and art.

Many of these characteristics which are found across the Caribbean can be found in Jamaica. For example:

- *ethnic groups* – the population is made up of a mix of people from many different ethnic groups. More than 80% of the population is either from East Indian or African ancestry, with the rest of the population made up of European, Chinese and mixed backgrounds
- *religion* – people practise a wide range of religions. Catholicism is the most popular form of Christianity. The next largest religious groups are Hindus, Pentecostals, Evangelical and Full Gospel Christians
- *language* – although the official language is English, Jamaicans speak Jamaican creole as well. Some people speak other languages, such as patois, Spanish, Hindi and Chinese.

Discussion

Discuss your understanding of the differences between national and Caribbean identity.

Steelpan players, Port of Spain, Trinidad

Exercise

4. Write your own definition of Caribbean identity.

5. Name three ways in which Caribbean identity can be shown. Give an example of each.

6. Describe what you can see in the picture and which features of Caribbean identity it shows.

Key vocabulary

Caribbean identity

ethnicity

Significant historical events that have shaped Jamaican culture

We are learning to:

- identify and outline the events in Jamaican history which have contributed to our culture.

The history of Jamaica is complex and rich. In this section, we explore some of the key events in Jamaica's eventful history by looking at a **timeline** of important dates in its history. Historical events play a powerful role in shaping Jamaica as we know it today. It is also important that we learn from these historical events, and remind ourselves of the past so that similar issues are not faced again in the future.

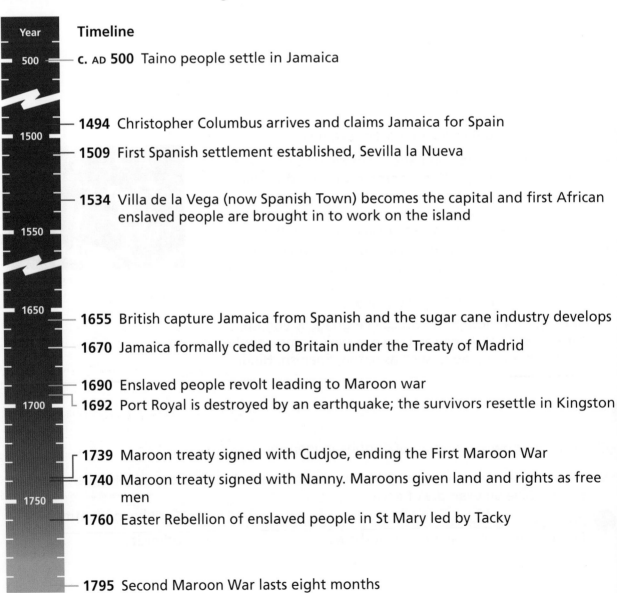

Year	Timeline
500	**c. AD 500** Taino people settle in Jamaica
1500	**1494** Christopher Columbus arrives and claims Jamaica for Spain
	1509 First Spanish settlement established, Sevilla la Nueva
1550	**1534** Villa de la Vega (now Spanish Town) becomes the capital and first African enslaved people are brought in to work on the island
1650	**1655** British capture Jamaica from Spanish and the sugar cane industry develops
	1670 Jamaica formally ceded to Britain under the Treaty of Madrid
1700	**1690** Enslaved people revolt leading to Maroon war
	1692 Port Royal is destroyed by an earthquake; the survivors resettle in Kingston
	1739 Maroon treaty signed with Cudjoe, ending the First Maroon War
1750	**1740** Maroon treaty signed with Nanny. Maroons given land and rights as free men
	1760 Easter Rebellion of enslaved people in St Mary led by Tacky
	1795 Second Maroon War lasts eight months

1800

1808 Slave trade Abolition Bill is passed

1831 Enslaved people revolt led by Sam Sharpe, who is hanged in 1832
1838 Emancipation of enslaved people

1850

1865 Morant Bay Rebellion led by Paul Bogle; Bogle and George William Gordon are hanged
1866 Jamaica becomes a crown colony

1900

1872 National capital is moved from Spanish Town to Kingston

1914 The Universal Negro Improvement Association (UNIA) is founded by Marcus Garvey

1938 Widespread rioting due to unemployment and the slow rate of political progress; the People's National Party (PNP) is founded by Norman Manley

1950

1943 The Jamaica Labour Party (JLP) is founded by Alexander Bustamante
1944 The first election is held under Universal Adult Suffrage
1958 Jamaica becomes a member of the Federation of the West Indies but withdraws three years later

2000

1962 Jamaica gains independence from Britain with Alexander Bustamante elected prime minister
1988 Jamaica is badly hit by Hurricane Gilbert
2006 Portia Simpson-Miller becomes Jamaica's first female prime minister
2013 Jamaica is given a loan by the International Monetary Fund of $1 billion to help with large debt payments

Did you know...?

The original inhabitants of Jamaica, the Tainos named the island Xaymaca, which meant "land of wood and water".

Exercise

1 Pick three events in this timeline which seem most significant in shaping the culture of Jamaica today.

2 Write a paragraph explaining why you picked each of these events.

Discussion

Which events beyond Jamaica, in the Caribbean may have shaped the culture of the people of Jamaica?

Key vocabulary

timeline

Political icons in Jamaica

We are learning to:

- outline the life and work of selected cultural icons in Jamaica.

There are many individuals who have contributed to Jamaica's political development. Some of these have been accorded the honour of National Hero, the highest award given to any Jamaican. We will explore some of these individuals and the work they did in this section.

National Heroes

The honour of the **Order of National Hero**, established in 1969, is the highest decoration awarded by the government of Jamaica. It may be given only to Jamaican citizens for "services of the most distinguished nature" to the nation.

Heroes are given the title "The Right Excellent" and allowed to wear the insignia of the order. This is a medallion of a fourteen-pointed gold and white star, surrounding the Jamaican coat of arms and the motto of the Order: "He built a city which hath foundations."

Seven people have now been awarded the honour of National Hero: Sir Alexander Bustamante, Marcus Garvey, George William Gordon, Norman Manley, Queen Nanny, Samuel Sharpe and Paul Bogle.

Paul Bogle

c.1822–1865

A Baptist deacon, Bogle led protests to end poverty and social injustice. After marching on the Morant Bay courthouse on 11 October 1865, he was captured and hanged, but this paved the way for more just treatment of people in the courts. There is some debate about whether the illustration here is actually Bogle himself.

Sir Alexander Bustamante

1884–1977

Bustamante began working to better the pay and working conditions of people when Jamaica was still a British colony. In 1943 he founded the Jamaica Labour Party, and in 1962 he became the first Prime Minister of independent Jamaica.

Marcus Garvey

1887–1940

Marcus Mosiah Garvey did much political work to improve people's lives. He founded the Universal Negro Improvement Association in 1914 and the People's Political Party in 1929.

George William Gordon

c.1820s–1865

George William Gordon was a businessman, politician, and landowner. He sold his land cheaply to free enslaved people and ensure they could earn a fair income. A friend of Paul Bogle, he was charged with complicity in the Morant Bay Rebellion of 1865, illegally tried, and executed.

Norman Manley

1893–1969

Norman Washington Manley founded the People's National Party in 1938 and was an advocate of universal suffrage. This was introduced to Jamaica in 1944.

Queen Nanny

c.1686–c.1740s

"Nanny of the Maroons" or "Queen Nanny" was a leader of the Maroons at the beginning of the 18th century. Not much is known about her life, but she is documented as a great military strategist against the British during the First Maroon War from 1720–1739.

Howard Cooke

1925–2014

Howard Cooke was a founding member of the People's National Party in 1938, elected to Parliament in 1958, and a Government Senator 1962–7. He was a member of the Joint Independence Constitution Committee, who drafted the Constitution in 1962 and became Governor-General in 1991. He was knighted in 1994 for services to Jamaican politics.

Other Heroes

Samuel Sharpe

1801–1832

Samuel Sharpe was the leader of the 1831–2 "Christmas Rebellion". He encouraged enslaved people to refuse to work on Christmas Day unless they were treated better and their pleas for freedom considered. The rebellion was quashed and Sharpe was hanged.

Edward Seaga

1930–2019

Edward Seaga was elected to the Legislative Council in 1959. Seaga was a member of the Joint Independence Constitution Committee who drafted the Constitution in 1962. Seaga was Minister of Development and Welfare from 1962 to 1967 and became Jamaica's fifth Prime Minister after the 1980 elections.

Exercise

1. Place the political icons in chronological order (date order) from the oldest.
2. Why do you think that there is only one female national political icon?
3. Carry out research into the political icon that you know least about. Write out 10 facts about their life and achievements.

Discussion

Which political icon made the greatest contribution to Jamaican culture, in your view?

Key vocabulary

Order of National Hero

Jamaican cultural icons and their contributions

We are learning to:

- outline the life and work of selected cultural icons in Jamaica
- evaluate the contributions of selected persons to Jamaican culture in the areas of music, art, dance, sports and language.

Music 》

Music is an important part of life in Jamaica. Many famous musicians were born in Jamaica including Bob Marley, Jimmy Cliff, Grace Jones, Dawn Penn and Lee "Scratch" Perry. Chronixx (born Jaymar Rolando McNaughton) is a young, versatile artist who received a Grammy award nomination in 2017 for his debut album, *Chronology*.

Singers and musicians in Jamaica have all contributed to cultural development. They have made the rest of the world more aware of Jamaican life and culture. This in turn has encouraged more people in Jamaica to take up music.

Profile

Bob Marley (1949–1981), Jamaican singer, songwriter, guitarist

- With his group the Wailers, he became famous for reggae music in the 1960s, 1970s and 1980s.
- The music became popular internationally and Marley sold more than 75 million copies of his songs.
- In 2004, Rolling Stone magazine placed him at number 11 in their list of the 100 greatest artists of all time.
- He is one of the bestselling artists of all time.

Bob Marley made a huge contribution to reggae music.

Profile

Marcia Griffiths (born 1949), singer

- Griffiths is one of the most successful female singers and most consistent hit makers.
- After five decades of being an international star on the world stage, she remains the most enduring presence in Jamaican music.
- Her solo career began in the 1960s. In the 1980s her single *Electric Boogie* began a worldwide dance craze 'The Electric Slide' that endures to today.
- In the 1970s Marcia became a member of 'I Threes', Bob Marley and the Wailers' backing singers, a harmony trio.

Marcia Griffiths, the famous singer.

The arts covers a wide range of subjects, including fine art, sculpture, writing and much more.

Profile

Marlon James (born 1970), novelist

- Marlon James is a Jamaican-born novelist who has written four novels, most recently, *Black Leopard, Red Wolf*, and before that *A Brief History of Seven Killings*, which won several awards, including the 2015 Man Booker Prize (Marlon James is the first Jamaican to win this prize).

- He teaches literature at St Paul, Minnesota, USA and is currently working on his next novel.

Marlon James is a famous Jamaican novelist.

Profile

Laura Facey Cooper (born 1954), sculptor

- Facey was trained at the Jamaica School of Art.
- In 1999 she completed 'Earth to Earth' for the University of Technology, a life-size mahogany carving of 'Christ Ascending' in 2000 for the St Andrew Parish Church, and the 2003 unveiling of 'Redemption Song' at the ceremonial entrance to Emancipation Park. 'Their Spirits Gone Before Them,' an installation of a 16-foot cottonwood canoe housing hundreds of the miniature resin figures of the 'Redemption Song' monument, is also an important work.
- Facey was awarded the silver Musgrave Medal in 2006 and in 2010.
- Facey was awarded the Order of Distinction in 2014.

Redemption Song, created by Laura Facey Cooper.

Exercise

1. What contribution has Laura Facey Cooper made to the cultural development of Jamaica? Find a picture of a sculpture of hers and show it to your class to support your answer.

2. How has Marlon James helped people in Jamaica appreciate and enjoy their own culture?

3. Discuss some of the people you have learnt about in this section. As a class, make a list of some people who have made an outstanding contribution to sports and arts in Jamaica.

4. Pick a person from the list who particularly inspires you and find out more about their life. Write a three minute PowerPoint about their life and achievements to share with the rest of the class.

Jamaican cultural icons and their contributions

We are learning to:

- evaluate the contributions of selected persons to Jamaican culture in the areas of music, art, dance, sports and language.

Dance

Dance is an important part of Jamaican culture. One traditional form is Bruckins, a member of the **creolised** group of traditional dances, which has a unique mixture of African and European influences. It was performed in the past mainly to celebrate the Anniversary of Emancipation from Enslavement on 1 August 1838. There are other forms of traditional dance such as Burru, Quadrille, and Tambu and Dinki-mini among others.

The Quadrille dance was introduced in Jamaica in the 19th century. It originally came from France, and the dance was developed in Jamaica to three styles – the Ballroom Style, the Camp Style and the Contra Style.

The Ballroom Style shares some of the features of the French and English ballroom style from in the 18th and 19th centuries. The Camp style includes African elements and is known as the Afro-Jamaican version of the Ballroom Style. The Contra Style is performed only to Mento music.

Quadrille was a popular dance after Emancipation, and was performed at weddings, family gatherings and tea parties. Nowadays, it is usually performed as part of the annual festival celebrations, as it is seen as an important part of our cultural heritage.

Discussion

Have a discussion in your class about the contributions made to Jamaican identity and development by sports people and people from the arts. How do you think that they contributed specifically?

The quadrille dance.

Profile

Bogle (22 August 1964 – 20 January 2005), born Gerald Levy.

- Also known as Bogle Dancer, Mr Bogle, Father Bogle, and Mr Wacky, was a Jamaican Dancehall star, dancer and choreographer.
- Bogle is recognised as part of the foundation and as an icon inside of dancehall culture.
- Bogle created more dancehall moves than any other figure, he is best known for creating the Bogle dance which is named after him.

Did you know...?

The stage name, Bogle, is a reference to Paul Bogle a National Hero of Jamaica.

Profile

Ralston Martin "Rex" Nettleford (1933–2010), dancer, choreographer and scholar.

- Professor Rex Nettleford was the co-founder of Jamaica's National Dance Theatre Company (NDTC).
- He made a remarkable contribution to his country, the Caribbean region and the world.
- Born in a village in Trelawny, Nettleford gained his formal education by winning a series of scholarships, including a Rhodes scholarship in 1953, to Oriel College, Oxford University.
- As soon as he had finished his studies, he returned to Jamaica and rejoined the University of the West Indies (UWI). He worked there for 40 years and was vice-chancellor from 1998 to 2004.
- Nettleford argued for people of African descent to empower themselves through education and social and economic development. He believed that black identity was strengthened through looking inward at the values drawn from people's African ancestry.
- Nettleford received numerous awards throughout his life, including the Order of Merit from the Jamaican government.

Ralston Martin 'Rex' Nettleford.

A Jamaican dancehall.

Sports

As well as Bolt and Fraser-Pryce, there have been several other recent Jamaican sprinting stars. Yohan Blake is the second fastest 100m and 200m sprinter of all time (behind Bolt). Veronica Campbell Brown won the Olympic gold; the first Caribbean woman to win this event and also retain the title.

Some of the world's most famous cricketers have come from Jamaica, including Michael Holding, Courtney Walsh and Chris Gayle.

Activity

Carry out research into a traditional Jamaican dance style. Find out what significance it has and how it contributes to Jamaica's national heritage. Present your findings back to your class.

Key vocabulary

dance

creolised

Exercise

1. What contribution has dance made to the culture of Jamaica?

2. Explain why dance is an important part of Jamaican cultural heritage.

3. What contributions have Usain Bolt and Shelley-Ann Fraser-Pryce made to the cultural development of Jamaica? Write 100 words to explain.

4. How do sports people contribute to the development of Jamaica?

5. Research two more examples of sports people who have made a contribution to Jamaica and explain how they have done this.

Jamaican cultural icons and their contributions

We are learning to:

- evaluate the contributions of selected persons to Jamaican culture in the areas of music, art, dance, sports and language.

Athletes ⟩⟩

Athletes head up the list of famous men and women who have made significant contributions, not only to their sports, but also to the culture, social and economic development of Jamaica.

Profile

Usain Bolt (born 1986)

- Said to be the fastest human ever, Bolt is the only sprinter to have won the 100m and 200m at three consecutive Olympic Games – in 2008, 2012 and 2016.
- From 2009 to 2015 (apart from the 100m in 2011) he won consecutive World Championship gold medals in the 100m, 200m, and 4 x100 m relay.

Usain Bolt is the fastest runner to date.

Profile

Shelley-Ann Fraser-Pryce (born 1986)

- Nicknamed the 'pocket rocket' Fraser-Pryce won medals for the 100m at three consecutive Olympics – gold in 2008 and 2012, and bronze in 2016, the first woman to have done this.
- She has won a number of awards in Jamaica and was named the IAAF World Athlete of the year in 2015.

Shelley-Ann Fraser-Pryce, known as the 'pocket rocket'.

Language ⟩⟩⟩

Patois is a speech, or language, which is used to describe non-standard versions of a local language. Jamaican patois is an English based language, which includes West African influences and is spoken by the majority of people on our island. It originated in the 17th century when people were transported to Jamaica began to adapt the English language. Jamaican patois is mostly used as a spoken language, but it is also used in reggae music, as it has its own rhythmic pattern. The Jamaican patois has a hugely significant role in our country's ethnic and cultural identity.

Profile

Festus Claudius 'Claude' McKay (15 September 1889 – 22 May 1948)

- A Jamaican writer and poet. He wrote five novels.
- He helped raise people's awareness of the Jamaican language of patois, by including it in his writing.
- His novels included *Home to Harlem*, *Banjo*, *Banana Bottom*, *Gingertown*, *Harlem Glory*.
- McKay also authored collections of poetry (including *Songs of Jamaica* and *Harlem Shadows*), a collection of short stories, two autobiographical books (*A Long Way from Home* and *My Green Hills of Jamaica*), and a non-fiction
- In 1977, the government of Jamaica named Claude McKay the national poet and posthumously awarded him the Order of Jamaica for his contribution to literature.

Festus Claudius 'Claude' McKay.

Profile

Louise Bennett-Coverley (7 September 1919 – 26 July 2006)

- A poet, writer, educator and folklorist, she preserves her poems and other works in Jamaican patois.
- Bennett-Coverley appeared in the films *Calypso* and *Club Paradise* produced a series of radio monologues, and hosted the children's TV program *Ring Ding*.
- Her books have included *Anancy Stories And Poems In Dialect*, *Laugh with Louise: A pot-pourri of Jamaican folklore* and *Jamaica Labrish*.
- She's won numerous awards including the Order of Jamaica, the Jamaican Order of Merit, and member of the Most Excellent Order of the British Empire.

Louise Bennett-Coverley.

Exercise

1. Why is it important to recognise outstanding individuals in sports, the arts, literature and language?

2. How have Jamaicans also contributed to science, in Jamaica and beyond? Carry out research into two important scientists in Jamaica.

3. Can you think of any other categories of important people that should be recognised in Jamaica's heritage?

Research

Carry out some research into the history and roots of patois and explain why it is an important part of Jamaican culture.

Key vocabulary

patois

Global recognition

We are learning to:

- justify how the contribution of these individuals help to create links with the rest of the world
- value the contributions of outstanding individuals locally and in the Caribbean region.

How individuals have contributed ⟩⟩

We have seen how individuals have contributed to the development of Jamaica. Now we will explore the contribution of individuals from the broader Caribbean region, exploring how they have created links with the rest of the world.

The Mighty Sparrow performing in New York, 13 August 2006.

Project

On the internet, research **three** of the outstanding personalities listed and list three or four ways they have helped create links with the rest of the world, as well as in the Caribbean. You should write 100–150 words. For example:

The Mighty Sparrow

As the Mighty Sparrow, Slinger Francisco has entertained audiences across the world for over 40 years as the unrivalled 'King of Calypso'. He has performed in Europe, Asia, Africa, North and South America and across the Caribbean islands.

In 1977, he was awarded the honorary title Chief of the Yorubas in Nigeria. In 1986, New York Mayor Ed Koch declared 18 March as 'The Mighty Sparrow Day'. In 1987, he was awarded an honorary doctorate degree, Doctor of Letters, from the University of the West Indies.

His reputation as the 'King of Calypso' reached worldwide. He was an 11-time winner of the Trinidad Calypso Monarch (the first one in 1956, the last in 1992) and he also won the 'King of Kings' competition, in which he defeated other calypso singers from across the world.

Choose from:

Politics: Michael Norman Manley, Dr Eric Williams

Economics: Sir Arthur Lewis

Sports: Hasely Crawford, Sir Viv Richards

The arts: Dr Derek Walcott, Peter Minshall

Entertainment: Toots Hibbert, Lee Perry

Science: Professor Courtenay Bartholomew; Thomas Lecky

Activity

Use the internet to research the accomplishments of two outstanding Caribbean personalities and their achievements at international level.

How we should value the contributions of outstanding individuals

How should we **value** the **contributions** these individuals have made to the Caribbean and beyond?

Their contributions vary because of the different fields that they have been involved in. They have all helped to contribute by improving society, winning medals and trophies for their country, making artistic statements, helping or making contributions to different sectors of the economy.

All of these personalities have had a positive social or economic effect on the Caribbean, as well as helping to make people feel good about themselves and their country.

- Dr Eric Williams contributed much of his life to politics and dedicated his life to creating a better society for the people of Trinidad.
- Sir Arthur Lewis dedicated his whole life to the study of economics and was able to help countries such as Jamaica, Trinidad, Ghana and Nigeria.
- Sportsmen like Hasely Crawford and Sir Viv Richards were dedicated to being the best in their sports and gained worldwide recognition for doing so.
- Peter Minshall knew from a very early age that he wanted to be an artist, which led eventually to him designing the opening ceremonies of the 1992 and 1996 Olympic Games.
- Toots Hibbert and Lee Perry both became internationally recognised for their music, and today their records are still influential to new generations of reggae fans.
- Professor Courtenay Bartholomew dedicated his medical career to the research into serious illnesses, which has had a worldwide impact.

Discussion

As a class, discuss which of the personalities has contributed the most to the region and why you think this is. Remember, each personality has excelled in different areas.

Activity

In pairs, plan a role-play between a TV reporter and a famous Caribbean personality. Write a list of questions you would ask during the interview about the achievements of the individual, and then act it out in front of the class.

Exercise

1. Which personality has contributed globally to
   a) economics b) sport c) entertainment d) medicine?

2. Choose one of these Caribbean personalities and write 100 words on how they have contributed both to the Caribbean and globally.

3. In groups, research texts and photos, and any other relevant illustrations, about any two Caribbean personalities. Create a 'wall of fame' in your classroom.

Key vocabulary

value

contribution

Questions

See how well you have understood the topics in this unit.

1. A _____ can be a symbol, logo, picture, name, face, person, building, or other image. It is recognised easily and represents an object or idea with great cultural significance to a wide cultural group.

   a) naturalisation

   b) hero

   c) culture

   d) cultural icon

   e) famous Jamaican

2. A/An _____ is a person who came before us, our relatives from the past.

   a) hero

   b) ancestor

   c) leader

   d) immigrant

3. The Order of National Hero was established in:

   a) 1988

   b) 1984

   c) 1969

   d) 2001.

4. True or False? Christopher Columbus arrived in Jamaica in 1594.

5. Correct this statement: The Spanish arrived in Jamaica after the British.

6. Outline three characteristics of an icon.

7. Write a short definition of the following terms:

   Culture

   Heritage

   Cultural icon.

8. Make a list of icons in Jamaica from the arts, including dance, art and language.

9. Which two of these are icons in language?

   a) Festus Claudius

   b) Usain Bolt

   c) Louise Bennett-Coverley

   d) Bob Marley

10. Give two examples of ways that icons are recognised in Jamaica.

11. Explain how icons inspire others.

12. Imagine that you work for an organisation that supports and inspires people to aim to become the very best in their field of interest. Write a paragraph of about 200 words describing your action.

13. Match the events to the dates.

   1) British capture Jamaica from Spanish and the sugar cane industry develops

   2) Port Royal is destroyed by an earthquake

   3) Easter Rebellion of enslaved people in St Mary led by Tacky

   4) Emancipation of enslaved people

   5) Jamaica becomes a crown colony

   6) The Jamaica Labour Party (JLP) is founded by Alexander Bustamante

   7) The first election is held under Universal Adult Suffrage

   a) 1866

   b) 1760

   c) 1943

   d) 1655

   e) 1944

   f) 1838

   g) 1692

14. Explain the achievements of Howard Cooke and Edward Seaga and their contributions to Jamaica.

Grade 8 Unit 3 Summary

Cultural icons

In this chapter, you have learned about:

- The meaning of culture and heritage
- How culture is shaped by ancestors
- The contribution of ancestors to the culture and heritage of Caribbean countries
- What the elements of a culture are
- What a cultural icon is
- The criteria used to recognise a person as a cultural icon
- The characteristics of an icon.

Cultural identity and the impact of history

In this chapter, you have learned about:

- What national identity means
- What Caribbean identity means
- The characteristics of Caribbean identity that are like those of Jamaican identity
- The significant historical events that shaped Jamaican culture.

The contribution of Jamaican icons

In this chapter, you have learned about:

- The national heroes as political icons in Jamaica
- Cultural icons who have contributed to music
- Cultural icons who have contributed to the arts
- Cultural icons who have contributed to dance
- Cultural icons who have contributed to sport
- Regional icons and their contribution to the Caribbean and the world
- How individuals have contributed to the development of Jamaica
- How we should value the contributions of outstanding individuals.

Checking your progress

To make good progress in understanding Jamaica's culture and heritage and our cultural icons, check that you understand these ideas.

Explain and use correctly the term *cultural icon*.

Outline factors used in deciding who is cultural icon of Jamaica.

Outline the characteristics of a national icon.

Explain and use correctly the terms *heritage* and *ancestors*.

Name the key stages in the history of Jamaica.

Explain the role of history in shaping Jamaica today.

Explain and use correctly the term *cultural heritage*.

Name three ways in which cultural icons are remembered and celebrated.

Explain why it is important to remember cultural icons.

Explain and use correctly the term *global citizenship*.

Describe the characteristics of culture.

Explain the contributions of the icons of Jamaica to the country.

End-of-term questions

Questions 1–6 >>>

See how well you have understood the ideas in Unit 1.

1. Explain why nationalism is important, giving examples.

2. Explain the difference between nationalism and citizenship.

3. Match the following terms with the correct definitions below.

   a) sovereignty

   b) development

   c) nation

   d) patriotism

   i) To value and feel loyal to your country

   ii) The authority of a country to govern itself

   iii) Economic growth in a sustainable way

   iv) A country or region that identifies itself as a separate entity

4. Briefly describe Vision 2030.

5. What are the four goals of Vision 2030?

6. Explain how each goal of Vision 2030 is being implemented or will be implemented.

Questions 7–10 >>>

See how well you have understood the ideas in Unit 2.

7. Explain what is meant by media literacy, using examples.

8. Give two examples of the positive effects of social media, communication and technology on the lives of people.

9. Outline some of the negative effects that mass and social media may have on individuals.

10. Give two examples of the recommendations you would make to encourage responsible use of social media.

Questions 11–14 〉〉〉

See how well you have understood the ideas in Unit 3.

11. Explain how Jamaica became a multicultural society.

12. Why is it important to accept and understand that people have different cultural backgrounds? Write a short paragraph to explain.

13. Explain why you think it is important to remember our national icons, past and present. Give at least three examples of icons in your answer, from different fields.

14. Create a spidergram showing:

    a) what culture is made up of

    b) Jamaica's important symbols and cultural icons
    c) Jamaica's past political icons
    d) Jamaica's present icons.

Unit 4: The Caribbean Landscape and Its Influence on Human Activities

Objectives: You will be able to:

The topography of the Caribbean

- explain the formation of the three types of rocks and give examples
- describe the characteristics of the main rock types found in the Caribbean
- describe major physical landforms: rivers, coastlines and beaches
- name and locate major landforms, land use and settlement patterns in Jamaica and the Caribbean.

Population distribution and density

- define terms and concepts related to population distribution and density
- interpret choropleth maps and dot maps
- account for the relationship between topography and settlement, communication and economic activities
- account for the population distribution and densities of Caribbean countries.

Negative effects of human activities on the landscape

- assess the different ways in which human activities impact the landscape
- propose solutions to remedy the negative impact of human activities on the landscape.

Map work

- define and use correctly the terms map, cartography and cartographer
- identify basic map features; explain the uses of maps; sketch and draw maps
- develop skills in observing geographic features; explore the immediate environment
- build competence in ICT
- distinguish between easting and northing grid lines and give grid references
- distinguish between large scale and small scale
- construct and interpret linear scales on a map
- use the cardinal points to give and follow directions.

Types of rock

We are learning to:

* explain the formation of the three types of rocks and give examples.

Key concepts

Rock is the solid mineral material forming part of the surface of the earth exposed on the surface or underlying the soil.

Topography is the study of the shape and features of land surfaces. The topography of Jamaica could refer to the surface shapes and features themselves, or could be a description of those features. There are many topographical features found in the Caribbean. These affect the landscape and the human activity that takes place there.

Soil is the upper layer of earth in which plants grow, a black or dark brown material typically consisting of a mixture of animal and plant remains, clay, and rock particles. Soil is essential for the growth of plants and is home to many types of life.

Soil is essential for the growth of plants.

Activity

Use the internet to research the term 'rock cycle', then draw a diagram to show the cycle.

Rock types

There are three main rock types found on the Earth: **igneous**, **sedimentary** and **metamorphic**. These rocks have been formed by different processes, known as the rock cycle – a process through which the major rock types change into each other.

Obsidian is an igneous rock.

Igneous rocks

Igneous rocks are the most common rock type found on Earth. They are formed when magma from the mantle cools beneath the surface or rises to the surface, then cools and hardens. This hardened rock is called igneous rock.

There are many examples of igneous rock, such as basalt, granite and obsidian. All igneous rocks contain crystals. Some rocks will have larger crystals than others – the size of the crystals depends on how quickly the magma cooled. The larger the crystal, the slower the magma **solidified**.

There are two types of igneous rock: **intrusive** and **extrusive**. Intrusive igneous rocks form inside the Earth – most igneous rocks are formed beneath the surface. These rocks have much larger crystals, because it has taken a long time for the rocks to cool.

Did you know...?

* Igneous rock can change into sedimentary rock or into metamorphic rock.
* Sedimentary rock can change into metamorphic rock or into igneous rock.
* Metamorphic rock can change into igneous or sedimentary rock.

Granite is the most well-known intrusive igneous rock. Extrusive igneous rocks form above the surface. These rocks generally form from a volcanic eruption as lava is ejected from a volcano. These rocks have much smaller crystals, because they have cooled very quickly. Examples of extrusive igneous rocks are obsidian, pumice and basalt.

Sedimentary rocks 》

Sedimentary rocks form under the seas and oceans. They form when the sediment that was **transported** (carried) by rivers into the seas and oceans is **deposited** (laid down) at the bottom of the sea floor. This sediment includes things such as sand and pieces of rock – even the skeletons of sea creatures.

The weight of the sediment squeezes down on the previous layer and squeezes out the water (**compaction**), which allows salt crystals to form. The crystals help to glue all the sediments together, forming a rock (**cementation**).

This process will continue with more layers added on top, so sedimentary rocks have very clear layers. Examples of sedimentary rock include limestone, chalk and sandstone.

Metamorphic rocks 》》》

Metamorphic rocks are formed by pressure or heat under the surface. They are formed from igneous and sedimentary rocks. Igneous and sedimentary rocks can be heated under the surface of the Earth. This will usually happen if they are close to rising magma. These rocks do not melt, but change chemically.

The heating of these rocks puts them under huge pressure and the crystals become arranged in layers. There are many examples of metamorphic rock. Slate and marble are possibly the most well known. Slate is formed from shale; marble from limestone.

Prehistoric fossil found in sedimentary rock.

Slate is a metamorphic rock.

Activity

Your teacher will give you 10 different rocks. Identify the different rock types.

Key vocabulary

rock

topography

soil

igneous rocks

sedimentary rocks

metamorphic rocks

solidified

intrusive rock

extrusive rock

transported

deposited

compaction

cementation

Exercise

1. Name the three main rock types.

2. Explain how igneous rocks form.

3. If an igneous rock has large crystals, has it cooled quickly or slowly?

4. What are the two types of igneous rock. How do they differ?

5. Give examples of both types of igneous rock.

The topography of the Caribbean

We are learning to:

* describe the characteristics of the main rock types found in the Caribbean.

The types of landscape, or topography of the Caribbean region is rich and varied. They include:

* Mountainous areas such as the Blue Mountains in eastern Jamaica, the Morne Diablotins in central Dominica, the Pitons in St Lucia, and the Northern Range in Trinidad. These are all covered with dense, evergreen rain forests and cut by fast flowing rivers.

* Hilly countryside, such as the high plateau of central Jamaica, or the islands of St Kitts, Antigua, and Barbados. There the hills rarely rise above 600 metres and are more gently sloped than the high mountains.

* Coastal plains are found around the edges of the hills and mountains, with their greatest areas on the southern or western sides of the mountains. Active volcanoes exist in Dominica, St Vincent, and St Lucia, and there are crater lakes formed by older activity in Grenada.

* All the islands of the Caribbean have rugged coastlines with innumerable inlets fringed by white or dark sands (depending on the layers of rock beneath them) of varying texture. The beaches of Negril, Jamaica, and Grand Anse, Grenada, have fine-textured white sands that extend for nearly eleven kilometres each.

Blue Mountains, Jamaica.

Hills in St Kitts.

Boiling Lake, Dominica.

Types of rock in the Caribbean

There are many types of rock in the Caribbean. These fall into the three main groups.

Type of rock	Example found in the Caribbean
Igneous	Granite, gabbro, pegmatite, basalt
Metamorphic	Marble, schist, serpentinite
Sedimentary	Sandstone, limestone, and shale

A section of coastline of Jamaica.

Cockpit Country

The Cockpit Country is located in the north west of Jamaica and is one of the most difficult to access parts of the island. It lies on an area of severely weathered limestone called **karst**, which is commonly found in the Caribbean.

Hiking area in the karst landscape at Alberfeldkogel in the Höllengebirge group.

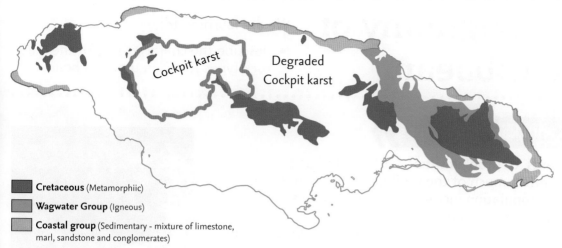

Cockpit karst

Degraded
Cockpit karst

■ **Cretaceous** (Metamorphiic)

■ **Wagwater Group** (Igneous)

□ **Coastal group** (Sedimentary - mixture of limestone,
marl, sandstone and conglomerates)

Rock types in Jamaica.

Karst is the term given to the distinctive landscape of and
features found in limestone regions; these features can be
found both on the surface and underground, such as sinkholes,
caves, stalactites, stalagmites. The landscape has a distinctive
series of round shaped hills, leading into valleys.

Sinkholes are a cavity in the ground caused by water erosion which
provides a route for surface water to disappear underground.

Karst is formed in rocks such as **limestone**. Limestone is a hard
sedimentary rock, composed mainly of calcium carbonate
or dolomite, used as building material, for example in the
making of cement.

Limestone.

Famous features in Cockpit Country include:

- the Windsor Caves which includes thousands of stalactites
and stalagmites, and has huge open underground caverns
such as Big Room, Royal Flat and Squeeze Up
- Marta Tick Cave, which includes the Jamaican flower bat
and the Jamaican fig-eating bat
- It is a major water resource for western Jamaica, and is also
the source for a number of rivers including the Montego
River and Great River.

Did you know?

According to the
Ministry of Transport
and Mining, 70% of
Jamaica's total surface
coverage consists of
limestone.

Exercise

1 What are the characteristics of each rock type?

2 a) Carry out some research into the characteristics of
rocks that are found in the Caribbean:

i) granite **ii)** talc **iii)** limestone.

b) For each of these rocks comment on the colour,
texture, form and if they are hard/soft.

3 Look at the map and write about how igneous,
metamorphic and sedimentary rock types are
distributed across the island.

Key vocabulary

karst

limestone

The topography of the Caribbean

We are learning to:

• describe the characteristics of the main rock types found in the Caribbean.

Problems with karst landscapes ⟩⟩

Karstic hazards, or problems that exist due to karst landscapes, affect much of the Caribbean mostly in rural areas. As the population increases, so does urbanisation (where people move into towns and cities), and as roads, cities and town are developed, karstic hazards are becoming more common. These include:

1. **seasonal drought**, which disrupts water supplies, particularly in rural areas where groundwater resources are poorly developed and residents depend on rainwater and springs

2. **seasonal flooding**, particularly that associated with tropical storms, causes property damage and human death, injury and displacement; ground surface subsidence and collapse threaten developing buildings and roads, houses and livestock

3. human impacts, which include quarrying, bauxite mining, extracting groundwater, urbanisation, agricultural development and tourism. Groundwater contamination is a serious human-induced hazard, particularly associated with the bauxite industry.

A sinkhole.

> **Did you know...?**
>
> Less than 10% of the karst area in Jamaica is within protected areas.

Discussion

Think about what you know about the topographical features of the Caribbean. What are the topographical features where you live?

Exercise

1 Explain what a karst landscape is.

2 Describe limestone.

3 What are karstic hazards and how might they affect people's lives?

4 Carry out research into the sinkholes in the Caribbean. Write down 10 facts about them.

Bauxite deposit area in Jamaica.

Bauxite ⟩⟩⟩

One important topological feature of the Caribbean is Bauxite. Bauxite is a clay type of rock that is the raw material that aluminium is made of. It consists largely of aluminium but also contains iron and oxygen, known as iron oxides. Bauxite is reddish-brown, white, tan, and tan-yellow. It is dull to earthy in appearance and can look like clay or soil.

One of the many uses of bauxite.

Aluminium is a silvery-white, lightweight metal. It is soft and malleable and is used in a huge variety of products, including cans, foils, kitchen utensils, window frames, beer kegs and aeroplane parts.

Case study

The commercial production of aluminium began only in the last decade of the 19th century. However, World War II greatly increased the demand for aluminium, During the 1940s exploration and development work was carried out in Jamaica, mainly by Alcan, Reynolds and Kaiser.

Jamaican bauxite was not used during the war, but these three North American companies (Alcan, Kaiser and Reynolds) came to the island to survey, buy land, and set up operations. Reynolds began exporting bauxite from Ocho Rios in June 1952, and Kaiser followed a year later from Port Kaiser on the south coast. Alcan built the first alumina processing plant near its mines at Kirkvine, Manchester, and in early 1952 began shipping alumina from Port Esquivel. This was the beginning of the industry in Jamaica.

After the first shipment of bauxite from Jamaica in 1952, production increased rapidly, and by 1957 Jamaica had become the leading bauxite producer in the world, with a production capacity of nearly 5 million tonnes of bauxite per year, almost a quarter of all the bauxite mined in the world in that year. Alcan built a second refinery in Jamaica at Ewarton, St Catherine, in 1959. In 1961, a fourth company, Alcoa, began mining bauxite in the island.

The production of alumina also increased, especially after the mid-1960s. By 1968, Alcan had brought the capacity of its two refineries to more than 1 million tonnes a year. In 1969 a new plant was commissioned at Nain, St Elizabeth, by Alpart, then a consortium of Kaiser, Reynolds and Anaconda, another U.S. company. In 1971, Revere Copper and Brass opened the island's fourth alumina plant at Maggotty, St Elizabeth. Two years later, Alcoa, which had been shipping unprocessed bauxite since 1963, built the country's fifth refinery, at Halse Hall, Clarendon.

Source: adapted from Jamaica Bauxite Institute website

A former bauxite mining site.

Alcoa, a bauxite mining company.

Key vocabulary
....

karstic hazards

seasonal drought

seasonal flooding

Exercise

5   Visit the Jamaica Bauxite Institute website and visit their 'Bauxite/Aluminium' page, then their 'Statistics' page. Describe the first three graphs you see.

6   What are the benefits of bauxite mining to the economy?

7   What is aluminium used for?

8   Provide three advantages of aluminium as a metal.

Physical landforms and features in the Caribbean

We are learning to:

- describe major physical landforms: rivers, coastlines and beaches
- name and locate major landforms in the Caribbean.

Rivers

Rivers are found all over Jamaica. The Rio Minho, which is the longest river in Jamaica at 92.8 km (57.7 miles). Other rivers can be short, such as Hectors River.

Whatever the length, rivers have the same characteristics. The start of a river is known as the **source**, which is often in hills and mountains. Rivers flow down hills and mountains with the gradient becoming less steep, often over flat plains, towards the sea, where they end. This is known as the **mouth** of the river. The longest river on a Caribbean island is the river Cauto on Cuba, which is 370 km.

Rio Minho.

In Jamaica, rivers are mainly used for irrigation and domestic purposes. They are also used for tourism (cruise trips) and for transporting trees to the ports for exports.

Coastline

A **coast** or **coastline** is an area of land beside the sea. All island countries have coastlines that form a perimeter around the land. Jamaica is completely surrounded by sea. Jamaica's coastline is about 248 km long. The coastlines of some Caribbean countries are very rugged and do not have as many beaches as others. These instead have cliffs and other erosional landforms. Along some coastlines there can be wetlands bordering the sea. Coastlines have various features.

- A **cape (headland)** is a narrow piece of land extending into the sea, and formed by glaciation, volcanoes but mainly by erosion of the land either side of the headland.
- A **bay** is an area where the coastline curves inland. Some of a coastline's best beaches are found in bays. The land beside the coast is not always flat. In fact, a lot of the coastline has tall cliffs beside the sea.
- **Beaches** are popular holiday destinations. There are often hotels, guesthouses, campsites and parks near sandy beaches, as they attract many tourists. Many of Jamaica's most beautiful and most famous beaches are on the north coast. These include Doctors Cave Beach, Las Cuevas Bay and Blanchisseuse. These beaches offer various activities, such as swimming, snorkelling and surfing. On the east coast are beaches such as Winnifred Beach. Jamaica's longest beach is Seven Mile beach, near Negril.

> **Did you know...?**
>
> Some of the beaches in Jamaica offer visitors the chance to enjoy activities such as kayaking and turtle-watching.

Mountains ▶▶▶

Mountains are large features that are usually very steep, over 600 m in height, and form a peak at the top. Mountains can be isolated or they may be part of a group called a mountain range.

In Jamaica, the central mountain chains, formed by igneous and metamorphic rocks, stretch across the island from west to east. Nearly half of Jamaica's land area is 300 m above sea level. The highest peak is in the Blue Mountains in the east at 2 256 m.

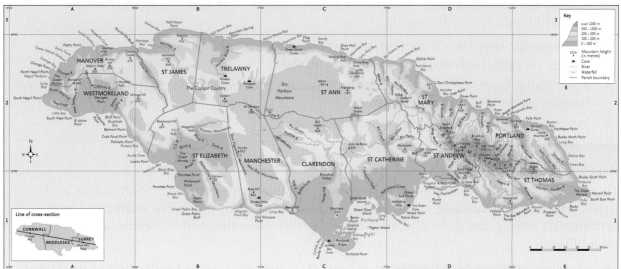

Exercise

1. Which is the longest river in Jamaica?

2. What is the term used for where a river starts?

3. Explain the difference between a cape and a bay.

4. What economic activity do the beaches in Jamaica attract?

5. Use the map to answer the following questions.

   a) On which coast of Jamaica is Orange Bay.

   b) To which mountain range is the Morant River closest to?

   c) Name three bays on the northern coast of Jamaica.

   d) Name a river in Jamaica.

6. Choose a beach that you have visited. Make a poster inviting tourists to this beach. On your poster, describe the natural features (for example, sand, bay) and list some activities that people can do there.

Parish	Peaks
Clarendon	Bull Head 848 m
Hanover	Dolphin Head 545 m
Manchester	Mount Denham 986 m
Portland	Blue Mountain Peak 2256 m
St Andrew	Catherine's Peak 1541m
St Ann	Albion 841 m
St Catherine	Juan de Bolas 836 m
St Elizabeth	Malvern 725 m
St James	Kempshot Hill 564 m
St Mary	Mount Telegraph 1301m
St Thomas	Macca Sucker 1335 m
Trelawny	Cockpit 748 m
Westmoreland	Orange Hill 641 m

Key vocabulary

river
source
mouth
coast/coastline
cape/headland
bay
beach
mountains

Land use in Jamaica

We are learning to:

• name and describe different settlement patterns in Jamaica.

Features of the human environment

The **human environment** refers to an area where humans live and work. The human environment contains the following:

• **settlements:** these are places where people settle down and live, including cities, towns, villages, hamlets, boroughs and counties
• agriculture: forms of agriculture include sugar cane, rice, cocoa, coffee, coconuts, market gardening and dairy farming
• industry: industrial estates and large factories.

Settlements

Thousands of years ago all that people looked for in a settlement was food, water and shelter. Settlements became larger if they were able to offer more. For example, some settlements were good defensive sites because they were situated somewhere safe, such as on a hill.

• The smallest type of settlement is a **hamlet**. A hamlet is just a small number of houses. All settlements start off as hamlets.
• A **village** is bigger than a hamlet, with a population of several hundred to several thousand people. Hamlets and villages are found in rural areas.
• **Towns** are larger than villages and are generally built up areas that have large populations.
• **Cities** are the largest type of settlement and have the highest number of buildings and people living there. Many cities and towns have rivers running through them. For example, The River Minho runs through the town of Frankfield.
• **Capital cities** are where the government of that country is located. They don't have to be the largest city in the country. Kingston is Jamaica's largest city and the capital.

Settlement patterns

The term **settlement pattern** refers to the shape of a settlement. Houses tend to be built close together at first and then, as the village grows, it grows into one of three patterns.

Linear settlement patterns are settlements where houses and buildings are built in lines. This might be along a river, which shows that the river was the main reason for the settlement to be built there. It might be along a road, where the road predates the settlement, so people have chosen to build there because this area most likely has good communications. In Jamaica, linear settlements along roads are the most common types of settlement pattern.

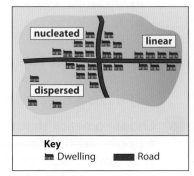

Settlement patterns.

Nucleated settlement patterns are where the houses and buildings are grouped closely together. The houses and buildings are generally clustered around a central point, such as a church, village green or town square. All sizes of settlements may follow a nucleated pattern. In Jamaica, nucleated settlements traditionally formed around areas of fertile land. Newer nucleated settlements tend to be grouped together if there are good communication links close by or where there are good amenities.

In **scattered** and **dispersed** settlements, the houses and buildings are spread far apart over a large area (the words scattered and dispersed both mean 'spread apart'). They are generally just individual buildings, so they do not form a specific settlement. These settlement types are found in mountainous and hilly regions of the country, such as in the Blue Mountains area of Jamaica. It is difficult to build on hilly land, so large settlements tend not to be built here.

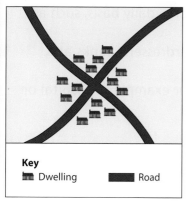

Key
🏠 Dwelling ▬▬ Road

A nucleated settlement.

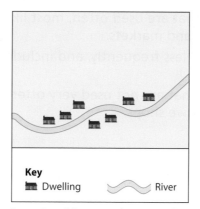

Key
🏠 Dwelling 〰️ River

Examples of linear settlements – the first shows a settlement built around two roads, the second by a river.

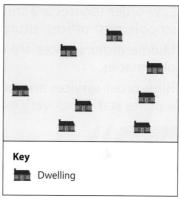

Key
🏠 Dwelling

A dispersed settlement.

Activity

Do you live in a village, town or city? What other villages, towns and cities, and other settlements, are close to where you live? Trace a map of Jamaica and add these places to the map.

Exercise

1. Explain, in your own words, the term *settlement pattern*.

2. What type of settlement pattern do you have where you live?

3. Talk to an older person (such as one of your grandparents) about the community where he or she grew up. What form of settlement was it? Ask the person why he or she thinks that particular form of settlement was established.

Key vocabulary

human environment

settlement

hamlet

village

town

city

capital city

settlement pattern

linear settlement

nucleated settlement

scattered/dispersed

Land use in Jamaica

We are learning to:

- identify and locate examples of human land use on a map of Jamaica.

Services ⟩⟩

Services are public utilities and amenities that are provided for settlements where people live. The number of services that are found in an area depends on the size of the settlement. Services can be divided into low-, middle- and high-order services.

- Low-order services are those that are used often, most likely on a daily basis, such as schools, post offices, churches and markets.
- Middle-order services are used less frequently, and include hairdressers, banks and pharmacies.
- High-order services are those that are not used very often – for example, a hospital or a police station, or very expensive shops.

Recreation ⟩⟩⟩

Recreational facilities are services or places where people go to enjoy themselves or visit as tourist destinations. Most settlements have some form of recreational facility, even if it is just a park. However, the main ones are found in large towns and cities.

- Museums such as The National Gallery of Jamaica in Kingston are examples of recreational facilities. These are very popular with tourists, so they are located in cities, as this is probably where tourists will stay.
- Major sporting venues are most commonly located in the largest settlements. Jamaica has some excellent sporting venues, such as Independence Park in Kingston and Montego Bay Sports Complex.
- Emancipation Park and Independence Park are two examples of large parks found in urban areas.

Agriculture ⟩⟩⟩⟩

Farming is an important human land use. There are two main types of farming:

- **livestock farming** is the rearing of animals such as sheep, cattle, pigs and hens
- **arable farming** is the growing of crops, such as sugar, coffee, cocoa, rice, bananas and paw paw.

As in many countries, farming in the Caribbean is becoming less important. In 2019, 16.4% of the Jamaican population was employed in agriculture and it counts as 7.5% of the country's income overall.

Industry ⟩⟩

Land is also used for industry. There are three main types of industry.

- **Primary industries** are those that involve extracting natural resources. Mining is a primary industry in the Caribbean, as is the extraction of oil, gas, limestone and bauxite.

- **Secondary industries**, otherwise known as manufacturing industries, are those that are involved with making things. Examples are rum, cement, metal, paper and chemical products.
- **Tertiary industries** are service industries that sell goods or provide a service.

Key vocabulary

services
recreational facilities
livestock farming
arable farming
primary industries
secondary industries
tertiary industries
communications

Exercise

1 Explain the differences between low-, middle- and high- order services, and give examples.

2 Why do you think we need recreational facilities?

Communications 》》

In geography, the term **communications** refers to transport facilities, such as roads, railways, ports and airports. If a country is well connected, it is said to have good communications. Cities have far better transport facilities than villages, because they have more people who need them.

Jamaica has good road networks. There are four primary A-roads and 15 secondary B-roads. Minor roads are found in the rural areas. These roads are generally no more than dirt tracks and connect the villages and hamlets in rural Jamaica. Railway systems are less well developed in the Caribbean. There are no public railway networks in Jamaica. In October 1992 public rail transport services finally stopped operating in Jamaica, although private industrial lines continue to operate in part today. There are a number of ports and airports in the Caribbean. There are five major ports in Jamaica. They are in Montego Bay, Ocho Rios, Falmouth, Port Antonio, and Kingston. Our two international airports are in Kingston and Montego Bay.

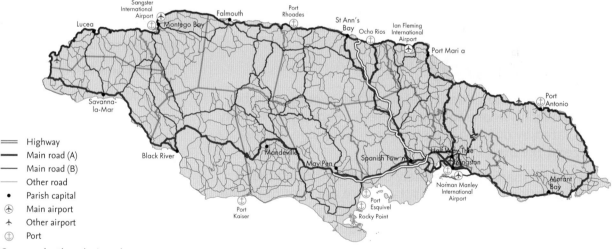

Communications in Jamaica.

Exercise

3 Look at the map and answer the following questions:

a) If you drove east from Ochos Rios, which town would you reach?

b) Where in Jamaica are the airports located?

c) Where in Jamaica would you catch a ferry?

Population distribution and density

We are learning to:

- distinguish between population distribution and population density.

In geography, we use different terminology when studying a specific topic. The topic of population has many new concepts that we need to understand.

Population

The word **population** refers to the total number of people living in a specific geographic area at a particular point in time. When we talk about population, we might refer to the population of a village, town, city, country or the world.

Census

A **census** is a way of collecting population information of a country. This is a questionnaire that is given out by the government every 10 years to every household in the country. Censuses ask questions regarding how many people live in the house the age of every household member and each person's occupation. The government uses the information to find the population of the country.

Population density

The term **population density** refers to the average number of people living in one square kilometre. Population density is calculated by dividing the number of people in an area by the size of the area.

Areas can be sparsely, moderately or densely populated. A high population density means that there are a lot of people living per square kilometre, while a low population density means there are few people living per square kilometre.

Did you know...?

The population of the 15 CARICOM members in July 2016 was as follows:

Antigua and Barbuda 96 286

The Bahamas 377 000

Barbados 286 000

Belize 383 071

Dominica 71 625

Grenada 111 454

Guyana 779 004

Haiti 11 123 176

Jamaica 2 934 855

Montserrat 5 267

St Kitts and Nevis 52 441

St Lucia 181 889

St Vincent and the Grenadines 110 210

Suriname 575 991

Trinidad and Tobago 1 389 858

Exercise

1. In your own words, explain the difference between population density and population distribution.

2. What is a census? How often does one take place?

3. What is the difference between a sparsely, moderately or densely populated area?

4. How is population density calculated?

We work out the population density so that we can understand how well populated an area is. This allows us to compare one area with another.

Population distribution

Population distribution refers to how the population is spread out. Population distribution is described as dense or sparse.

We know the world has a population of approximately 7 billion people. However, these people are not evenly spread out across the world. Some counties, such as China and India, have approximately 1 billion people each. Other countries have much fewer people. Jamaica has a population of approximately 3 million.

Urban and rural

Urban areas are built-up areas such as towns and cities, which have many shops and services. They tend to have a lot of people living there, with moderate and high population densities.

Mumbai, is the most populous city in India. In 2017, its population was estimated to be 22 million.

Rural areas are villages and hamlets with not many services. These settlements have few people living there and therefore have low population densities.

Project

Carry out a project to learn about the population of the region where you live, or another region in the Caribbean that you know well. Follow these steps:

1. Choose a region to study.

2. Make a glossary of words related to population. These are the aspects of population that you are going to research.

3. Do some online research. Find out about the population of your region. Learn about:

   - the total population
   - the population density
   - the population distribution.

4. Write two paragraphs about the population in your region.

Key vocabulary

population

census

population density

population distribution

urban areas

rural areas

Choropleth and dot maps

We are learning to:

- define terms and concepts related to population distribution and density
- interpret choropleth maps and dot maps.

Choropleth maps ⟩⟩

A **choropleth map** is a type of map that uses colour to show data, such as the population density of an area or country. In the map below, each country is coloured according to population density, and the darker the colour, the denser the population. A choropleth map can be a very effective way of comparing areas and countries.

The disadvantages of using this type of map are:

- it can be difficult to interpret, as it might be hard to distinguish between similar shades
- they give the false impression that abrupt changes occur at the boundaries of shaded areas, where quite often the change is more gradual
- they are often unsuitable for showing total values, for example, the map below does not give any indication about the total population of a country.

Key vocabulary

choropleth map

dot map

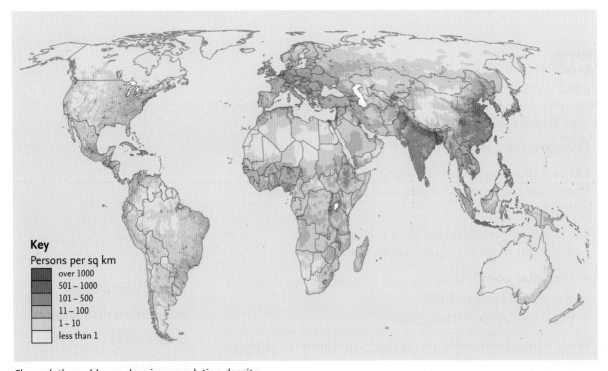

Key
Persons per sq km
- over 1000
- 501 – 1000
- 101 – 500
- 11 – 100
- 1 – 10
- less than 1

Choropleth world map showing population density.

Dot maps ▸▸▸

A **dot map** is a type of map that can be used to show population distribution and population density. Each dot symbol represents a certain number. In the map below, 1 dot = 2 000 people.

There are many advantages of using dot maps to show population distribution. They can be used to compare population patterns within a country or between countries. They are easy to interpret by counting the number of dots.

The main drawback of using dot maps is that they can be quite time-consuming to construct.

When making a dot map, there are a couple of things that need to be considered. First, you must think about the size of the dot and what value the dot will have. Using many small dots to represent smaller values can be more effective than using fewer larger dots.

4.8

Activity

In the previous lesson you carried out a project about population distribution in the region of a country of the Caribbean region or where you live. From the data collected in that project, make a dot map to show the population distribution in your region.

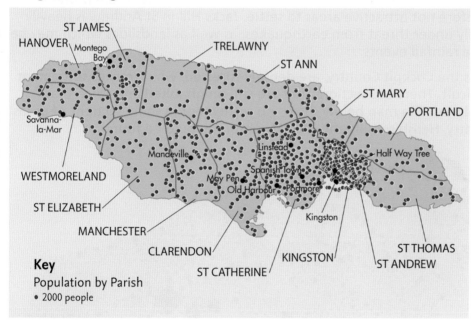

Dot map of Jamaica.

Exercise

1. How do choropleth and dot maps show data?

2. Make a table showing the advantages and disadvantages of using choropleth maps and dot maps.

3. Look at the dot map and answer the questions:

   a) Where in Jamaica is there the greatest and least population density and distribution?

   b) Why do you think those areas have the greatest population density and distribution?

   c) Comment about the population density and distribution in another Caribbean country.

Relief and settlement: population distribution in Jamaica

We are learning to:

* account for the relationship between topography and settlement, communication and economic activities.

Relief plays a major role in determining where people settle and how population is distributed.

Mountainous and hilly terrains ⟫

Areas that are mountainous and hilly tend to have lower populations than flatter areas. This is mainly because hilly land is difficult to build on. Some of these areas may have hard rocks that are difficult to excavate when building homes, some have poor soils which makes farming difficult and some are prone to hazards such as landslides due to faulting. These rugged areas also usually lack or have limited amenities. The nature of these areas means settlement will be scattered or dispersed. Many parts of the Blue Mountains are prone to landslides and are therefore not attractive areas to settle. Jacks Hill in St Andrew is heavily faulted and is continually under threat from earthquakes, as well as landslides which may be triggered during intense rainfall events.

Some hilly areas, such as the Cockpit Country, are densely forested, which makes settlement and other activities difficult. There are sections that are still uninhabited and some that have not been fully explored. The map below shows no settlement in some sections of areas where the Cockpit Country, Hellshire Hills and Blue Mountains would be found.

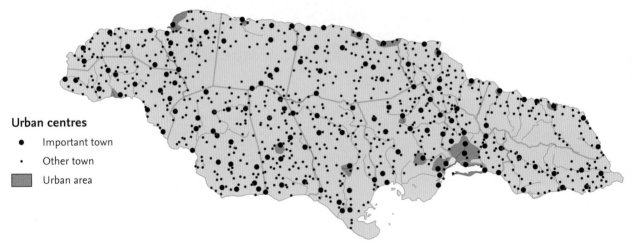

Urban centres
* Important town
* Other town
▪ Urban area

The physical features of Jamaica affect the way that the land is used.

Wetlands ⟫⟫

Some areas in Jamaica are less well populated, because they have a harsh environment that is not attractive to people or features that making setting up settlements difficult.

Similarly, wetlands, are places that are regularly flooded with fresh, brackish or salty water. Wetlands are often found on the coast, on coastal plains or on near-shore islands.

They are also known as swamps (when they have more trees) or marshes (more grass). One of the most common types of wetland in Jamaica is the mangrove wetland, which is found along coasts, coastal rivers, around ponds, lagoons and on small islands (cays). These are almost impossible to build on and therefore discourage settlement.

Coastal areas >>>

Coastal areas are more densely populated in the Caribbean. This is because the land tends to be flatter around the coast and is easier to build on. The climate is also more hospitable. The map shows how Jamaica's population is spread out.

The majority of Jamaica's parish capitals are coastal towns (except Mandeville, Spanish Town, May Pen and Half Way Tree). This means it was much easier to establish these main towns in these areas and people are more attracted to these settlements due to the services they offer. There are other coastal towns such as Ocho Rios and Negril that are of great significance in Jamaica as resort towns and attract large numbers of people to settle there.

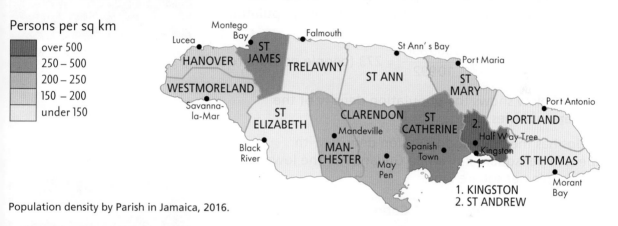

Population density by Parish in Jamaica, 2016.

Parish	Population (2016, est.)
St Andrew	580 626
St Catherine	522 057
Clarendon	248 087
Manchester	192 178
St James	185 985
St Ann	174 473
St Elizabeth	152 074

Parish	Population (2016, est.)
Westmoreland	145 854
St Mary	115 045
St Thomas	95 087
Kingston	90 184
Portland	82 771
Trelawny	76 099
Hanover	70 374

Population by Parish.

Exercise

1. Consider the distribution of towns in Jamaica. Look back in the unit and explain why you think the population is distributed the way it is.

2. If you were planning to build a new town in Jamaica, where would you build it? Explain your reasons.

Key vocabulary

relief

101

Relief and settlement in the Caribbean

We are learning to:

- calculate the population densities of Jamaica and other Caribbean countries
- account for the population distribution and densities of Caribbean countries.

Calculating population density

Population density is calculated by dividing the population by the size of the area:

$$\text{Population density} = \frac{\text{Population}}{\text{Area}}$$

Jamaica has a population of approximately 3 000 000 and an area of 10 992 square km. So, to work out the population density:

$$\text{Population density of Jamaica} = \frac{3\,000\,000}{10\,992} = 273 \text{ (people per square km)}$$

Barbados has a population density of 638.

The table below shows the population density of the Caribbean countries.

Barbados has the highest population density with 638 people per square km, while Guyana has the lowest, with 4 people per square km.

Country	Density
Antigua and Barbuda	195
The Bahamas	25
Barbados	638
Cuba	102
Dominica	96
Dominican Republic	220
Grenada	300

Country	Density
Guyana	4
Haiti	409
Jamaica	273
St Kitts and Nevis	192
St Lucia	270
St Vincent and the Grenadines	259
Trinidad and Tobago	264

Guyana has a population density of 4.

Reasons for the differences in population densities

There are many reasons why some Caribbean countries are more densely populated than others. If we look at two Caribbean countries in more depth, the reasons should become clear.

The landscape of Barbados is made up mainly of gently sloping plains and rolling hills; compared to other Caribbean islands which are quite mountainous, Barbados would be described as flat. The most dense area in Barbados is found in the parishes of St Michael and Christ Church which are both lowland areas between 0–100m; the least dense areas are found in those parishes with relatively higher terrains (highest point is 340m). These include parishes such as St Thomas and St John. The majority of towns, including the capital Bridgetown, are found on the lowland areas and along the coastline.

There are several reasons why Barbados has a high population density.

- It has an appealing climate. It has a tropical monsoon climate, which means it has two seasons, one of which is wet. It doesn't experience too many natural disasters, such as hurricanes.
- A good climate means productive agriculture. Tobacco, cotton, ginger and sugar cane have been grown on Barbados and exported across the world.
- Barbados has large cities and towns such as Bridgetown and Oistins. The country is very small and is very well connected.
- Barbados is a rich country. It is ranked as the 53rd richest country in the world, and its people enjoy a moderate **standard of living**, with good services and amenities. This has attracted a lot of **migration** over the years. Barbados continues to receive many immigrants today from countries such as Syria and Lebanon.
- Historically, Barbados has had a problem with its high birth rate, which means lots of babies were born. This has led to an unusually high population for such a small country.

Guyana's landscape is charactised by four distinct regions: the hilly region, the interior savannah region, the forested highlands and the low coastal plains. More than 90% of the population lives on the low coastal plains which are relatively fertile but only consist of about 5% of the entire land area. Settlements are also strongly influenced by the Berbice and Demarara rivers.

Guyana, on the other hand, has the lowest population density of all the Caribbean islands. There are several reasons for this:

- More than 80% of the country is covered in tropical forest, which is protected by the government. There are a number of indigenous groups that live inside the tropical forests, but these numbers are low.
- Only 2% of the land is used for agriculture. This is partly because most of the land is forested, but also because the climate is not very suitable for productive farming.
- Guyana is a relatively poor country and the people living in the settlements there have a relatively lower standard of living, particularly those living in rural areas. Not all households are equipped with clean, running water, and **sanitation** is very poor.

Exercise

1. In your own words, explain why Barbados has a higher population density than Guyana. Use a graphic organiser to help you.

2. Look at the table. Put the countries in order according to their population density, from the highest to the lowest. Where is Jamaica?

Key vocabulary

standard of living

migration

sanitation

Relief and economic activities and communication

We are learning to:

- account for the relationship between relief and agriculture, tourism.

Relief and agriculture »

Relief influences the type of agricultural activities that take place. Large-scale agriculture tends to take place on the plains and in some valleys. The plains of Jamaica are found in the south. For example, Georges Plain in Westmoreland, Pedro Plains in St Elizabeth and Vere Plain in Clarendon all have large sugar estates, as do Luidas Vale and the Nassau Valley.

Most banana growing occurs on the east coast of Jamaica, where the conditions are most suitable. Areas that have thin soils, such as mountainous and hilly regions, are not suitable agricultural land, so little or no farming takes place there.

A farmer attends his crops, in Georges Plains.

In other mountainous areas, farming takes place mainly on a small scale due to the steep slopes and rugged terrain, which creates different challenges for farmers. The crops grown on these small farms are mainly cash crops such as yam, potato, cassava, tomato, carrots. One crop grown on medium to large scale in mountainous areas is coffee, and this is due to the climate in these elevated areas, especially the Blue Mountains.

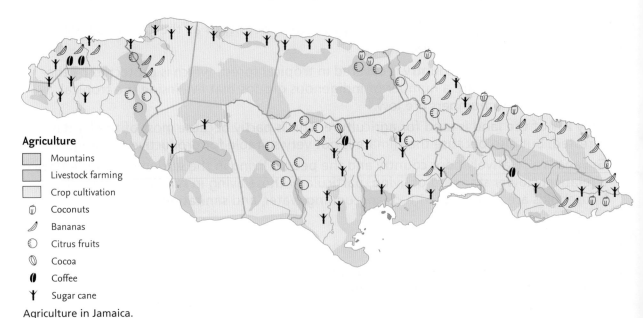

Agriculture

- Mountains
- Livestock farming
- Crop cultivation
- ⓤ Coconuts
- ⫽ Bananas
- ◔ Citrus fruits
- ◍ Cocoa
- ◖ Coffee
- Ψ Sugar cane

Agriculture in Jamaica.

Case study

The Jamaica Blue Mountains provide the perfect conditions to grow one of the world's best coffees! The Blue Mountains have very fertile soil rich in phosphorous and nitrogen, which are perfect for growing the coffee. The coffee is known as Jamaica Blue Mountain coffee, because it is grown in the parishes of Portland, St Andrew, St Mary and St Thomas.

Jamaica Blue Mountain coffee is one of the finest coffees in the world.

Relief and tourism ▶▶▶

Tourist activities in Jamaica take place mainly on the coast, especially in areas that have, or are close to, stretches of white sand beaches. This is the main relief feature influencing the development of resort towns and tourist attractions along the north coast, the western end of the island, and some sections of the south coast. The majority of hotels, especially large, all-inclusive ones, are located in these areas. Many tourist activities, however, take place away from the coast and occur inland. Many of these are influenced by Jamaica's rivers (rafting, waterfalls, river safari), mountains and forests (hiking, sight-seeing, adventure parks).

Mountains and forests (hiking)	Blue Mountain Peak Hike, Hollywell Nature Walk, Mystic Mountain Rainforest Adventure
Rivers and hot springs	Bamboo rafting (Martha Brae River), Dunn's River Falls, Black River safari, Blue Hole Mineral Spring,
Caves	Doctor's Cave Beach, Green Grotto Caves, Windsor Cave

Examples of tourist activities using Jamaica's natural features.

Exercise

1. In your own words explain the term relief, and its role in agriculture and industry in Jamaica.

2. Look at the agriculture map. Explain why so many crops are grown near the coast.

3. Why are the Jamaica Blue Mountains good for coffee cultivation and not banana cultivation?

Relief and economic activities and communication

We are learning to:

- account for the relationship between industry and communication.

Relief and industry

Industrial activities in Jamaica are concentrated on the **plains** or on flat lands along the coast. This is because mountainous areas with steep **rugged** terrains are not suitable for accommodating factories, warehouses and other facilities used in manufacturing and processing. Some industrial activities take place in the interior **valleys**, as shown on the map, and almost all can be found close to a reliable source of water.

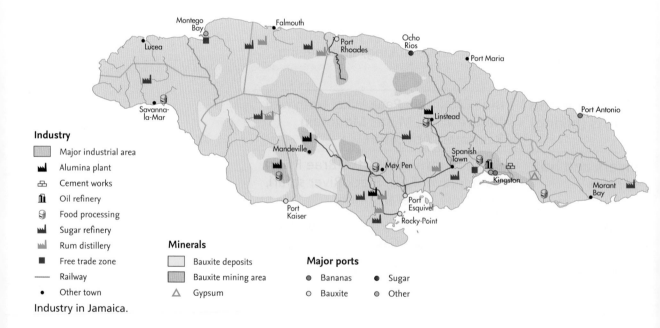

Industry

▨ Major industrial area
▙ Alumina plant
⌸ Cement works
🏛 Oil refinery
🍶 Food processing
▙ Sugar refinery
▙ Rum distillery
■ Free trade zone
— Railway
• Other town

Industry in Jamaica.

Minerals

▢ Bauxite deposits
▨ Bauxite mining area
△ Gypsum

Major ports

● Bananas   ● Sugar
○ Bauxite   ● Other

Relief and communication

Several highways and main roads run through Jamaica, connecting the larger settlements. People want to live near areas that are well connected to cities and towns, so that they are able to access services and amenities more easily.

Where there is greatest population, there are generally good communication systems. Roads in Jamaica are however largely influenced by its physical features. For example, the rivers have already carved routes into the landscape as they find their way to the sea, so many roads follow the path of rivers, which is easier than cutting a route through the mountains. A typical example is the Junction roadway which connects Kingston with the north coast through St Mary by following the route of the Wag Water River. A large section of the Class A Main Road follows the flat land along the coast for all the parishes except St Catherine, Clarendon, Manchester and a part of St Elizabeth; the road runs inland through these parishes as the coastlines are mainly rugged or have wetlands.

There is no road in some parts of the Blue Mountains and the Cockpit Country. Only foot trails allow access to these areas.

Communications

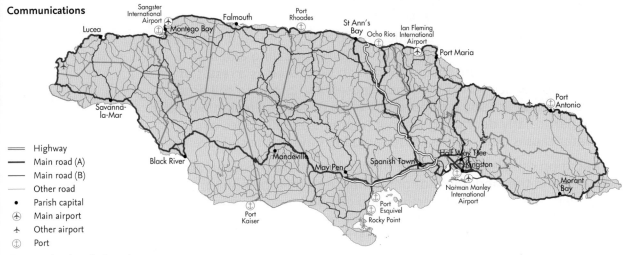

===	Highway
—	Main road (A)
—	Main road (B)
—	Other road
•	Parish capital
✈	Main airport
✈	Other airport
⊥	Port

Communications in Jamaica.

The road network in Jamaica is made up of almost 21 000 km (13 000 miles) of roads, of which over 15 000 km (9 300 miles) are paved. The roads are classified into freeways, primary (or A) roads, secondary (or B) roads, parochial roads and unclassified roads.

Exercise

1. Look at the industry and communications maps. Why do you think major industry is located around the Kingston area?

Key vocabulary

plains

rugged

valleys

Negative effects of human activities on the landscape

We are learning to:

- assess the different ways in which human activities impact the landscape.

As we establish settlements, carry out our various activities and build our communication networks, the landscape can be impacted in a lot of ways. These impacts may range from degraded landscapes to polluted water bodies. These activities all require that we modify the landscape in some way, and in doing so, some negative effects may be seen.

Land degradation and soil erosion

Land degradation when the productive capacity of the land has been reduced and also when it is no longer visually appealing and may be considered an eyesore. Degradation can be caused as a result of deforestation which leaves the land exposed and prone to soil erosion, the process in which soil is removed by wind or water. **Erosion** by water can be particularly degrading when it happens on hill slopes when rainwater causes deep gullies to be carved in land as the soil is removed.

Degradation can also be the result of farming where chemicals are overused and the land does not get a chance to be replenished; the land, over time, may lose its fertility and can no longer support farming activities. Mining requires digging into the earth and hillsides to remove the materials needed. These areas are left scarred and even where attempts are made to refurbish them, they never regain their original character.

Destruction of forests

One of the clearest examples of man's negative impact on the landscape is the destruction of forests. In 1950, tropical forests covered approximately 15% of the Earth's surface. Today, this has been reduced to about 6%. In terms of impact on the landscape, deforestation has led to the deterioration of more than a third of Jamaica's watersheds, drying up streams and rivers.

Other impacts include shortage of water in towns and city areas, loss of animal habitat and loss of plant and animal species. Deforestation results from clearing trees to make way for new settlements, new farmlands, road expansion and also to carry out mining activities.

As much as 320 sq km of forest are lost every day, and in 100 years' time rainforests could be completely destroyed.

The destruction of tropical forests can have detrimental effects on our planet.

Key vocabulary

land degradation

erosion

Case study

The effects of mining

Bauxite mining is the single largest contributor to deforestation in Jamaica. In 50 years of operation the industry has stripped 5 099 hectares land of trees, including some 3 218 hectares of forest. It has also caused the destruction of an undetermined number of hectares by opening access roads into forests. Bauxite is the island's second largest foreign exchange earner after tourism.

The price of those earnings, however, is a high one. Bauxite is extracted using a type of mining which requires the complete removal of vegetation and topsoil. Most affected are the parishes of St Ann and Manchester. Bauxite mining may also have other longer terms – the large scale removal of vegetation may be causing abnormal rainfall patterns and prolonged droughts in some areas.

In recent years Manchester, St Elizabeth and Trelawny, three of the parishes with severely degraded mining areas, have experienced abnormal weather patterns including prolonged droughts and changes in the rainy season. Island-wide, rainfall has decreased by 20% over the last 30 years, dry spells are longer and harsher and the temperature has risen by 1%.

The National Environmental Protection Agency (NEPA) says bauxite mining may have done some environmental damage to the island given the range of interlocking activities. The agency listed dust, which causes health and property damage, and noise pollution as possible environmental problems.

Bauxite companies are required by law to return the land to a productive state, once a mine closes. Land restoration involves filling the cavities and laying some 38 centimetres of topsoil. So far, the land recovered has been suitable for only housing, the planting of food crops such as vegetables and for pasture for cattle.

Pollution >>>

Mining and processing, especially of bauxite, produce waste which cannot be easily discarded. This waste is stored on the land and sometimes causes pollution, even when the precautionary measures are put in place. Water resources (rivers and groundwater) have also been affected by waste from bauxite mining and processing, as well as the waste from sugar factories. Farming, both large and small scale, can result in pollution of water resources also. This stems largely from the pesticides, herbicides and some fertilisers that are used on the farms.

After the excavation of bauxite, red sludge waste is produced during the refining process; red mud lakes now cover many areas of Jamaica where alumina refining has taken place.

Exercise

1. Explain the impact on Jamaica of the destruction of the forests.

2. Create a list of the advantages and disadvantages of mining Bauxite. Give reasons for your answer.

3. Why is the pollution caused by bauxite mining such a problem?

4. How are bauxite extraction companies expected to treat the land after they have finished mining?

Effects of human activities on the landscape: solutions

We are learning to:

- propose solutions to remedy the negative impact of human activities on the landscape.

There are a number of possible solutions for the negative effects of human use of the landscape.

Reduce mining inputs and outputs

Reducing inputs – some mining activities use large amount of land and water for their operations. These can be reduced where possible with application of new technologies and modernised techniques.

Reducing outputs – new technologies and modernised techniques can help reduce waste materials, especially where the potential pollution exists. Recycling should be practised where possible. For example, considerations have been to reusing the red mud waste in making cement or pig iron. Research is also being done on producing zero waste during the processing of the mineral.

Reforestation and selective tree removal

Where trees have been removed to facilitate human activities, they should be replanted, especially in areas that are prone to land slippage and to prevent soil erosion.

Where possible, only selective trees should be removed so that the land is not left completely exposed or a habitat is completely lost. This technique was used by the operators of Mystic Mountain Rainforest Adventure when setting up the park.

Replenishing the environment

- Mining companies sometimes overlook the importance of replenishing the environment. There are simple solutions that can be followed, such as replenishing native soils and grasses, cleaning excess waste, proper waste removal, site inspections and replanting trees and natural forestry.

Discussion

What are the best ways for mining companies to reduce their impact on the environment? Imagine you are in the government, what laws would you create to make sure that these ideas are put into practice?

Forest reserves and protected areas ▶▶▶

These are areas declared by law for **protection** from misuse and to preserve the various resources (such as plants and animals) in the area. This helps to reduce pressure on these areas and, in turn, protect the landscape.

There are a number of government agencies including the Fisheries Division, the Forestry Department, Jamaica National Heritage Trust and the Natural Resources Conservation Authority, who work to protect Jamaica's natural resources.

In total, Jamaica has 249 protected areas including:

Montego Bay Marine Park is a protected area.

- Montego Bay Marine Park, including mangroves, white sand beaches and corals
- Cockpit Country Reserve which has a high diversity of plants and animals
- Negril Marine Park, including mangroves and corals
- Black River Morass, which is a large freshwater system
- Palisadoes Port Royal Protected Areas, which includes the protection of animals such as the American crocodile, the green turtle and the West Indian Manatee
- Hellshire Hills
- Gourie Forest Reserve.

Protecting hill slopes ▶

For farming activities, farmers can practise contour farming or terracing to reduce the likelihood of erosion and keep hill sides intact. For road construction, sound engineering techniques and principles should be applied, such as building retaining walls and ensuring proper drainage in place to prevent collapse.

The Black River Morass is a protected area.

Activity

Imagine you own a mining company. Produce a PowerPoint which shows how you are going to minimise the damage on the local environment during and after mining bauxite in Jamaica. Include images.

Research

Research how some of the agencies in Jamaica help to protect our natural resources.

Exercise

1. Describe how mining companies can 'replenish the environment' once mining has finished.

2. Explain why areas in Jamaica are designated as 'protected'.

3. Write a paragraph discussing the benefits and disadvantages of mining.

Key vocabulary
....

protection

111

What is a map?

We are learning to:

- define and use correctly the terms map, cartography and cartographer
- explain the role of a cartographer
- identify basic map features
- explain the uses of maps.

Uses of maps

What is a map? A **map** is a diagram that shows a particular place on Earth, usually on a flat surface. It may show the whole or part of an area. When you look at a map, you have to imagine you are looking at the ground from directly above it in the air. This is called a **bird's-eye view**. If the map is showing a room or building, this view is called the **floor plan**.

The purpose of a map is to show the relationship between specific features that are represented on the map. A map is usually much smaller than the area it represents, so it is impossible to show every feature of a real place on a map. For this reason, different types of map show different information.

- Political maps show the shapes of countries and their main cities.
- Physical maps show natural features such as mountains, rivers, lakes and deserts.
- Road maps show the roads in an area.
- Tourist maps show tourist destinations, hotels and other places of interest for tourists.
- Resources maps show where particular natural resources occur, or where particular kinds of industry take place.

Cartography is the study of maps, and the art of drawing maps. A **cartographer** is someone who plans and draws maps as their profession.

Activity

Trace a map outline of Jamaica. Use symbols to fill in the main mountains, rivers and cities on each island. Draw a key or legend.

Exercise

1 Match each type of map to the closest description.

Type of map	What it might show
a) physical	**i)** oil fields, crops grown
b) road map	**ii)** borders, capital cities
c) resources map	**iii)** streets, roads, highways
d) political map	**iv)** rivers, lakes, mountains

Activity

Create a map of a local area, such as your school or community and show basic map features.

Maps follow **conventions**. A convention is the usual way of doing something. In mapping, the main conventions are:

- a title – tells you what the map shows
- a map **scale** – shows the relationship between the size of the map and the size of the area in real life
- symbols – give information about real objects
- a **legend**, or **key** – shows what each symbol represents
- a direction arrow that points north
- a border for the map.

Discussion

What is a cartographer's job and why is it important? How do symbols make it easier for cartographers to show things on maps?

Jamaica

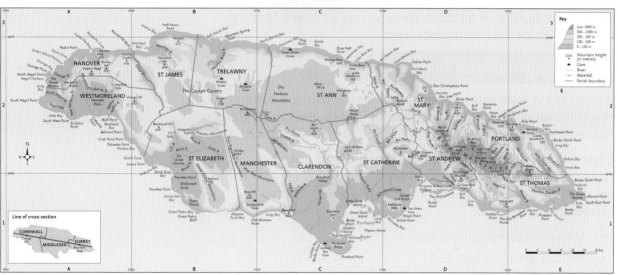

Relief Map of Jamaica.

Exercise

2 Write one example of something represented on the map using the colour blue.

3 Write two examples of things represented by shapes on a map.

4 Draw a symbol for a:

    a) golf course   **b)** bird sanctuary
    c) art gallery/museum **d)** airport.

5 Describe four different ways we use maps.

Key vocabulary

map

bird's-eye view

floor plan

cartography

cartographer

convention

scale

legend/key

Observing and drawing maps

We are learning to:

- sketch and draw maps
- develop skills in observing geographic features
- explore the immediate environment
- build competence in ICT
- extract relevant information from images.

Placing features on a map 〉〉

In order to draw maps, you need to know how to place the map features – title, scale, key, use of symbols, north arrow and a map border. If a map is missing any of these features, it is likely to be an incomplete map.

Observing geographic features 〉〉〉

If you take a walk around your community, you will observe many features, both natural and built. Roads, buildings, trees, hills and other features all form part of your environment.

Observation is another word for looking and noticing. Observing the world around us gives us a good idea of the **location** of the features around us. When we observe our environment, we ask:

- What features can we see?
- Where are they located?
- How are they arranged in relation to each other?

Measuring 〉〉〉〉

It can be difficult to work out the distances between different features. A useful way of measuring is by using **paces**. A pace is a long step. Usually we use one pace to equal approximately one metre. You can pace out your classroom or school grounds to work out the approximate distances between places.

Exercise

1 What do you understand by 'observation'?

2 Why is observation the first step in drawing maps?

3 Work in groups. Find out the dimensions of your classroom. You can measure using paces (large steps), or by using a metre rule, tape measure or any other instrument. Use your measurements to make a sketch of the classroom.

Activity

Work in groups. Each group chooses a particular part of your neighbourhood.

a) Use a camera to take reference photos of the area.

b) Use the reference photos to help you draw a sketch of the area.

c) Present your sketch and photos in a neat, labelled wall display.

Representing your environment

There are a range of techniques you can use to represent your observations – drawn sketches, diagrams drawn on a computer, videos, photographs and spoken or written descriptions.

When you walk around your neighbourhood, you can use sketches, videos, snapshots and written notes to help you capture what you see and how the features are arranged in relation to each other.

There are many different kinds of computer software you can use to help you make maps, for example, scribblemaps.com

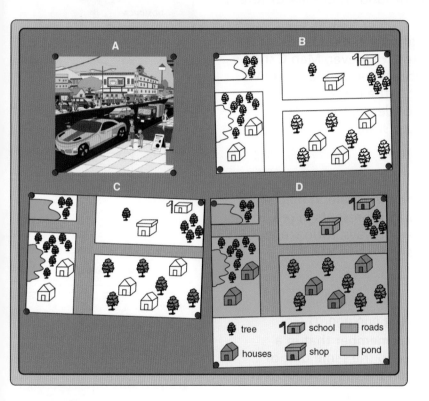

Activity

In groups, collect at least five different kinds of maps. You can use atlases, city road maps, tourist maps or any other maps you can find.

a) Do any of the maps NOT use the basic map features?

b) Are there any maps that do not show north? How do you know where north lies on these maps?

c) Note any differences in the symbols used on each map.

d) What other differences do you notice?

Project

Use a computer to generate a diagram of one of the following:

a) your school grounds

b) your house and the surrounding buildings in your street

c) any area of your choice in your neighbourhood.

Exercise

4 List the main features you would need to show in a map of:

    a) the inside of your classroom **b)** your school grounds

    c) your street.

5 Look at the pictures above. Match each description below with one of the pictures:

    rough sketch   photograph

    computer drawing   neat hand drawing

6 How can photographs help you make a map of your neighbourhood?

Key vocabulary

observation

location

paces

Types of map scale

We are learning to:

- distinguish between large scale and small scale
- identify the types of scale.

Scaling up, scaling down ⟩⟩

A map is a reduced (or scaled down) representation of a place in the real world. Accurate maps are drawn **to scale**. That means that each unit you measure on a map represents a certain number of units on the ground. There are different ways of writing map scales.

Look at the three maps to the right. Each map takes up the same amount of space on the page. However, Map C shows the whole of the Caribbean region, whereas Map B shows a more detailed part of this region (the Lesser Antilles) and Map A shows a higher level of detail: the island of Dominica. Each map has a different scale.

Types of scale ⟩⟩

Above each map, you can read the **map scale**. A map scale tells you what each unit on the map represents in real life. We can show a map scale in different ways: ratio scales, linear scales and scale statements.

Ratio scale ⟩⟩⟩⟩

Look at Map A. The **ratio scale** is 1: 3 000 000. This is a number ratio. It is important to remember that in a ratio scale, both the numbers refer to the same unit of measurement, for example, 1 cm on the map is equivalent to 3 000 000 cm on the ground.

There are 100 000 cm in 1 km. So, to work out this distance in km, divide by 100 000.

3 000 000 ÷ 100 000 = 30.

So 1 cm on the map shows 30 km on the ground.

Linear scale ⟩⟩

Under the number scale, you can see a **linear scale**. A linear scale makes it easier to work out the relationship between a unit on the page and distances in real life. The linear scale shows you the real-life distance represented by each centimetre on the map.

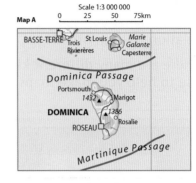

Map A
Scale 1:3 000 000

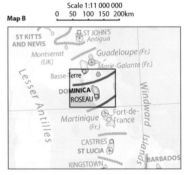

Map B
Scale 1:11 000 000

Map C
Scale 1:50 000 000

Examples of maps at different scales.

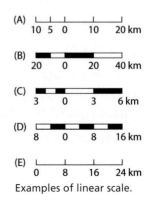

(A) 10 5 0   10   20 km

(B) 20 0   20   40 km

(C) 3 0   3   6 km

(D) 8 0   8   16 km

(E) 0   8   16   24 km

Examples of linear scale.

Sometimes scale is expressed as a **scale statement**, for example: 1 cm = 25 km. This is not a ratio scale, because the units are not both in the same unit of measure. It tells you the relationship between units on the map and units in real life.

The larger the scale of a map, the more detail it shows in real life. So, Map A is the largest scale of the three maps here. Map C is the smallest scale map.

Exercise

1 Write the number scale for each of the three maps on this page, and then write in words what the scale means.

Map A   1:_____   1 unit on the map represents ___ units on the ground.

Map B   1: _____   1 unit on the map represents ___ units on the ground.

Map C   1: _____   1 unit on the map represents ___ units on the ground.

2 In pairs, work out how to complete these rules about scale.

   a) Larger scale maps represent (more/less) detail than smaller scale maps.

   b) The higher the number of units that each unit on the map represents in real life, the (larger/smaller) the scale of the map.

3 Look at the following maps in an atlas. Write down the scale of each one as a number scale:

   a) the world

   b) Africa

   c) the Caribbean.

4 Work in pairs. Choose one of the maps. Measure the distance between two cities on the map. Calculate the distance in kilometres using the scale.

5 Go back to the measurements you took of your classroom. Draw a scale map of your classroom. Show the positions of the doors and windows, as well as at least one item of furniture. Show your scale on your classroom map.

Discussion

The distances on maps do not always give us an idea of how long it takes to travel between two places. Discuss some of the reasons for this.

Key vocabulary

to scale

map scale

ratio scale

linear scale

scale statement

Working with map scales

We are learning to:

- measure the distance between two places using the linear scale.

Measuring distance between two places ❯❯

There are 100 000 cm in 1 km. There are 100 cm in 1 m.

Let's say that you want to work out the distance between Point A and Point B in your country. On the map, the distance is about 2 cm and the scale is 1:600 000.

- Multiply by the map scale: 2 cm × 600 000 = 1 200 000 cm.
- Now we need to divide by 100 000 in order to work out the distance in km: 1 200 000 ÷ 100 000 = 12 km.

  2 cm on the map represents 12 km on the ground.

- To work out a distance in km, you can measure the distance in cm on the map, and use this formula:

$$1 \times s/100\ 000$$

If a map scale is 1: s, where s represents the number scale.

Activity

You will need a ruler and an atlas.

a) Find a map of Africa in your atlas.

b) Measure the length of the continent. Calculate it in km.

c) Measure the width across the continent at its widest point. Calculate it in km.

d) What do you notice?

Exercise

1 What is the number scale of the map opposite?

2 Copy and complete: 1 cm on the map represents _____ in real life.

3 Use the map to work out the distance between the following places:

   a) Haiti to Cuba

   b) Puerto Rico to the Dominican Republic.

4 Name five countries that are within 1000 km of Jamaica.

5 The map opposite is not very useful if you want to work out distances within Jamaica.

   a) Why not?

   b) Would you need a map with a larger or smaller scale? Explain your answer.

Activity

Use an atlas of the Caribbean and compare maps of five different countries.

a) Write the names of the five countries and the map scale of each.

b) Which country is shown at the largest scale?

c) Why do you think the countries are shown at different scales?

The Caribbean

4.18

Using map scales

We are learning to:

- construct and interpret linear scales on a map
- use templates of maps.

Scaling up or down

A map cannot be the same size as the area it shows. so a map is always smaller than the area it shows. You have learned about map scales. They tell us how much smaller the map is than the area it represents.

In order to be able to draw your own maps to scale, you need to be able to construct and interpret linear scales. A **template** is an outline or grid that makes it easy for us to see the relationships between positions on a map or diagram.

If you take a piece of grid paper and trace the outline of your hand, the drawing will be life-size. 1 cm on the drawing represents 1 cm in real life. This means the scale is 1:1.

You can then copy this drawing onto paper with smaller squares in order to scale it down.

The drawing below is a scale drawing of a single page in this book. The scale is 1:5, or 1 cm represents 5 cm.

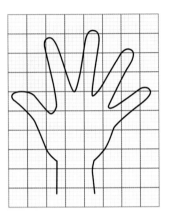

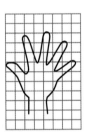

Grid paper with hand outline drawings.

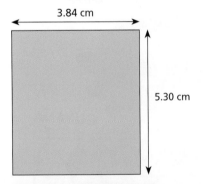

3.84 cm

5.30 cm

Map templates

You can make a map of a book by following these steps:

- Step 1: measure the length and width of the book in cm.
- Step 2: change the real measurements to the scaled-down measurements. For a scale of 1:5, we divide each measurement by 5.
- Step 3: draw a map of the book using your new measurements. Remember to write the scale under your book.

Activity

In groups, choose three books of different sizes. Draw maps of your books using a number scale of 1:5.

Here is a map of a classroom, using a scale of 1:100. The students measured the length and width of the classroom in metres. They also showed the door, windows, board and desks.

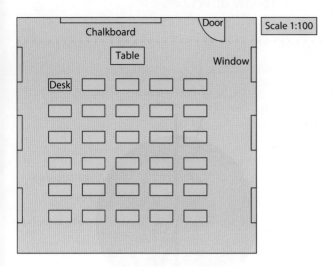

Work in groups. Make your own classroom map similar to the one in the picture. Use a scale of 1:100. Measure the length and width of the classroom in metres, using a ruler or tape measure. Also measure the door, windows, board and desks or tables.

The following outline of Jamaica is drawn at a scale of 1:1 000 000.

Scale 1 : 1 000 000

Exercise

1 What do you understand by:

   a) scaling up?   **b)** scaling down?

2 Describe how you would scale the above map up to draw it at a scale of 1:600 000. Use grid paper to do this.

3 Choose another island from your atlas.

   a) Identify the scale.

   b) Draw it at a smaller scale on grid paper.

Key vocabulary

template

121

Cardinal points

We are learning to:
- use the cardinal points to give and follow directions
- identify eight cardinal points.

Magnetic north and true north 》

On a map, when you see an arrow pointing towards the letter N, it is showing the direction of north. It is known as the north point. A **compass** is an instrument used to show direction. The pointer always shows the direction of north.

When you hold a magnetic compass, the arrow always pulls in the direction of **magnetic north**. This is the direction of the magnetic North Pole. The magnetic North Pole is constantly moving. Currently, it is located at about 86°N, 160°W.

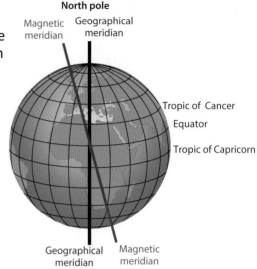

Compass Points 》》

There are four main **cardinal points** – north, south, east and west. In the diagram, these are the larger arrows. We usually show north at the top, south at the bottom, west towards the left and east towards the right.

We can divide the compass further into four more directions, midway between each of the cardinal points. These are called the intermediate points – northeast, southeast, northwest and southwest.

If we draw eight more lines, midway between each of the cardinal and intermediate points, we get the secondary intermediate points – north-northeast, east-northeast, east-southeast, and so on.

You can work out other directions according to the position of north.

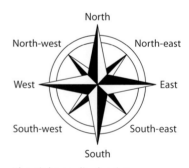

The eight cardinal points.

Exercise

1 Name the:

   a) four cardinal points
   b) four intermediate points
   c) eight secondary intermediate points.

2 Find a map of Africa in your atlas. Copy the table and fill in three countries that belong to each region of the African continent. Explain to a friend how you decided where each region was.

Region	Countries
North Africa	
Southern Africa	
East Africa	
West Africa	

Make your own direction finder. Cut out a small square of clear plastic. Draw a diagram of the sixteen-point compass rose on the plastic. Use your direction finder to help you work out the direction on the map below:

a) from Old Road Town to Basseterre   **b)** from Cotton Ground to Brick Kiln   **c)** from Cayon to Frigate Bay.

Relief Map of St Kitts and Nevis

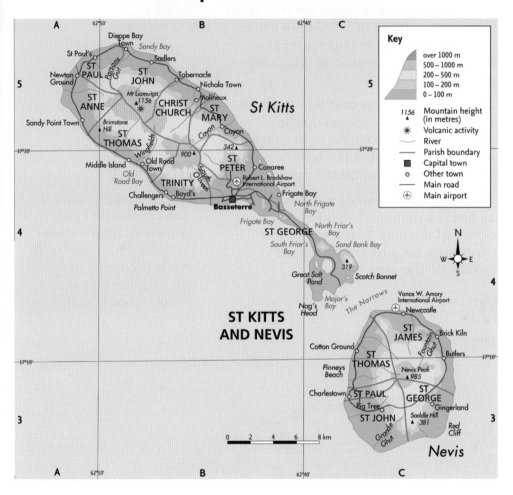

Key

	over 1000 m
	500 – 1000 m
	200 – 500 m
	100 – 200 m
	0 – 100 m
1156 ▲	Mountain height (in metres)
❋	Volcanic activity
～	River
—	Parish boundary
■	Capital town
○	Other town
—	Main road
✈	Main airport

---

3 Look at a Caribbean map. Identify an island:

    a) towards the north and
    b) south of the Caribbean.

4 Look at a world map. Identify continents:

    a) in the northern and southern hemisphere and
    b) in both hemispheres.

Key vocabulary

compass

magnetic north

cardinal points

Finding places on a map

We are learning to:

- distinguish between easting and northing grid lines
- explain the purpose of grid squares and grid lines
- give grid references.

Easting and northing grid lines

When you look at a map, you will notice **grid lines** that form blocks over the area of the map. These grid lines are often blue, brown or black and they help us to find exact places and locations. For example, tourists can use the grid lines on tourist maps to find a museum or beach.

The vertical lines on a map are known as **eastings**. Centred between each line is a letter. The letter moves up the alphabet from the left side of the map to the right side of the map. They are called eastings because the letters move up the alphabet as you move to the east on the map.

The horizontal lines on a map are known as **northings**. Centred between each line is a number. The number increases from the bottom of the map to the top of the map. They are called northings because these numbers increase as you move north on the map.

Discussion

Online maps (maps on the internet) do not usually have grid lines. Why do you think these maps do not need grids in the same way that maps in books do?

Using grid lines

Look at this map of Jamaica.

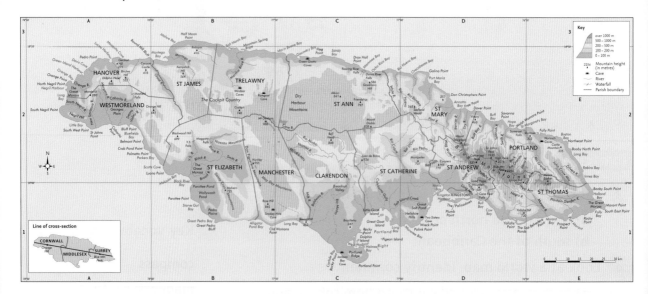

Imagine that you want to find Little Goat Island on the map of Jamaica but you cannot remember where it is. You could spend a long time looking for the name on the map, and you may find it after a while. Or you could look up Little Goat Island in the index at the back of the atlas. You would find the following **grid reference**:

Little Goat Island   C1

Find the letter C along the bottom of the map, and place your finger in that block. Now find the number 1 along the left side of the map, and place another finger in the block numbered 1. Move the two fingers along the grid lines until they meet. This locates block C1. Look carefully inside the block. Can you find Little Goat Island?

Exercise

1 What are the two kinds of grid lines shown on maps?

2 Why do we use these lines on maps?

3 **a)** Name the harbour found in D1.
   b) Name three bays found in E1.
   c) Name two parishes found in A2.

4 Write down the grid references for:

   a) Kingston
   b) Port Antonio
   c) Montego Bay.

5 Draw a grid like this one. Now choose any three of the blocks. Draw a different shape in each block. Have a partner write the grid references for each of your shapes.

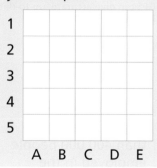

Key vocabulary

grid lines

eastings

northings

grid reference

Maps of today

We are learning to:

- describe recent developments in uses of maps
- compare maps of today with those of 20 years ago
- develop research skills.

Using maps to get around ❯❯

The maps we use today are very different from the charts that explorers used in the past. Think about what you do when you need to go to a new address, or if you get lost. If you have a smartphone, you can simply click on the maps and find your way using electronic maps and a **GPS** system.

The most widely used printed maps are **road maps**. People who are travelling long distances can use these maps in the car to keep track of where they are going and how far they have travelled. However, electronic maps are taking over from printed maps for most purposes.

A geographer studying maps for her work.

Case study

Making maps in the 21st century

Georgina Stevens-Jones is a geographer. She studied geography at university, graduating with a bachelor's degree in 1997.

"At that time, we had to collect information by **surveying** areas and making measurements. Then we drew maps by hand on sheets of clear **acetate**. We carefully layered the sheets, and took photographs to create the final map. Nobody does that anymore. Today you would just use a GPS!

GPS can give accurate, up-to-date information.

A map was something printed on paper. You folded it up and carried it with you. If the information became out-of-date, you had to look for a newer one and throw away the old one.

Today, people just update their smartphones and computers via the internet. You can carry a world map, to any degree of detail, with you in your pocket."

After Ms Stevens-Jones graduated, she worked with social services organisations to map outbreaks of tuberculosis. Later jobs included mapping ecosystems. Many of her fellow students now work for national intelligence agencies that fight crime and terrorism.

> **Did you know...?**
>
> The USA had more than 400 000 people employed in the mapping industry in 2010. Researchers predicted that this industry would grow by 35% to employ 550 000 people by 2020.

"Traditionally, geographers studied the natural environment and its relationship with human society. Cartographers focused on creating and drawing maps. This has changed since the 1990s. A new field, called **Geographical Information Systems (GIS)** has emerged. This combines the fields of cartography and geography."

Ms Stevens-Jones says that geography opens up a world of fascinating career fields. Some of her fellow students have done the following kinds of work:

- built models of the Earth using GPS, in order to draw maps
- studied volcanic activity to predict future eruptions
- studied earthquake patterns
- used photographs and other digital images to create 3D models of places
- carried out environmental impact assessments to discover whether buildings and developments are sustainable for the environment
- studied outbreaks of diseases in different environments.

Activity

Work in groups. Use a mapping application on a computer, such as Google Maps.

a) Find a map of the whole of your country.

b) Zoom in to find the location of your school.

c) Find the locations of each group member's home.

d) On your own, get the directions from school to your house. Then get the directions using the online map. What differences did you notice?

Exercise

1 Copy and complete the table to show ways that maps have changed since the 1990s.

	Before 1990s	Today
How cartographers collect information		
How maps get drawn		
How people store or carry the maps		
How we update the information		
Any other differences		

2 Why do you think people still use road maps?

3 Unscramble the names of the different fields of study:
  a) ohpyregag
  b) cragharptoy.

Discussion

What are the benefits of new technology for students of geography?

Key vocabulary

GPS (Global Positioning System)

road map

surveying

acetate

GIS (Global Information Systems)

127

Questions

See how well you have understood the topics in this unit.

1. What are the three main types of rock?

2. Correct this statement: Sedimentary rock can change into igneous rock only.

3. Identify three negative effects of Bauxite mining on the environment.

4. Identify three ways of reducing negative environmental effects on the environment.

5. Apart from Bauxite, what else is mined in Jamaica?

6. True or false: Quarrying refers to where minerals are replaced in the land.

7. Match the key vocabulary word with its definition.

   i) primary industries
   ii) secondary industries
   iii) tertiary industries

   a) industries that involve selling products
   b) involve extracting natural resources
   c) involved with making things.

8. Write definitions for the following terms:

   a) Linear settlement
   b) Nucleated settlement
   c) Scattered and dispersed settlements.

9. Identify these settlement forms:

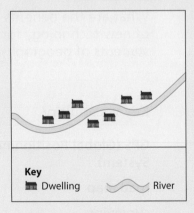 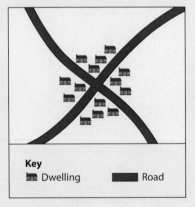 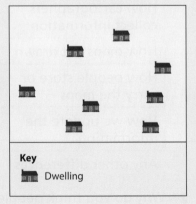

10. Explain the difference between a chloropleth map and a dot map.

11. Describe how the population is distributed in Jamaica.

12. Explain how population density is calculated.

13. Explain the term relief, and how it determines where people settle.

14. Which is the most populated parish in Jamaica?

15. Explain the role of land relief on agriculture.

16. Name two possible solutions for the negative effects of human use of the landscape.

17. Name two agencies in Jamaica who work to protect Jamaica's natural resources.

18. Explain the main conventions of maps using the following words: key, scale, symbols, direction arrows.

19. Explain what is meant by 'cardinal points'.

20. What is the difference between easting and northing grid lines?

21. Explain what GIS stands for.

22. Explain the kinds of jobs that geographers do.

23. Match the types of maps with their definitions.

   1) political maps
   2) physical maps
   3) road maps
   4) tourist maps
   5) resources maps

   a) show natural features such as mountains, rivers, lakes and deserts
   b) show the roads in an area
   c) show where particular natural resources occur, or where particular kinds of industry take place
   d) show the shapes of countries and their main cities
   e) show tourist destinations, hotels and other places of interest for tourists.

24. Describe the differences between livestock and arable farming.

25. Explain the differences between primary, secondary and tertiary industries.

26. Draw a graphic organiser to show how primary, secondary and tertiary industries are organised.

Grade 8 Unit 4 Summary

Caribbean topography

In this chapter, you have learned about:

- The three main types of rock found on the Earth
- Differentiating between igneous, sedimentary and metamorphic rocks
- The rich and varied topography of the Caribbean region
- The categories of rocks found in the Caribbean
- Karst in the Cockpit Country and the features that make the area famous and valuable
- The mining of bauxite for commercial purposes in Jamaica
- Natural physical landforms of the Caribbean such as rivers, coastlines and mountains
- Features of the human environment such as settlements, agriculture and industry
- What settlement pattern means and the features of it
- The importance of a good communications network in a country.

Population distribution and density

In this chapter, you have learned about:

- The role of census in knowing a country's population, its density and distribution
- The differences between urban and rural areas
- The benefits and challenges of using choropleth maps and dot maps
- The relationship between relief and settlement in Jamaica and the Caribbean
- The reasons for the differences in population densities and how to measure them
- How relief affects communication and economic activities such as industry and tourism
- Land degradation and soil erosion, deforestation and pollution, and the possible solutions for these problems.

Map work

In this chapter, you have learned about:

- The features of maps, the requirements for drawing them and using scales
- How to use cardinal points to give directions
- Using easting and northing grid lines to locate places on a map
- Using GPS to navigate in unfamiliar places.

Checking your progress

To make good progress in understanding the Caribbean landscape and its influence on human activities, check that you understand these ideas.

Explain and use correctly the terms: *rock, soil, topography*.

Describe how there are different topographies in Jamaica.

Explain the differences and similarities between different settlement types.

Explain and use correctly the terms *mining, quarrying*.

Name the three types of rocks.

Explain how the different rock types are formed.

Explain the relationship between relief and human activities.

Name three ways in which human activities impact the landscape.

Explain how we can reduce the effects of human activity on the landscape.

Explain and use maps, scales and cardinal points.

Describe the population distribution in Jamaica.

Explain the formation of volcanoes.

Unit 5: Economic Institutions

Objectives: You will be able to:

Understanding social, economic and political institutions

- distinguish between social, economic and political institutions
- describe the functions of each institution in Jamaica.

Money, Savings and Investments

- value savings
- understand the difference between a need and a want
- understand reasons for saving, classification of savings, benefits of saving
- identify factors that may hinder a person from saving.

Examples of economic institutions

- describe the characteristics and functions of different types of financial institutions
- describe the characteristics and functions of credit unions in Jamaica
- identify unregulated and informal financial institutions.

Financial responsibility

- participate in activities to develop the values and attitudes needed to live prudent financial lives.

Planning for the future

- value savings and investment.

Understanding social, economic and political institutions

We are learning to:

- distinguish between social, economic and political institutions.

An institution is an organisation that helps society to function smoothly. There are many institutions in society, for example, the family, education, the law. In this section we will explore the role of the economy in particular. Here is a summary of the main types of institutions in society today.

Institutions are there to help organise complex, modern societies. They are influenced by both formal and informal rules and norms, and are enduring, but may change over time. For example economic reform is necessary because the way that business is carried out changes.

Institutions are often governed by laws, that are created by governments. Think about the institution of education, for example. The rules about how long a child stays in school are decided by the government. Politicians work together with the education system to make sure that schools are run smoothly.

Even informal institutions are shaped by the government; for example, there are rules and laws about marriage and divorce.

Activity

Imagine you are involved in a plane crash and land on an uninhabited island. You need to organise the group of people you are with. How will you organise social life, and take political decisions and economic decisions? Give reasons for your answers. What would happen if your group was not organised?

Discussion

In small groups, discuss which set of institutions is most important, and why. Should the government be involved with setting rules and organising all of these types of institutions? Explain your answer, giving examples.

Exercise

1 In your own words, define the term institution.

2 What are the differences between a social institution and a political institution?

3 Give an example of each type of institution – social, political, economic – that you may see every day in Jamaica.

Key vocabulary

social institutions

political institutions

economic institutions

Institutions

1 Social institutions relate to areas of life that govern our relationships with other people. For example, the family helps us to manage and regulate relationships, raise children, share resources, make sure that we have financial and emotional security. Other examples of social institutions include school and the church.

A church is one of our social institutions.

2 Political institutions help ensure that a country is governed and runs smoothly. The government in Jamaica is democratic, which means that politicians are voted in by the people to speak on their behalf. This ensures that decisions are made about how Jamaica is run that reflect the needs and wants of the people.

Government buildings are one of our political institutions.

3 Economic institutions relate to how goods and money are distributed in society. This involves regulation by the government, private companies and businesses but also by informal schemes and private schemes. Jamaican society is based on the idea that individuals should and can pursue their own financial arrangements.

A bank is one of our economic institutions.

Activity

Decide if the following are connected to social, political or economic institutions. They may be connected to more than one institution:

- social services
- the police
- schools
- banks
- housing offices.

Entrance to Kingston College All Boys High School in Jamaica.

Exercise

4 Explain the difference between formal and informal rules and norms. Give examples of each.

5 What is meant by institutional reform and why is it needed?

6 How are economic institutions different from other types of institutions?

What role does each institution play in the Jamaican society?

We are learning to:

- describe the functions of each institution in Jamaica.

Now that we know what the main forms of institutions are in society, we are going to explore in more detail what each form does, what role or function it plays in society.

Institution	Roles/functions	Examples
Social	<ul><li>ensuring that relationships in the family function correctly, between adults, and between adults and children</li><li>ensuring that people have a home</li><li>ensuring that people have financial support</li><li>ensuring that children learn how to behave</li><li>making sure that children are ready to start school and supporting them through school</li><li>ensuring that adults and children are able to share their problems, have someone to listen to them</li></ul>	<ul><li>giving advice</li><li>listening to people's problems</li><li>helping with homework</li><li>providing food and shelter</li><li>table manners</li><li>encouragement and support with decisions</li><li>learning about relationships</li></ul>
Political	<ul><li>ensuring that political decisions are taken so that the country is run smoothly</li><li>making sure that the government is made up of representative individuals who were voted in by the public</li><li>making sure that people who need help are given it, through creating laws and policies</li><li>making sure that rules are made for businesses to ensure that they behave in morally correct ways</li><li>creating laws and policies such as Vision 2030 and ensuring that these are carried through</li><li>running day to day government, organising voting and elections</li><li>deciding on citizenship rules</li><li>creating guidance for the education system</li></ul>	<ul><li>writing a constitution</li><li>creating laws and policies</li><li>writing rules about elections, organising and administering these to make sure they are fair</li><li>business and trade laws</li><li>taxation laws, making sure that everyone pays tax fairly</li><li>immigration services provided to ensure people have citizenship</li><li>education ministers help the education system run smoothly</li></ul>

Institution	Roles/functions	Examples
Economic	• ensuring the fair distribution of wealth and goods • ensuring that people who are poorer are given support • writing laws to support these decisions • making decisions based on the changing needs of the economy • responding to changes such as the climate change, and globalisation • ensuring that sustainable development takes place • ensuring that Jamaica conducts trade with other countries • making sure that people save and have pensions • providing resources for those who can't work • providing banking services	• tax is greater for those who earn more • the government provide financial help to those who need it • regulations for banks and businesses • Vision 2030 to ensure that Jamaica is fairer and has a plan to develop its economy as well as encourage sustainable, environmentally friendly practices • membership with other Caribbean countries, e.g. CARICOM • providing guidance and support in banking, investing and saving

The roles of different institutions.

Discussion

In your class, discuss the role the institutions in our society play. Do they help to structure our society, provide support to individuals and families, and if so, how?

Exercise

1 In your own words explain what are 'economic functions'.

2 Explain how the government is involved with all three institutions.

3 Are the functions of each institution always carried out? Give examples of where this might not occur.

4 Write a short essay describing the functions of each institution.

Did you know...?

The allocation to the Ministry of Education, Youth and Information for financial year 2018/19 increased by $2.7 billion, moving to $101.6 billion from $98.9 billion in 2017/18.

Project

Create a model that represents an institution of your choice. Write a brief history about the institution selected, outline its functions and give examples of ways in which the institution has helped to build the Jamaican society.

Money, savings and investments

We are learning to:

- value savings
- understand the difference between a need and a want
- understand the reasons for saving.

Money ❭❭

Money is anything widely regarded as valuable that is acceptable in a transaction between two or more parties. Cash, credit cards, cheques, gold, scarce commodities and even salt are different forms of money that have been used over time. A new type of money called **bitcoin**, or virtual money, is beginning to attract attention. It may become the money of the future.

Jamaican dollar bills.

Money must have certain qualities:

- it must be acceptable to all parties, meaning that the parties to a transaction must agree to accept it as a means of payment
- it must be scarce for it to have value, for example, we cannot use leaves for money, as they are found everywhere and easily accessible
- it must be durable and not deteriorate, because people will lose confidence in it. Would you accept a torn crumpled dollar?
- it must be in different sizes or divisible to enable small transactions; this is the reason for large and small bills and coins
- it must be portable in order for it to be easily carried around
- it must be difficult to copy, to prevent people from reproducing it illegally
- it must be uniform – all bills and coins of equal value must look exactly the same.

The functions of money include:

- it can hold its value over time (store of value)
- it enables transactions (medium of exchange)
- it rates the value of goods to each other (measure of value)
- it allows payments in the future to repay credit given (standard for deferred payment).

Exercise

1 In your view, what are the five most important qualities that money should have?

2 In your own words, explain the functions of money.

Needs and wants ⟩⟩

Human beings have many needs and wants that together contribute to a satisfying standard of living.

A **need** is a necessity that sustains basic life, and having to do without it will cause suffering or in extreme cases even death. For example, food, water, shelter, clothing and good health are basic human needs. We can live without food for two weeks. but we will die if we do not have water for a few days.

A **want** is a human desire not considered necessary to sustain life, but which human beings desire to fulfil their lives – for example, a new pair of shoes or trainers, or a new mobile phone.

Savings refers to money that is set aside and not spent in the present but which may be used in the future. For example, you may have a piggy bank which you use to put away money for a future use. Many people have savings in the bank or other financial institutions.

Project

Working in groups, find five pictures in magazines or catalogues of items that you want and five pictures of items that you need. Then order them from 1 to 10 the most essential (1) to the least essential (10).

The need for money ⟩⟩⟩

The need or demand for money can be placed into three categories.

- The **transaction need** for money is seen where individuals require money to make everyday purchases such as a soft drink or paying for a taxi.
- The **precautionary need** for money is seen where money is required for emergencies or for unexpected events such as sudden illnesses or a leaking roof.
- The **speculative need** for money is seen when individuals chose to keep their wealth in the form of assets instead of money. For example, a good substitute for money is a house, land or gold coins which can be converted into money.

Activity

Write a reflective piece in which you discuss your needs and wants. Which is greater at this time? Explain.

Exercise

3. Explain the difference between a need and a want.

4. Name two everyday items that you consider a need.

5. Name two items of your own that you consider a want.

6. Why should people save their money?

7. In your own words, explain the difference between transactional, precautionary and speculative needs for money.

8. Identify three examples of a transaction, precautionary and speculative need for money.

Key vocabulary

money

bitcoin

need

want

savings

transaction need

precautionary need

speculative need

Saving our money

We are learning to:

- understand reasons for saving, classification of savings, benefits of saving
- identify factors that may hinder a person from saving.

Reasons for savings

Money is usually saved for known or unknown events in the present and in the future. This is known as savings.

An unknown event may be an unexpected illness, such as cancer, which is costly to treat. A known event could include the purchase and maintenance of a new house or car.

Retirement is another reason why people save. After retiring individuals will still need income on which to live comfortably in their senior years. Future family needs that enhance quality of life – such as yearly holidays, servicing debts, education and special milestones, like special birthdays and anniversaries – are added needs that require savings.

The Jamaica Stock Exchange.

Classification of savings

In Jamaica, individuals save using both formal or informal facilities.

The **formal savings** sector consists of commercial banks, such as the National Commercial Bank (NCB), into which we make regular deposits in a savings account to earn interest over time. There are also credit unions, insurance companies and the Jamaican Stock Exchange. They all offer opportunities for long-term savings products to clients wishing to save.

The **informal saving** facilities include the "partner plan" and "round robin". The partner plan is a system where members contribute a weekly sum to a pool of money, which is paid to a different member every week or month. This payment is called a "hand". Round robins are similar to the partner plan but are usually used by business persons to boost their income. Private moneylenders and saving at home are also part of the informal means through which people save.

> Did you know...?
>
> The Jamaica Stock Exchange (JSE) began its operations in 1968.

> **Discussion**
>
> "There's no point in saving. I want to enjoy my money today and have fun." As a class, discuss what you would say if your friend told you this.

Barriers to saving

Factors that hinder savings include:

- lack of financial education by family members; if parents do not stress the value and importance of careful spending and saving, this will not form part of a child's upbringing and persist into later life

- with high costs of living it is difficult to save, because almost all income earned is used to meet basic needs
- the lack of a budget and poor spending habits – a budget is a disciplined way to make sure that planned income is equal to planned spending, with money left over for savings
- high levels of debt leave very little over to save – saving can only be achieved if some spending is given up
- although low income owners pay less tax on their earnings, they pay indirect taxes such as on goods bought at supermarkets, which can reduce their spending power.

Project

Students work in groups to complete this project. Each person has been 'given' $400 to use as their budget for one month.

Identify a target amount that you would like to save after one month, for example $50, for something special, such as a holiday. You also have to travel to work each day (own car or public transport), and pay for food and electricity. You also want to spend some money on entertainment, such as going to the cinema, and pay mobile phone costs.

In your groups, discuss factors that may have hindered your saving and make a plan of expenditure and saving for your total monthly allowance, then discuss it with the class to start a debate on saving.

Exercise

1. Explain in your own words why we should save money.

2. What types of saving institutions are there in Jamaica?

Activity

Visit your local bank and ask for an application form for a savings account. Practise filling in the forms. What have you learnt about the process? What information do they need from you?

Key vocabulary

formal savings

informal savings

Examples of economic institutions

We are learning to:

- describe the characteristics and functions of different types of financial institutions.

Jamaica has a **mixed economic system**. This means there is mixture of businesses and organisations, some of which are owned privately and others are owned and operated by the government.

Government economic institutions

Ministry of Finance and the Public Service

The Ministry of Finance and Public Service is the main body responsible for the country's economy. The primary focus of this part of the government is to help make sure that financially sound policies that will help the economy grow and the country develop are put into place. It also monitors these policies and provides useful information to the government on how best to achieve sustainable economic growth.

Discussion

Think about what sustainable economic growth means. Discuss how policies such as Vision 2030 ensure sustainable economic growth?

The Ministry of Finance and Public Service oversees important government bodies such as the Bank of Jamaica, Tax Administration Jamaica, the Financial Services Commission and the Accountant General's Department.

Case study

The Financial Services Commission (FSC)

During the mid 1990s Jamaica's financial sector experienced a period of instability and the Government of Jamaica had to intervene to help several financial institutions. This crisis resulted in changes and recommendations for the improvement in regulation and supervision of the financial sector. The FSC was created after the Financial Services Commission Act to oversee the regulation of Jamaica's insurance, pension and securities industries.

The Financial Services Commission website.

The FSC, a self-financing regulatory body, was given wide-ranging powers to supervise, investigate and punish businesses if they did not respond to rules and regulations.

Case study

The Bank of Jamaica

The Bank of Jamaica was founded in May 1961. It was set up so that there was a regulated financial structure to encourage economic development in Jamaica after its independence in 1962. The role of the bank was to:

- issue currency (notes and coins)
- administer the financial reserves of Jamaica

- supply credit so as to encourage production, trade and employment
- develop money and capital markets in Jamaica
- act as banker to the Government.

In recent years, the bank has become much proactive in the Jamaican economy and has increased its role in helping economic growth and development. In 1985, the Bank introduced a programme for financial reform – The Financial Sector Reform Programme (FSRP) – with the main aim for it to be more effective helping economic development.

Source: adapted from Bank of Jamaica website

Private economic institutions

There are a range of privately owned institutions in Jamaica. These are different from publicly owned financial institutions because they seek to make a profit. All privately owned economic institutions are monitored by the Bank of Jamaica and the Financial Services Commission.

These include banks and building societies. Banks are generally listed on the stockmarket (a collection of markets and exchanges) and have external shareholders whereas building societies have members and no external shareholders. Banks also usually offer a wider range of products compared to building societies.

Case study

The Development Bank of Jamaica (DBJ)

The DBJ is a government institution that drives private sector development and contributes to economic growth in Jamaica.

The bank's mission is to provide 'opportunities to all Jamaicans to improve their quality of life through development financing, capacity building, public-private partnership and privatisation solutions in keeping with Government policy'.

This means that as an organisation, the DJB helps businesses grow, develop and follow the rules as set out by the Jamaican government.

> **Did you know…?**
>
> The Bank of Jamaica, established by the Bank of Jamaica Law (1960), began operations in May 1961. Today it employs 2 700 people in Jamaica in 58 branches.

Activity

Find out who the current Minister for Finance and the Public Service is.

Exercise

1. Explain the difference between public and privately owned companies.

2. Explain what is meant by Jamaica having a 'mixed economy'.

3. Which ministry is in charge of regulating financial services in the country?

4. Describe the role of the Bank of Jamaica.

5. Write a short essay explaining why the economy needs regulations.

The Jamaican government aims to grow the economy over the coming years.

Key vocabulary

mixed economic system

Credit unions in Jamaica

We are learning to:

• describe the characteristics and functions of different types of financial institutions.

A credit union is a member-owned financial cooperative, controlled by its members and operated with the idea of people helping people, providing its members loans or credit at good rates as well as other financial services.

The first credit union in Jamaica was established in the 1940s. This was developed to help people get loans and other financial services who might not get these from banks or other financial institutions. They work because members work together by pooling their resources, so the relationship between credit unions and their members is built on the people-helping-people philosophy.

How are credit unions different to other financial institutions?

• Credit unions have a unique structure. Other financial institutions are owned by stockholders who seek to profit from their investment in the organisation, credit unions are owned co-operatively and democratically controlled by all of their members without regard to the amount of money that a member has in the credit union.

• Credit unions are directed by a board which is a group of volunteers selected from within the membership.

• Credit unions return profits to their members in the form of dividends, competitive loans rates and services.

• Credit unions do business with their members only.

How do credit unions benefit members?

• Every credit union member is a co-owner of the credit union.

• Each member has equal voting power, (one vote), the same as all other members in the credit union irrespective of the amount of his savings.

• Each member has the power to exercise his/her democratic right in determining by whom and how the credit union is run.

• A credit union member shares in any annual surplus.

• Credit unions now offer a range of financial services, in some instances the same as those available in other financial institutions.

> **Did you know...?**
>
> As of 31 December 2019 there were 25 credit unions in Jamaica.

Activity

Carry out research into one of Jamaica's Credit Union, find out what services they offer. How does it help its members? Which groups of workers does this union protect?

- Members can determine the type of financial services the credit union should provide.
- Members are helped to save through the habit of thrift that is encouraged by credit unions.
- Members can save directly and transact business at their credit unions through salary deduction facilities.
- Life savings and loan protection insurance at no cost to members.

Source: taken from Credit Unions of Jamaica website

Case study

Jamaica Co-operative Credit Union League

The Jamaica Co-operative Credit Union League (JCCUL) was founded in 1942. The JCCUL was founded as a democratically voluntary organisation, which was financed by its member credit unions. The objectives of the JCCUL included:

- represent its members about issues such as legislation
- making loans to its member credit unions
- undertaking investments for its member credit unions
- organising new credit unions

Over the years the JCCUL grew in size and influence, and by 1972, along with a number of other credit unions, formed the Caribbean Conference of Credit Unions. Today, the JCCUL has over 1.5 million members, and offers a whole range of services including support services, corporate branding, advocacy and public relations. The mission of the league is 'To enable the growth and development of Co-operatives in Jamaica through representation and services'.

Activity

Visit the Jamaica Co-operative Credit Union League website. Find out what the organisation does today in Jamaica. Write 100 words on why this organisation is important.

Exercise

1 Using your own words, explain what a credit union is.

2 Explain why credit unions were established in Jamaica.

3 Write a paragraph explaining the benefits of credit unions.

Unregulated and informal financial institutions

We are learning to:

- identify unregulated and informal financial institutions.

Regulated and unregulated financial institutions 》》

Public financial institutions are **regulated**. This is where a bank, a credit union or a savings association operate under the authority of the country that they are based in.

Financial regulation refers to the rules and laws that they operate under. The reasons for financial regulation are to protect the public who use those services, but who may not have enough information or knowledge of the services or products they are being offered, or for when they hand over their money. The regulations also make sure that a country's financial system is stable and helps to maintain the validity of those institutions. Overall, if something goes wrong with the institution the customers money is protected – they will get it back.

Apart from the public and private financial institutions, there are also **unregulated** and informal institutions. These are likely to be unchecked, possibly arranged between people without formal agreements, such as borrowing money or selling goods without being officially registered. These have grown in recent years as a result of many things including slow economic growth in Jamaica. They are appealing because they avoid formal regulations such as paying tax or filling in paperwork.

Informal savings facility 》》

Saving at home

Saving at home means putting aside small portions of earnings in parts of the home that are considered to be safe. It used to be common to hide savings beneath mattresses. This practice has declined but there are many who still do not trust the banks and so prefer to save at home.

The 'partner plan'

One popular informal savings plan in Jamaica is called a partner plan. This involves members who are required to make a small monthly contribution to the community fund. A banker is assigned to collect the money and supervise the distribution. The banker is usually paid a small fee for their role in the group. Withdrawals are done by taking monthly or weekly deposits from each member of a group and then giving the whole sum to one member of the group. The person receiving the monthly or weekly sum is based on a rota, ensuring each participant will eventually receive a large payout. Benefits include:

- allows members to reduce worries about money; makes sure that their free cash is saved
- enables people to commit their surplus cash towards future purchases with the potential to improve their quality of life
- in emergency cases of unforeseen illness, members can rely on their group members and the resulting group fund to quickly take out a loan, so it is a flexible arrangement
- avoids complex applications for a loan from a bank.

There are risks to using this kind of informal savings plans as there are fewer rules to govern the practice.

- Corrupt persons can make withdrawals then disappear without paying their portion of the loan.
- Bankers for these types of saving plans might also be dishonest and arrange the finances so that they get a bigger 'cut' than originally agreed.
- If the money is lost there is no insurance for savers.

Here are some examples of other unregulated and informal financial facilities or arrangement:

- street hawkers selling goods
- buying and selling goods second hand
- borrowing money without a formal contract, from friends, or someone local.

There are many potential problems with these kinds of institutions including:

- customers are not protected by financial regulations, such as being able to terminate the loan
- customers can not complain if they feel that they have been unfairly treated.

If a person works for an informal or unregulated institution, there are also issues:

- the informal economy tends to employ lower-skilled and less productive workers. As a result, workers in the formal economy earn, on average, about 19% more than workers in the informal economy
- workers' rights are not protected by the same laws, for example, no pension and no sick pay
- workers/employers may not pay tax
- workers may not be protected by health and safety laws as the would be in formal work arrangements.

Street markets are part of the informal economy.

Did you know...?

The informal economy is estimated to be around 30% of the total economy in Jamaica.

Exercise

1 Explain the difference between the formal and informal financial institutions.

2 What are the problems with unregulated work?

3 What are some factors that contribute to development of unregulated financial facilities and businesses?

4 What can the government do to reduce the amount of unregulated and informal financial regulations?

Key vocabulary

regulated

unregulated

The role of economic institutions

We are learning to:

* explain the functions of economic institutions.

As we saw in the previous lesson, economic institutions play a range of important roles. This is to ensure that the economic system in Jamaica runs smoothly and fairly.

The role of economic institutions ⟩⟩

Public economic institutions are run and monitored by the government of Jamaica. Therefore they reflect the values of the government, and are not run to make a profit. Some of their key functions are:

* to ensure that the economy of Jamaica is secure and stable
* ensuring opportunities to set up businesses and for employment
* ensuring public funds are protected and used wisely for the benefit of all
* making sure that taxes are paid
* making sure that all financial transactions are transparent and legal.

Private economic institutions are self-governed and seek to make a profit but they are checked by the government too. Along with public economic institutions, private economic institutions carry out some of the following functions:

* satisfy the needs and wants of individuals by offering goods and services
* offer employment opportunities so some persons can earn an income and satisfy their needs and wants
* offer opportunities for individuals to apply their knowledge, skills and talents by creating jobs requiring different abilities at different levels
* provide funds and economic assistance to other institutions so they can function effectively.

Discussion

Discuss the differences and similarities between public and private economic institutions.

What are the key risks threatening banks today? ⟩⟩

Banks today face a number of risks that threaten their business – and their customers money. One of the most serious is **cybercrime**.

As people begin to use online banking more and more, and rely on ever changing technology, it creates more opportunities for criminals to attack their banking systems.

Some of the most serious cybercrimes affecting banks are outlined below.

- Credential stuffing – this is when a cyberattack targets customers' personal data. Hackers can get unauthorised access to customers' accounts using software to find out login details. They then use this information to try and gain access to other online accounts.

- Phishing – tricking people into giving financial information by sending emails that look as if they come from organisations such as banks. This information is then used to steal their money or identity. Phishing can also be used when a link is sent by email which installs **malware** to steal login details and other data. Hackers can attack banks in this way to get into sensitive areas of the banks' data. Phishing can be directed at both bank employees and customers.

Cybercrime is a growing problem.

- Ransomware – this is a type of malware that gets into computer systems, and freezes the systems, unless a fee is paid to release it. Smaller banks, which may not have large IT resources, or have out of date security technology are especially vulnerable to this kind of attack.

- Identity theft – this is a very serious, but common problem. This is when a person's personal details, which may include their name, address and bank details, are stolen. This can happen when someone accesses personal information on websites that the person uses, for example to buy a book from.

Phishing, hacking and identity theft are big issues for the banking industry.

So, what can banks do to protect their business and our money? Technology is improving all the time to help banks with these problems ranging from stronger firewalls and security, the use of artificial intelligence to scan for cyber threats, and asking their customers to regularly change their own security details.

Exercise

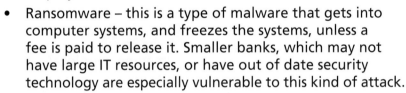

1. Explain the difference between public and private economic institutions.

2. Give two examples of public and two examples of private institutions in Jamaica.

3. Write three paragraphs explaining some of the problems facing banks today from cyber attack.

Key vocabulary

public economic institution

private economic institution

cybercrime

malware

Financial responsibility

We are learning to:

- participate in activities to develop the values and attitudes needed to live prudent financial lives.

The importance of planning a budget

A **budget** is an itemised summary of expected **income** (earnings) and **expenditure** (what you spend). A person, family, country or business can have a budget. A budget can also refer to how much money you have available to spend on something – for example, some clothes, a car or a house.

A budget is also a detailed financial plan of the way planned income is able to finance planned expenditure over a given period.

A family working out a budget.

Why is a budget important?

- A budget is important because it guards against unplanned spending, which causes us to spend more than we should. It further helps us to decide, in advance, how income can achieve future goals through the discipline of a financial plan.

- A budget also prevents financial instability over time. Financial instability occurs when financial debts exceed income over an extended period. A budget therefore promotes careful spending and prevents overspending.

Here are some tips as to how you could draw up a monthly budget plan:

- get organised and take your time when you plan your budget
- add up all your income
- work out your essential spending – for example, for families it will be rent/mortgage, bills, food and clothing
- work out your need spending and reduce it
- work out the gap between your income and spending
- be honest about how you spend on needs.

Activity

Imagine your local community leaders have told you that they are concerned about levels of debt in your neighbourhood. Make a poster for display in your community centre that explains why budgeting is important.

Exercise

1. Explain what a budget is. Who can have one?

2. Why is it important to have a budget?

Case study

Daniel decided that he wanted to create a monthly budget, as he found that he did not have enough money at the end of each month. Here is the budget Daniel came up with.

PLANNED INCOME	END OF MONTH
Monthly salary	$14 000
Other earnings	$2 000
Total income	**$16 000**

PLANNED EXPENSES	
Utilities and rent	$6 000
Food	$5 000
Auto Fuel	$2 000
Other	$2 000
Total planned spend	**$15 000**

DISPOSABLE INCOME	
Going out/leisure	$200
Phone	$250
Clothes	$300
Total spend	**$750**

UNPLANNED EXPENSES	
Plumbing repairs	**$500**
Total expenses	**$16 250** ($15 000 + $500 + $750)
Net Income	−$250 ($16 000 − $16 250)

Questions

1. How much money does Daniel have left over this month?

2. What could he save on to make sure that his monthly budget worked?

3. Of the disposable income items, which one do you think Daniel needs to keep? Why?

4. What do you think Daniel should do **a)** for this month and **b)** for future months?

Activity

Copy a blank version of the budget plan and create a personal budget.

Add your income (for example, your allowance, birthday money, chores money and school allowance) and spending to the budget.

Compare your budget with a partner's and then share with the class.

Activity

In pairs, do a role-play where one of you is Daniel and the other is Daniel's friend. Act out what his friend would advise him about his spending and budget.

Key vocabulary

budget

income

expenditure

Planning for the future

We are learning to:

- value savings and investment.

Financial stability

Financial stability refers to the prudent use of our financial resources to meet our future goals over an extended period without becoming indebted.

Financial stability is therefore achieved when, over time, our income is equal to, or exceeds, expenditure in a sustained manner and our goals have been achieved.

Budget planning and financial stability go hand in hand. A budget plan matches planned spending to planned income, preventing the creation of large debts over time. It also helps to identify savings that may be used to reduce debt and maintain financial stability.

It further creates a pool of savings to fund emergencies and unplanned events, as an alternative to costly borrowing from the bank. Financial stability is achieved through the discipline provided by a budget.

Saving over a long period of time can help meet our future goals, such as going to university.

The benefits of planning a budget

The benefits of having a budget include:

- it provides financial stability over a long period
- it can identify ways to save income, which over time which can be used for investment, pay medical bills and finance unplanned events
- it enables us to pay debts on time and avoid the stress caused by debt creation
- it leads to the achievement of financial independence (this can apply to an individual, a family, a business or a country).

Research

Conduct research to find out about different types of savings or investments that can be done to finance future needs.

Exercise

1. Define in your own words the terms budget planning and financial stability.

2. How may budget planning achieve financial stability?

3. What are the benefits of planning a budget?

4. Why do you think it is important to be able to achieve financial independence?

Planning for the future >>>

We all wish to be successful in the future. Importantly we possess the ability to influence the quality of our future by devising a plan to achieve this goal.

Planning for the future is a roadmap for future success for the short-term (five years), medium-term (ten to fifteen years) and long-term (fifty years).

Needs planning >>

Perhaps the best way to plan for the future is to conduct **needs planning**. Needs planning identifies our future needs and the source of future income to pay for these needs when they arise. Some of our future needs include:

House repairs are often costly – money should be set aside to pay for these needs.

- basic physical needs such as food, shelter, clothing and health, which persist well into our advanced years. We must therefore have money planned for meals, a place to live, clothes to wear and a health plan for medical care
- primary, secondary and tertiary education in the present and future. We should have the income in place to finance these important future needs
- special occasions in the future, such as landmark birthdays, anniversaries, weddings and family vacations. We must carefully plan to avoid borrowing for these needs. A savings plan for these occasions is therefore necessary
- building renovation and maintenance. Since it is costly to carry out house repairs, a separate fund should be set up to finance these needs
- saving for our retirement years. This is a critical need, since our income from employment will cease. This predictable future need can be achieved by saving throughout our early working years.

Discussion

In groups of five students, choose one benefit of budget planning. Then consult your parents to help you to understand how budget planning contributes to financial stability. Use the information for a class discussion.

Exercise

5 Define in your own words the terms short-, medium- and long-term goals.

6 In your own words, explain the term needs planning.

7 Why is it necessary to plan for the future?

8 State three benefits related to future planning.

9 Place the following needs/wants into the short-, medium- or long-term periods:

    a) retirement   **b)** tertiary education

    c) silver anniversary   **d)** wedding   **e)** food.

Key vocabulary
....

financial stability

needs planning

Questions

See how well you have understood the topics in this unit.

1. A _____ is an organisation that is owned and run by members, that offers financial services.

   a) bank
   b) credit union
   c) building society
   d) stock market

2. A social institution is one that focuses on:

   a) peoples personal and relationship needs
   b) people's legal and citizenship needs
   c) people's financial needs
   d) people's health needs.

3. Why is money necessary? Give three reasons.

4. Explain the difference between a need and a want.

5. Explain why saving is important.

6. Which of these are examples of private financial institutions?

   a) Banks
   b) Government ministries
   c) Schools
   d) Credit unions

7. True or False? The role of the Bank of Jamaica is to help regulate the economy of Jamaica.

8. Describe the role of credit unions in Jamaica. How do they benefit its members?

9. Correct this statement: Gross Domestic Product measures the value of social activity within a country.

10. Explain the difference between regulated and unregulated financial institutions.

11. Write a short definition of the following terms:

    Budget
    Income
    Expenditure

12. Explain why it is important to have a budget.

13. Which two of these are problems associated with the informal finance sector?

  a) Lack of paperwork
  b) Workers are unable to complain about pay
  c) There is no regulation
  d) Workers pay too much tax.

14. Name three tips to help someone draw up a monthly budget plan.

15. Explain the role of the government in regulating financial institutions in Jamaica.

16. Explain the term financial stability.

17. Explain the terms 'needs planning'.

18. True or false?

A need is a human desire not considered necessary to sustain life, but which human beings desire to fulfil their lives – for example, a new pair of shoes or trainers, or a new mobile phone.

A want is a necessity that sustains basic life, and having to do without it will cause suffering or in extreme cases even death.

19. Match the institution to their role.

  1) Social
  2) Political
  3) Economic

  a) ensuring the fair distribution of wealth and goods
  b) ensuring that relationships in the family function correctly
  c) ensuring that political decisions are taken so that the country is run smoothly

Grade 8 Unit 5 Summary

Social, economic and political institutions

In this chapter, you have learned about:

- What an institution is
- How to distinguish between social, political and economic institutions
- The roles and functions of social, political and economic institutions in a society.

Money, savings and investments

In this chapter, you have learned about:

- The qualities and functions of money
- The differences between a need and a want and how they relate to saving
- The three categories for the demand for money
- What the reasons for saving money are
- Classifying saving facilities as formal and informal
- The factors that prevent savings
- The functions of government economic institutions
- The functions of private economic institutions
- What a credit union is and how it differs from other financial institutions
- The benefits that members get from their credit unions
- The differences between regulated and unregulated financial institutions
- The informal saving facilities that people in the Caribbean use
- The main risks that banks face in today's technologically advanced world.

Financial responsibility

In this chapter, you have learned about:

- What is meant by financial stability
- The importance of using a budget
- What financial stability is and the benefits of planning a budget
- The factors to consider when planning for the future.

Financial responsibility

In this chapter, you have learned about:

- What is meant by financial responsibility
- The importance of using a budget
- What financial stability is and the benefits of using a budget
- The factors to consider when planning for the future.

Checking your progress

To make good progress in understanding economic institutions, check that you understand these ideas.

Explain and use correctly the term *social*, *political* and *economic institution*.

Describe the functions of economic institutions.

Outline the characteristics of economic institutions.

Explain and use correctly the term *financial institution*.

Describe issues facing economic institutions.

Outline advantages and disadvantages of unregulated and informal saving schemes.

Explain and use correctly the terms *money*, *need*, *want*, *saving*, *precautionary*, *thrifty*.

Name three formal economic institutions in Jamaica.

Explain the importance of economic institutions on our lives.

Explain the different forms of need or demand we have for money.

Consider the reasons for saving and hinderances to saving.

Examine the role of money in society.

SOCIAL STUDIES
Unit 6: Consumer Affairs

Objectives: You will be able to: ▶▶▶

Key concepts in understanding consumer affairs
- develop working definitions for key terms.

Factors that influence consumer demand
- analyse the factors which influence consumer demand
- design a product, develop a plan to market the product and design success criteria.

Rights and responsibilities of the consumer

- analyse the rights and responsibilities of the consumer
- evaluate the role of government and consumer protection agencies in protecting the rights of the consumer
- take steps to seek redress when rights have been violated.

Understanding globalisation

- define and explain relevant terms and concepts: globalisation, global village, economy, trade, technology
- discuss the impact of globalism on the consumer and consumerism.

The impact of globalisation on the consumer and consumerism

- discuss the impact of globalisation on the consumer and consumerism
- examine the impact of technology on consumerism.

Key concepts in understanding consumer affairs

We are learning to:

- develop working definitions for key terms.

Consumers and producers

A **consumer** is a person who uses goods and services, which may satisfy the consumer's needs or wants. A large proportion of what many people buy may satisfy their wants rather than their needs.

We need clothes to cover our bodies and keep us warm when it is cold. But most consumers buy more clothes than they need such as buying several pairs of shoes, jackets and jeans because they want or like them. They may also buy new clothes every year because of changes in fashion. The older clothes are discarded as the consumer wants new, fashionable clothes.

This is why many people describe the society we live in today as a **consumer society** (a society based on **consumerism**) which relies on consumers buying more than they actually need.

Distinguish between needs and wants

The difference between a need and a want can be summarised as follows:

- A need relates to human requirements that nurture the body and mind and help us to survive. These determine a basic quality of life. For example, food, water, clothing, shelter and health care are basic human needs.

- A want is a human desire that increases satisfaction of life beyond basic bodily needs. For example, we would like to have holidays, swimming pools and jewellery, but they are not essential to our basic needs.

Factors that influence what we consume are determined by several factors:

- We make personal choices – for example, we buy a certain brand of footwear.

- Peer pressure can create want – we may buy something that is popular among our peers so we are part of the crowd – for example, branded clothing.

- Bodily needs cause us to buy food and water.

Having a meal is an example of a need.

- Habits determine our wants – for example, if we buy something every day (say, bottled water), it becomes a habit.
- Information can help us to make better choices – for example, we may buy a bottle of water instead of a soft drink because we have been told that soft drinks have sugar and additives that may be harmful to our bodies.
- Advertising persuades us to spend on wants, because advertisers use psychology to influence our choices – for example, the picture of the burger that looks more appealing than the actual burger.

Having a swimming pool at home is an example of a want.

Types of consumers

There are three types of consumer:

Consumers of goods (primary and secondary goods)

These are people who buy either materials to create a final product, primary goods, or people who buy finished foods, known as secondary goods. So for example, lumber bought to make a chair is a primary good, while a ready-made chair bought for use at home would be an example of secondary goods.

Consumers of services

This refers to where people buy a service, which is an experience, a process or support that helps them in some way. For example, getting a haircut, paying for delivery services or daycare services.

Consumers of credit

These are people who take on personal debt in order to purchase goods and services. For example, paying for an item over a period of time. This is sometimes known as higher purchase. This can make it easier for people to buy expensive items, as the cost is spread over a period of time.

Discussion

In groups, discuss the differences between a consumer and consumerism. Share your ideas with the whole class.

Exercise

1 Identify whether each of the following is a want or a need:

   a) bottled water   **b)** cheese sandwich
   c) T-bone steak   **d)** pair of khaki pants
   e) designer footwear **f)** bus travel
   g) visit to the health centre.

2 Why do you think peer pressure can make you spend?

3 Identify an advertisement that influenced you to make a purchase.

Key vocabulary

consumer

consumer society

consumerism

6.1

161

Factors that influence consumer demand

We are learning to:

- analyse the factors which influence consumer demand.

There are a number of factors that influence consumer **demand**; the things that affect what consumers want. These change over time and from place to place. In fashion, for example, some styles of clothes are considered fashionable. People then want to buy more of these products, which creates increased demand. Other factors affecting demand include:

Factors	Influence on demand
Consumers' tastes and preferences	One factor which determines the demand for things is the tastes and preferences of consumers. People's tastes and preferences for various goods often change and as a result there is change in demand for them. The changes in demand for various goods occur due to changes in fashion and also due to the pressure of adverts by manufacturers and sellers of different products. When certain goods go out of fashion or people's tastes and preferences no longer favour them, the demand for them decreases.
Consumers' income	Demand for goods also depends upon people's incomes. The greater people's incomes, the greater their demand for goods. Greater income means greater purchasing power. Therefore, when incomes increase, people can afford to buy more.
Changes in the price of goods	If the price of a good rises beyond what consumers are able to afford then the demand for the good will decrease. If the price of the goods falls or decreases, consumers can afford more and so demand for these goods will increase.
Advertising	Advertisements to promote the sale of a product are an important factor in determining demand for a product. The purpose of advertisements is to influence consumers to purchase a product, which is sometimes done by appealing to people using celebrities or influencers to promote goods or services. This will influence the demand for a good or service. Advertisements are placed in various media such as newspapers, radio, and television and are repeated several times so that consumers are convinced about their superior quality. When advertisements prove successful they cause an increase in demand for the product.
Market size	Market size for a good is determined by adding the current number of customers to the number of possible future customers. The greater the number of consumers of a good, the greater the market demand for it.
Quality of goods or services	Another factor which influences the demand for goods is consumers' expectations of the quality of the goods or service. If people feel they are getting a high quality good or service, the demand for it will be great.

There are several factors that make a product successful.

1. A high quality product that benefits the user
2. A thoroughly planned product
3. Attractiveness to the intended consumers
4. Good marketing (strategy for selling of the product).

Marketing »»

Marketing is the process through which producers, wholesalers or retailers create a demand for the goods or services that they produce or provide. Marketing involves the **advertising**, distribution and sale of goods. Marketing usually involves a number of procedures:

- identifying a product which is in demand by prospective consumers; if it is a new product, this is usually done through market research in the form of surveys
- agreeing on a selling price to make sure that the product is competitive with similar products on the market
- identifying where the product will be sold to consumers
- advertising the product to help increase sales and awareness of its availability
- following the distribution chain to get the product to the point of sale.

Advertising »»»

Advertising is when a producer tries to persuade consumers to buy their goods or services. Advertising usually takes the form of an advertisement (or advert) that looks to persuade consumers to buy the product by making it a desirable item, or service, to have.

Advertising can take the form of newspaper and magazine advertisements, flyers, posters on billboards, ship fronts, television and radio advertising, and also on social media. Today, you can see advertisements almost everywhere you go.

Exercise

1. In your own words, define the terms marketing and advertising.
2. Draw a graphic organiser to show the process of marketing and advertising.
3. Count how many examples of advertising you see on your way to school.

Did you know...?

There are two main types of advertisement. *Informative advertising* informs consumers about a product and its benefits, whereas *persuasive advertising* tries to persuade consumers to buy the product.

Advertising is when a producer tries to persuade consumers to buy their goods or services.

Project

Work in groups to create a product (for example, pepper sauce, patties) and develop and implement a marketing strategy to sell the product to other students and teachers. At the end of the exercise, submit the strategy that was used to market the product, as well as a report on the challenges experienced.

Key vocabulary

demand

marketing

advertising

Factors that influence consumer demand

We are learning to:

- analyse the factors which influence consumer demand
- design a product, develop a plan to market the product and design success criteria.

The importance of distribution ⟫

The **Four Ps of Marketing** are the main things that you have to consider when marketing your goods. The four Ps are shown in the graphic. Distribution (Place in the four Ps) is important because:

- if a product cannot reach the customer, or consumer, then the company who owns the product cannot sell any goods or make money – customers will just buy a rival product

- the price of a product is worked out according to several factors, including the cost of making and marketing the product, but effective and efficient distribution can help to keep the price down and therefore make the product more affordable to more people

- some online companies are more attractive to buy from, because they promise quick delivery – companies such as Amazon offer next-day deliveries; fast and efficient deliveries help to increase customer satisfaction and encourage repeat business.

The 4Ps of marketing

Product
What are we selling?

Price
How much will the product or service cost?

Place
Where will we sell it and how will we get it there?

Promotion
How will we let people know we are selling the product/service?

Key vocabulary

Four Ps of Marketing

Activity

In groups you are going to design a product.

1. Decide what sort of product you are going to design.
2. Decide what kind of consumer(s) you are going to try to appeal to and why.
3. Create a document which explaining the use of your product and why your product is going to be successful. If the product is a food item, state all of the ingredients it contains.
4. Draw a picture showing the design of your product, explaining all the parts if applicable.
5. Design your marketing campaign which includes how and where you will market your product and create an advertisement or jingle to showcase the product.

Present your product and marketing plan to the rest of the class. Decide whose product is most likely to be successful, giving reasons why.

Research

Carry out some research into a marketing company in Jamaica. Find out:

a) What they do: the types of marketing they do online and offline
b) Some of the brands they represent
c) When was the company established?
d) What are the aims of the company?
e) How many people do they employ?
f) What kinds of skills do you think a person would need to be good at marketing?

Presenting is a skill which you will improve the more you do it.

Online marketing 》》》

As more and more people gain access to the internet there are more and more forms of advertising online. This includes:

- blogging
- YouTube videos
- advertising on websites
- text messages
- emails.

However, not everyone has access to the internet in Jamaica. Also, people may get overwhelmed with advertisements online and pay little attention to them.

Discussion

What are the pros and cons of using the internet to advertise a product?

How can blogging help promote your business?

Exercise

1. Explain the four P's of marketing, using your own words.

2. Think of a popular consumer product and explain what made it so successful.

3. Write an essay explaining the factors that affect consumer demand.

Rights and responsibilities of the consumer

We are learning to:

- analyse the rights and responsibilities of the consumer.

What are consumer rights?

Consumer rights are a set of laws that protect consumers when they are buying goods or services. This means that there are things that people who sell goods and services must do to protect consumers from harm or exploitation.

You can get help if you're treated unfairly or when things go wrong. This includes problems with:

- *credit and store cards:* if for example, you are charged for something you did not buy, you are entitled to a refund
- *faulty goods:* if you buy something that is broken or damaged, you have the right to have it replaced or fixed
- *counterfeit goods:* if you have been sold a stolen or fake item, you are entitled to a refund or to have it replaced
- *poor service:* you have the right to ask for a refund or discount if you feel that service has been poor, or some form of compensation
- *contracts:* if you enter a contract or agreement with a trader or provider of service, and they break the terms of this contract, you are entitled to challenge this and seek some form of solution
- *builders:* if you employ builders and they do not produce a high quality of work, you are entitled to request an improvement to that work
- *rogue traders:* people who offer goods or services that are fake or counterfeit should be reported.

If service is poor, you can ask for compensation.

Rogue traders who sell fake goods should be reported.

Exercise

1 In your own words, explain the term consumer rights, and give four examples where a consumer is within their rights.

Consumer rights in Jamaica

Consumers in Jamaica are protected by both national and international consumer rights laws. These are summarised below.

United Nations (UN) Guidelines on Consumer Protection

In 1985 Jamaica signed up to the United Nations (UN) Guidelines on Consumer Protection recognising the eight basic rights of the consumer, namely:

1. The Right to Safety
2. The Right to Choose
3. The Right to be Informed
4. The Right to be Heard
5. The Right to Redress
6. The Right to the Satisfaction of Basic Needs
7. The Right to a Healthy Environment
8. The Right to Consumer Education.

The Consumer Affairs Commission

In 1990 The Consumer Affairs Commission (CAC) was established in Jamaica. The focus of this agency was on consumer education, providing a variety of information to better equip the consumer to cope with all of the choices they had in buying services and products.

Information provided as part of this education programme include:

- Rights of the consumer
- Responsibilities of the consumer
- Budgeting and shopping hints
- Food safety
- Consumer vigilance
- Matters relating to the environment
- Laws and agencies providing consumer protection.

The CAC tries to reach individuals at all levels and age groups; for example, it has an active school programme.

Consumers have the right to seek compensation if the goods they buy are not to standard.

Case study

In 2020, The Consumer Affairs Commission (CAC) managed to secure a total of $6.8 million in refunds and compensation on behalf of their clients in just six months (1 April–30 November).

In that period, the CAC received 1 235 cases of which they were able to successfully get compensation for 796 of them. The categories of goods that saw the most claims were electrical equipment and appliances (30%), utilities (19%) and cable services, as well as miscellaneous which covers other services (14%).

A common claim was related to telecommunication (phone) providers, where either their credit had run out, the data plan was not working correctly or they had not received enough information from the provider about their plan.

The CAC Chief Executive Officer (CEO), Dolsie Allen, said that they were asking telecommuniation providers to "be a little more mindful [of their] responsibilities to the consumers in terms of how you respond to your consumers, how long it takes to respond to a complaint, and how you communicate changes to your consumers".

Mrs Allen encouraged people to "utilise our services as we are here to serve you, and we try our best to ensure that you get the compensation or redress that you deserve".

Source: adapted from Jamaica Information Service website

Exercise

2 Which organisation offers guidelines for international consumer rights, and which organisation offers guidelines for Jamaica?

3 How does The Consumer Affairs Commission (CAC) helps Jamaica's citizens? Give some examples.

Rights and responsibilities of the consumer

We are learning to:

- evaluate the role of government and consumer protection agencies in protecting the rights of the consumer.

What services does the Consumer Affairs Commission provide?

There are a number of services that consumers can access at the Consumer Affairs Commission free of charge:

- market research information on prices of grocery, petrol, agricultural and hardware items
- tips on issues such as budgeting, disaster preparedness, sustainable consumption, back to school preparation, and others
- consumer education initiatives such as presentations to schools, businesses and social clubs and participation in expositions, fairs and other events of this nature
- workshops and seminars for members of the business sector
- complaints resolution.

Jamaica Public Services Limited (JPS), the sole distributor of electricity in Jamaica.

As well as laws, consumer protection groups have led to a number of consumer protection agencies including the Bureau of Standards Jamaica (BSJ) and the Office of Utilities Regulation (OUR).

The Office of Utilities Regulation (OUR) was set up in 1995 in Jamaica by an Act of Parliament to regulate the operations of the **utility** companies on the islands. The OUR began operations in 1997. The utility companies include telecommunications, water, sewage, electricity, road, rail and ferry.

Their role is to provide a route for customers to complain about any grievances that they may have with any of the utility companies, while also working with the utility companies to make sure that they get a commercial return for their investment. They also make sure that cost and services for regulated sectors are fair to both the consumer and the company.

The Bureau of Standards Jamaica was established in 1969 to oversee that and encourage **standardisation** in relation to goods, processes and practices. This relates to making sure that organisations within particular sectors or services all work to the same standards.

Its main role is to make sure that standards are met, monitoring to make sure that they are met, conducting tests and **certifying** that businesses meet the standards, and provide training where necessary to educate about standards. As the Bureau is a legislative body, it works to various Acts of Parliament including The Standards Act (1968) and the more recent CARICOM Regional Organisation for Standards and Quality Act (2005).

Case study

The National Consumers' League (NCL) Jamaica

The National Consumers' League (NCL) is the oldest consumer organisation in the Caribbean and Latin America. The National Consumers' League was founded in 1966 and has been a member of Consumers International since 1967. Membership has risen to 5 000 overall, with 1 800 active.

The National Consumers' League provides consumers with information and advice on goods and services. It also **lobbies** government and business on behalf of customers.

NCL has been involved in all activities relating to consumer protection and advocacy, and recently has campaigned on Genetic Modification of Foods, Intellectual Property Rights and Consumer Education.

Their mission is to advance consumer knowledge, awareness about products, services, prices, market trends, their rights and responsibilities to enable them to make informed choices in a liberalising economy.

Case study

Joyce P Campbell

Joyce P. Campbell has spent most of her life serving her country and fellow citizens. As a consumer rights advocate and past president of the National Consumers' League (NCL), Campbell has been noted for her work in consumer rights advocacy, which spans five decades.

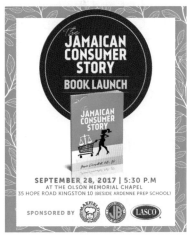

Joyce P Campbell's book on consumerism.

Exercise

1 Explain in your own words what is meant by consumer rights.

2 What role does the Bureau of Standards Jamaica (BSJ) and the Office of Utilities Regulation (OUR) have in consumer rights in Jamaica?

3 What is meant by 'complaints resolution'?

4 Carry out research into the Fair Trading Commission and explain their role.

5 What role does the National Consumers League play?

Key vocabulary

utility

standardisation

certify

lobby

Rights and responsibilities of the consumer

We are learning to:

* take steps to seek redress when rights have been violated.

What happens when consumer rights have been violated?

The CAC provide a Complaints Resolution service through a Complaints Bureau, with the focus on difficulties being experienced by consumers such as refusal or delays in repairing, or replacing defective goods; breach of contract, among others.

Are you being treated unfairly by a vendor?

If you have complained to a vendor about a service or product and the matter was not satisfactorily resolved, the Complaints Department at the Consumer Affairs Commission will be able to help. Through the use of the Consumer Protection Act among other pieces of legislation, the Complaints Department team will seek to resolve your complaint.

Research

Visit the government website for consumer affairs, and see what information is required to file a complaint. In pairs, imagine one of you is filing a complaint and the other is an agent at the CAC trying to resolve it. How would you try to resolve the problem?

Case study

Recalled products

When a product is found faulty, a consumer can contact the consumer affairs website and file a complaint. If several complaints are made, a product can be recalled, which means that people can take it back to the shop and ask for a refund. For example, a brand of popcorn was found to be dangerous because it caught fire when put in the microwave, as instructed. Consumers complained to the consumer affairs website and a notice was put out about this brand of popcorn as a 'recalled object'. Consumers were encouraged to contact the vendor for a new bag which was safe, free of charge, to replace their unsafe products.

Recalled products are products that are found to be dangerous or faulty.

Research

Carry out some research into recalled products in Jamaica. Find out what action is required, and what the consumer can do to get their item replaced or their money back.

As well as having rights, consumers also have responsibilities or obligations.

Consumer

1. Check before you buy

Make sure you know what you are buying. Do your research and make sure you understand what the product or service will provide, and compare it against other products or services that are available.

2. Read and follow instructions

Products and services tend to come with instructions and fine print. It is your responsibility to read everything the company gives you. Often products break or are mis-used, and customers are even injured, due to not reading the instructions and fine print.

3. Use the product or service as intended

Even after reading all the instructions, it is your responsibility to use the product or service as instructed. Sometimes deliberate mis-use can be punishable by law.

4. Make a complaint

You have a legal right to speak out when you feel you have been wronged by a company or organisation. Most companies have a complaints department that you can contact.

5. Your responsibilities for purchasing

Your consumer rights may be void if you have purchased or used a product or service illegally or not as it was intended. For example, if you stole a product, or you bought prescription drugs from a friend or street dealer – this would impact your consumer rights.

Exercise

1. Who should you contact if you feel you have been treated unfairly by a vendor?

2. What is a recalled product?

3. Summarise your responsibilities as a consumer into a paragraph.

Understanding globalisation

We are learning to:

- define and explain relevant terms and concepts: globalisation, global village, economy, trade, technology
- discuss the impact of globalism on the consumer and consumerism.

Globalisation ▶▶

The word **global** means worldwide or relating to the whole world. **Globalisation** relates to things that take place all over the world. For example:

- opening up of world trading **markets**, through improvements in transport, communication and the removal of barriers to **trade**
- commercial activities – many businesses have branches in different countries and/or trade products all over the world
- social interactions in person or through social media like Facebook, X and Instagram
- climate change and pollution are global problems
- **communicable diseases** can affect communities all over the world, and the whole world is responsible for trying to control them. A communicable disease is passed from one person to another – for example, hepatitis, influenza or HIV/AIDS.

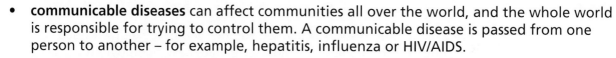

People connected in a global village.

An economy is a system of how industry, trade and finance are organised in a country, region or worldwide. In the Caribbean, globalisation offers opportunities such as:

- a greater range and quality of goods
- chances to export to new and bigger markets
- more exports leading to an increase in employment
- more exports resulting in increased business investment
- increased wages and standards of living.

While economic globalisation has many positives, it can also mean that cheaper, imported goods can be bought by the population at the expense of locally produced goods. This can result in some companies going out of business. Other disadvantages of globalisation include the loss of labour from markets to other countries (so skill sets are lost to some countries), there is no guarantee that income filters down to the local community, which can cause another issue that there could be a widening gap between richer and poorer countries.

Exercise

1. In your own words define globalisation and communicable diseases.

2. What are the advantages of globalisation in terms of trade?

Discussion

Do you rely on technology in your everyday life? What would happen if you were no longer able to use technology? Discuss this topic in groups.

Global village

The term **global village** is used to describe the way people all over the world have become connected through technology.

People who live in a village all know each other and communicate regularly with each other. In the same way people all over the globe are now able to communicate with each other with technology, through social media such as Facebook and X.

Distance is no longer a barrier to communication. The availability of news at our fingertips has encouraged us to become more involved in events around the world.

People in an internet café in the Philippines.

Technology

Technology consists of devices and systems which have been created for practical purposes. The technology that allows us to communicate with people all over the world is vast and complex. Satellites orbit the globe to relay weather reports and televised images to all parts of the world and the internet connects people with friends and family as well as with business partners.

It is estimated that more than 59% of the world's population now use the internet to communicate and do research. The increase in access and usage over the last 20 years is quite staggering. In 1994 only 0.4% of the world's population used the internet.

Many people have internet access in their homes or through their mobile phones. Others make use of public internet cafés to access the internet.

All big- and medium-sized enterprises rely on the internet to communicate with their customers and suppliers.

Activity

Make a poster or a drawing to illustrate your understanding of the term global village.

Did you know...?

In 2017 around 55% of the population of Jamaica had access to the internet.

Activity

Create a concept map to explain the meaning and features of the term 'globalisation'.

Exercise

3 In your own words, define the terms global village and technology.

4 Why do you think the term global village is used?

5 Why do you think social media make it easier to keep in touch with people in different parts of the world?

6 How many people in the world today have access to the internet?

7 What are the advantages and disadvantages of globalisation for developing economies such as Jamaica's?

Key vocabulary

global

globalisation

market

trade

communicable diseases

global village

The impact of globalisation on the consumer and consumerism

We are learning to:

- discuss the impact of globalisation on the consumer and consumerism
- examine the impact of technology on consumerism.

Online shopping

In countries where there is sufficient internet connectivity, the economy can change significantly with the growth of e-commerce, or **online shopping**. People started using the internet to buy goods and services in the 1980s. This type of commerce has grown significantly since then, with many people relying on the internet to purchase things like train and air tickets, holidays and books, and to do their banking.

E-commerce businesses have websites with details of all the goods and services they sell. In order to buy goods online, a customer usually needs a debit card or a credit card, and a secure internet connection. This is a quick and easy way to shop, as goods purchased are delivered to your office or home, or via a post office.

Globalisation has helped to increase the number of cheaper goods that are available in supermarkets.

Imports of cheaper goods ⟩⟩⟩

One effect of globalisation is that it has increased the number of cheaper goods and services that are available. There can be a variety of reasons for this, including lower production costs, lower cost of raw materials and lower labour costs.

Large **transnational companies** (organisations that have business interests in more than one country) are able to use economies of scale to their benefit. This is where bigger companies are able to lower their unit costs, because they are selling more products. Having cheaper goods and services can be a good thing for the consumer, but the quality of goods may suffer, or the level of service may be lower than if you paid a little bit more elsewhere.

Research

Do your own research on the meaning of the term market. This will broaden your understanding of how this term is used.

Exercise

1 What does e-commerce rely on to operate successfully?

2 How has online shopping changed the way people buy their goods?

3 Explain why having cheaper goods is not always a good thing.

Competition ⟩⟩⟩⟩

Globalisation and removal of barriers to international trade has led to increased **competition**. Competition exists when there are several producers who make the same or similar items, or who offer similar goods or services.

These producers compete with each other to make their products and services attractive to customers. Factors that affect competition include the quality, price and availability of goods and services.

Competition between producers can sometimes mean that:

- local producers who cannot compete against the buying power of big companies could go out of business
- local products can be thought of as too costly or they may become unavailable, limiting consumer choice.

Understanding consumerism ⟩⟩

Consumerism refers to the concept of buying goods and using services based on the idea that owning and having access to things leads to a better quality of life.

The main advantages of consumerism are:

- it helps economies to grow and creates jobs
- demand from consumers means that products and services have to be constantly innovated to stay competitive
- it fuels global trade – different countries import and export from one another.

The main disadvantages of consumerism are:

- the demand for materials and resources, and the movement of them across the world, is not good for the environment
- it can lead some people to get into debt because they spend beyond their means
- it can create greater social inequality between those who can afford material things and those who cannot.

Consumerism can create a trade imbalance. For example, if consumers in Jamaica buy lots of imported goods, it can mean that the overall value of imports becomes higher than exports. This can negatively impact the national economy.

The impact of technology on consumerism »»

E-commerce, or online shopping is shifting the way people purchase their goods and services. Consequently, traditional retailers, aware of these changes, have developed strategies to keep up with the continuously evolving marketplace. These strategies vary from creating virtual stores (i.e. websites) and developing digital social networks to gathering data about potential customers and advertising online.

Be careful who you give out your information to when shopping online.

Project

Create a table to log whether the goods and services you use over the next week were locally manufactured or imported.

Share your findings with the rest of the class.

Activity

Work in groups to develop an awareness campaign for teenagers. The campaign should explain how to choose products and services to minimise the negative impacts of consumerism on the Jamaican economy.

Research

Survey friends and family to find out what they think about consumerism. Ask whether they like to spend their money or save, what they like to spend their money on, and how spending money makes them feel.

When shopping online make sure you follow these safety measures:

- check that the website you are shopping from is legitimate
- use a credit card for online payments, as major credit card providers are obliged to refund consumers if either the supplier goes bust or does not deliver the goods
- other payment methods you can use safely are PayPal or GooglePay
- if there is a form online to fill in your own personal details, only fill in the ones relevant to the purchase – you shouldn't have to provide security details to complete your purchase
- make sure your password is secure and is regularly changed
- watch out for suspicious text messages, texts or emails from online stores – some fraudsters are very good at making fake messages or websites.

Exercise

4 Explain the advantages and disadvantages of competition.

5 What are the advantages of shopping online?

6 What are the disadvantages of shopping online?

7 How can the government ensure that consumer rights and responsibilities are upheld online?

8 How might E-commerce affect marketing strategies?

Key vocabulary

online shopping

transnational company

competition

Questions

See how well you have understood the topics in this unit.

1. Identify different types of consumer.

2. A _____ is someone who buys particular products or services.

   a) shopper
   b) migrant
   c) consumer
   d) minister

3. _____ are people who manufacture or create a particular good or service

   a) Producers
   b) Consumers
   c) Ministers
   d) Advocates

4. In which year was the CAC set up?

   a) 1990
   b) 1988
   c) 1980
   d) 1967

5. True or False? A rogue trader is a consumer who buys fake goods.

6. Correct this statement: Globalisation is a process where the people live more locally, using less technology.

7. Explain in your own words how globalisation can make goods cheaper for the consumer.

8. How is technology affecting consumerism?

9. What is marketing?

10. Write a short definition of the following terms:

    Consumerism
    Demand
    Consumer society

11. Explain what happens when a product is found to be faulty or dangerous.

12. Match the 4Ps of marketing.

    1) Product
    2) Place
    3) Price
    4) Promotion

    a) How will we let people know we are selling the product/service?
    b) How much will the product or service cost?
    c) What are we selling?
    d) Where will we sell it and how will we get it there?

13. Give two examples of consumer responsibilities.

14. Give three examples of consumer rights.

15. Explain the role of the National Consumers League.

16. Imagine that you work for an organisation which helps consumers file complaints about faulty products. Write a paragraph of about 200 words describing your action.

17. What do you understand by the terms globalisation and global village?

18. Match the type of consumer with its definition.

    1) Consumers of goods
    2) Consumers of services
    3) Consumers of credit

    a) people who buy a service
    b) people who take on personal debt in order to purchase goods and services
    c) people who buy either materials to create a final product

Grade 8 Unit 6 Summary

Consumer affairs and demand

In this chapter, you have learned about:

- What is meant by consumer and producer
- The habits that lead to consumerism
- How to distinguish between wants and needs
- The factors that influence what we consume
- The three categories of consumers
- The factors that influence consumer demand
- What the factors of a successful product are
- Using marketing and advertising to create demand for products and services
- The four main marketing procedures
- The impact of online marketing in creating consumer demand.

Consumer rights and responsibilities

In this chapter, you have learned about:

- What consumer rights are
- National and international consumer rights laws
- The eight consumer rights covered by the United Nations Guidelines on Consumer Protection
- The functions and services of the Consumer Affairs Commission in Jamaica
- Channels available to consumers when their rights are violated
- The responsibilities of the consumer.

Globalisation and the consumer

In this chapter, you have learned about:

- What globalisation is and the benefits and drawbacks of it
- How technology has enabled communication and created a global village
- The impact of globalisation on the consumer and consumerism
- How technology has enabled consumerism.

Checking your progress

To make good progress in understanding consumer affairs, check that you understand these ideas.

Explain and use correctly the terms *consumer, consumer rights* and *responsibilities*.

Describe examples of consumer rights.

Outline the main responsibilities that a consumer has.

Explain and use correctly the term *e-commerce*.

Outline advantages and disadvantages of technology based shopping.

Explain what makes a good marketing strategy.

Explain and use correctly the term *consumer demand*.

Name 2 consumer rights laws that exist in Jamaica.

Explain the role of consumer affairs in resolving consumer complaints.

Explain and use correctly the term *globalisation*.

Describe the Charter of Fundamental Rights.

Explain the functions of the C.A.C.

End-of-term questions

See how well you have understood the ideas in Unit 4.

1. Explain the difference between the three types of rocks.

2. Match the following terms with the correct definitions below:

   a) hamlet

   b) town

   c) city

   d) capital city

   i) larger than villages

   ii) the largest settlement type

   iii) a small number of houses

   iv) a large settlement where the government of a country in located

3. Briefly describe the difference between linear and nucleated settlement patterns.

4. Describe how the physical environment shapes where the population is greatest.

5. Explain the difference between physical and human-made features.

See how well you have understood the ideas in Unit 5.

6. Explain what is meant by political, social and economic institutions, using examples.

7. Provide two examples of ways the government of Jamaica ensures the economy is stable.

8. Give two examples of the potential problems with informal financial institutions.

9. Explain the role of credit unions.

10. What is the role of the Bank of Jamaica?

Questions 11–15 >>

See how well you have understood the ideas in Unit 6.

11. Explain the difference between consumers and producers.

12. Why is it important that consumers understand their rights? Write a short paragraph to explain.

13. Write a short essay of six paragraphs in which you explain how consumers are protected in Jamaica.

14. Explain why you think technology and globalisation are affecting consumerism. Give at least three examples in your answer.

15. Create a spidergram showing the responsibilities of the consumer.

Unit 7: Climate Change: The Impact of Human Activities

Objectives: You will be able to: ▶▶

The difference between weather and climate

- differentiate between weather and climate
- define and correctly use key concepts.

How the climate affects how we live

- differentiate between weather and climate
- define and correctly use key concepts.

Climate graphs

- differentiate between weather and climate
- define and correctly use key concepts.

Climate change and global warming

- gather, synthesise and evaluate information from multiple sources which represent different views on climate change
- examine the impact of human activities on climate change
- examine the greenhouse effect
- predict the consequences of climate change on different environments and different groups of people.

Organisations which manage and monitor climate change

- analyse the role of local and international organisations and agreements which manage and monitor climate change.

How can you reduce your carbon footprint?

- propose strategies to mitigate the effects of climate change on Jamaica.

The difference between weather and climate

We are learning to:

- differentiate between weather and climate
- define and correctly use key concepts.

Weather and climate 》

Weather is a set of conditions in the atmosphere at a particular time and place. It changes all the time, and the weather in one place is different from the conditions elsewhere. For example, it may be dry in the morning, then rainy in the afternoon, or it may be calm at your home but windy at your school.

Climate is pattern of weather in a place over a longer period. The climate of a place controls the weather. For example, it would be very unusual to have a snowstorm in the Caribbean, because our climate is generally warm and mild.

The weather is a set of conditions at a certain time and place – for example, it may be windy and rainy one day, and sunny and hot the next day.

Research

Using the internet, research which countries have the following:

a) highest and lowest recorded temperatures

b) wettest and driest rainfall figures

c) windiest conditions.

The weather 》》

Most people watch, talk about and look up the weather daily. This is because the weather is so important to our everyday lives. We might only check the weather so that we can decide what to wear that day or see whether we should take an umbrella out with us.

For other people, the weather is more important, however. For example, it is vital that a farmer knows what is going on with the weather, so that he knows when to plough his fields or harvest his crops.

He might also need to keep up to date with the weather in case there is a risk of flooding, which might drown his crops or endanger his animals. Regardless of the reason we need to know the weather, the fact is, we check it on an ever-increasing basis.

Examples of some extreme weather phenomena in the Caribbean, include:

- A **cyclone** is a tropical storm with a closed, circulating wind pattern.
- A **hurricane** occurs when a tropical cyclone moves faster than 119 km per hour. The area of a hurricane can measure more than 950 km across, and wind speeds can reach 300 km per hour.
- A **tornado**, also known as a twister, is a spinning column of air that forms under thunderclouds. Tornadoes can be extremely violent and destructive, with wind speeds of more than 480 km per hour.

The climate in Jamaica >>>>

Jamaica lies within the tropics and has a tropical maritime climate. The prevailing winds are from the east and northeast. These bring rain throughout the year with the greatest rainfall in the mountains facing the north and the east. In contrast, the southwest of the island, protected at the foot of the mountains, has a semi-arid climate. Temperatures vary very little throughout the year but the height of the land above sea level has an influence on the temperature causing the mountains to be cooler than the lowlands.

Exercise

1. What is the difference between weather and climate?

2. Look outside. What is the weather like today?

3. Is today's weather usual or unusual for this time of year? Give reasons for your answer.

4. Look at the photo on page 186. Describe the weather in the photo.

5. Look at a map of Jamaica showing the climate on the island. Which climate do you live in?

Key vocabulary

weather

climate

cyclone

hurricane

tornado

How the climate affects how we live

We are learning to:

- differentiate between weather and climate
- define and correctly use key concepts.

How do the weather and climate affect us day to day?

What the weather is like affects us in our everyday lives. It influences our decisions about what we wear and what we do each day. Weather and climate affect people, industries and the environment all over the world.

Clothes worn

If you live in a very warm country, you will want to wear loose clothes made from cotton or linen, as these are cooling in warm temperatures. You will most likely wear shorts and T-shirts in warm countries, to try to stay as cool as possible.

In contrast, if you live in cold countries you will want to wrap up really warm and wear as many layers as possible. In some of the coldest countries in the world, such as northern Russia, people wear **animal hides** (skin) to keep warm. The hides of animals such as caribou and hares can be worn to protect people from the very cold air, because if you wore short sleeves in these countries you could very easily get **frostbite**. There is a phrase used in Iceland that says, 'There is no such thing as bad weather, just bad clothing.'

Warm clothing in essential in cold climates such as in Iceland.

Health problems

Climate affects what diseases are found, and spread, in different countries. Most diseases are very heavily influenced by the weather, and many diseases need specific weather conditions. For example, malaria is a very dangerous disease spread by mosquitoes. Mosquitoes are found all over the world and they are not all harmful. However, tropical areas, where temperatures are warm and the air is **humid** (moist), make excellent breeding conditions for mosquitoes and for this reason malaria is a problem in these areas.

Not only does warm weather cause disease, but it can also lead to other serious medical conditions such as sunburn, heatstroke and even skin cancer. Colder temperatures can cause illnesses such as frostbite, pneumonia and hypothermia.

Sporting activities »

The climate affects the different sporting activities that are possible in a country.

For example, countries that have snow in the winter months can be very popular ski and snowboarding destinations. Countries such as New Zealand, France and the USA (for example, in Colorado) are all very popular ski areas. Many people visit these countries from all over the world.

Sports such as cricket are heavily influenced by the climate. In the Caribbean, the cricket season takes place between November and May, whereas in the UK – which has far less reliable sunshine – the season can only be played in the warmer months, between April and September.

The sunny climate in Jamaica means that the cricket season takes place between November and May.

Crops planted »»

Farming is a very important industry around the world. It is not necessarily a big industry in many countries now, but it is still a very important industry and one that is highly dependent on the climate. Not all crops need the same weather conditions.

While it is true that most crops need sunshine and rain to grow, too much sunshine or too much rainfall will not produce many crops.

Countries that are very hot, such as Ethiopia, struggle to grow crops because the temperatures are so high and there is very little rainfall.

Some regions, such as certain states in the USA (for instance, Alaska), cannot grow crops easily because there are very low temperatures and very little rainfall.

Some of the best regions to farm are where there are no extreme weather conditions.

Farming is an important industry and highly dependent on climate.

Exercise

1. How do the weather and climate affect our decisions about what to wear?

2. What health problems may be caused by the weather?

3. Give examples of sports that need specific weather conditions.

4. How is farming affected by the weather?

Key vocabulary

animal hide

frostbite

humid

Climate graphs

We are learning to:

- differentiate between weather and climate
- define and correctly use key concepts.

Climate graphs ➤➤

Climate information is shown using **climate graphs**. These are graphs that show temperature and rainfall statistics for a country or area over a period of time. The most common type of climate graph shows the annual temperature and rainfall over a one-year period. Temperatures are shown as a line graph and rainfall is shown as a bar graph. A climate graph can help us to understand the climate of a place and also the type of weather to expect at different times of the year. A climate graph can also help us to monitor changes that may be taking place in the climate.

> **Did you know...?**
>
> Someone who studies the weather and climate is known as a meteorologist.

Interpreting climate graphs ➤➤➤

When studying climate graphs, there are a few things that you must take into consideration:

- What is the **range** of temperatures across the year? (To find this out, you subtract the minimum temperature from the maximum temperature.)
- What month(s) of the year are the hottest? What is the temperature?
- What month(s) of the year are the coldest? What is the temperature?
- Is there rainfall in every month of the year?

Average rainfall graphs

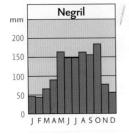
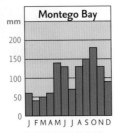
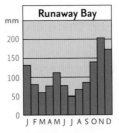

Average temperature graphs

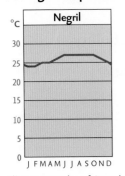
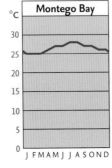
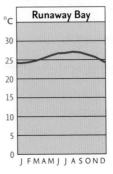

Climate graphs of Jamaica.

- If a month is dry, what month of the year is it?
- Is there a lot of rain?
- What is the total annual rainfall? (To find this out, you add up all the rainfall in every month of the year.)

Interpreting isohyet maps ▶▶▶

Isohyet maps are maps that are used to show rainfall figures. They connect different places on a map that have the same amounts of rainfall at a specific time.

When studying isohyet maps, there are a couple of things that need to be considered:

- What is the overall pattern of rainfall like? Are some areas much wetter than others? What are the figures?
- Are there any extremes – for example, some areas that have a lot of rainfall, compared to others that have none? What are the figures?

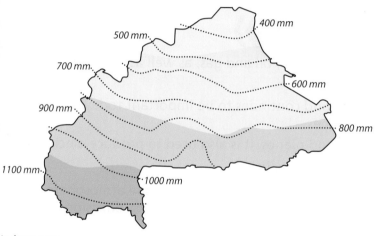

Isohyet map.

Activity

Using an atlas and other sources, gather and interpret information on temperature and rainfall in Jamaica. Create a PowerPoint presentation to show what you have found.

Exercise

1 What do climate graphs show?

2 Look at the climate graph above.

    a) Which months have the least and most rainfall?

    b) Which six months form the 'wet season'?

3 What do isohyet maps show?

4 From the isohyet map, can you give reasons as to why some areas are wetter or drier than others?

5 What should you consider when interpreting climate and isohyet maps?

6 In your own words, explain how graphs are used to show temperature and rainfall.

Activity

Your teacher will arrange a visit to your class from a meteorologist. They will discuss why it is important to be able to provide climate data to citizens.

Key vocabulary

climate graphs

range

isohyet maps

Climate change and global warming: causes

We are learning to:

- gather, synthesise and evaluate information from multiple sources which represent different views on climate change.

Climate change is a change in global or regional climate patterns, in recent decades, mainly due to the increased levels of carbon dioxide produced by the use of fossil fuels.

The Earth's climate has changed numerous times in the past, for example, long ago during the last Ice Age. The climate change that is being experienced today is as a result of increased warming of Earth's atmosphere. Climate change can also happen naturally, but climate change today is believed to be a result of human activities.

Global warming a gradual increase in the overall temperature of the Earth's atmosphere generally attributed to the greenhouse effect caused by increased levels of carbon dioxide and other pollutants.

The use of natural resources and global warming

The overuse and burning of fossil fuels such as coal, oil and gas, as well as destruction of rainforests, can lead to global warming.

- Coal has been used for many centuries and continues to be important today. Coal is mainly used for power and heating homes.
- Oil is used as a fuel, to power vehicles and planes. It is also used to produce electricity.
- One of the main uses of gas is to create electricity.

When all of these fuels are burned, they release dangerous gases into the atmosphere. One of the most dangerous of these is **carbon dioxide**. This is known as **carbon emission**.

Global warming and climate change

Burning fossil fuels increases the carbon levels in the atmosphere, which is gradually causing the atmosphere to retain more heat. This causes average temperatures to rise, a process known as warming, which could cause disasters for life on Earth.

- The ice caps at the north and south poles are melting at a fast rate, causing a rise in sea levels.
- Higher sea levels could cause the flooding or disappearance of coastal cities and low-lying islands.
- Warmer temperatures also mean the oceans are warmer, causing increases in storms and the different hazards associated with them.
- Temperature changes cause a change in the climate in different places, such as more intense rainfall in some areas and increased drought and desertification in dry areas.

Global warming can be defined as a gradual increase in the overall temperature of the Earth's atmosphere generally agreed to be a result of an enhancement of the **greenhouse effect** caused by increased levels of carbon dioxide and other gases in the atmosphere.

Here are some facts about global warming:

- With the start of industry (factories and technology) in the 18th century, humans began emitting more fossil fuels from coal, oil, and gas to run our cars, trucks, and factories.
- There is more carbon dioxide in the atmosphere today than at any point in the last 800 000 years.
- Since 1870, global sea levels have risen by about 8 inches.
- Global climate change has already had observable effects on the environment. Glaciers have shrunk, ice on rivers and lakes is breaking up earlier, plant and animal ranges have shifted and trees are flowering sooner.
- Heat waves caused by global warming present greater risk of heat-related illness and death.
- Global warming puts coral reefs in danger as the ocean warms, and scientists fear that coral reefs will not be able to adapt quickly enough to the resulting changing conditions.

Source: DoSomething website

Greenhouse gases ⟩⟩⟩

Carbon dioxide is a **greenhouse gas**. This means that it is a gas that forms naturally in the atmosphere.

Small amounts of greenhouse gases in the atmosphere are a good thing, as they keep the temperatures in the atmosphere warm enough to sustain human life. However, it's because of the enhanced greenhouse effect that we are experiencing global warming, and consequently, climate change.

Too much carbon dioxide, methane, nitrous oxide and the other greenhouse gases in the atmosphere leads to an increase in global temperature, otherwise known as global warming.

Global warming can have very negative impacts on the environment, such as melting of glaciers, increase in sea levels, higher temperatures, drought and an increase in hurricanes.

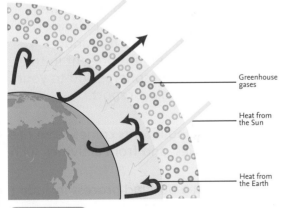

Greenhouse gases

Heat from the Sun

Heat from the Earth

Key vocabulary

climate change
global warming
carbon dioxide
carbon emissions
greenhouse effect
greenhouse gas

Exercise

1. Give two examples of activities that lead to global warming.

2. In your own words, define greenhouse gas and global warming.

Human activities and climate change

We are learning to:

- examine the impact of human activities on climate change
- examine the greenhouse effect.

Climate change is the change of the Earth's temperature and weather patterns as a result of increased carbon dioxide in the air caused by human activity. Many human activities have harmful effects on the environment and contribute to climate change, for example air travel contributes 4–9% of climate change, and vehicle use is one of the biggest contributors to carbon dioxide emissions.

Carbon dioxide (CO_2)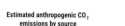

Carbon dioxide, which is emitted whenever coal, oil, natural gas and other carbon-rich fossil fuels are burned. Carbon dioxide is the largest contributor to climate change because it is so common

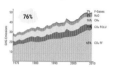

Estimated anthropogenic CO_2 emissions by source

Agriculture

As the world's population grows, more food is needed, but agriculture is one of the sectors that produce the most CO_2 emissions. Deforestation, soil erosion and machine intensive farming all lead to increased levels of carbon in the atmosphere, while farming releases greenhouse gases, such as methane and nitrous oxide into the atmosphere. Livestock produces methane during digestion and is released by belches. Methane also escapes from stored manure and organic waste in landfills. Nitrous oxide emissions are an indirect product of organic and mineral nitrogen fertilisers.

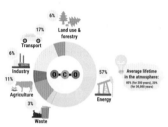

Greenhouse gas emissions by economic sector.

Deforestation

Deforestation is the removal of trees and vegetation to create open spaces for human activities – this can be harmful for the environment, as it can lead to increased global warming and climate change. It is estimated the damaging and clearing of forests is responsible for around 10% of global warming.

Industry

Industry is responsible for up to 65% of CO_2 emissions into the atmosphere. It comes from many different human activities:

- fire produces smoke, dust and soot. The main source of these pollutants comes from fire used in industrial processes, for example in sugar cane factories, and from activities such as burning waste materials
- internal combustion engines burn gasoline. By-products of the burning process include carbon monoxide, lead and particulates, which are released into the air
- some factories release gases such as sulphur oxides, sulphur dioxides and nitrous oxides
- cement and chemical factories, as well as quarries and mines, emit large quantities of dust into the air.

Project

Research the main greenhouse gases. Draw up a table using the information. Show the name and abbreviation of the gas, a short description of which activities produce the gas and what kinds of problems it produces when it is present in the atmosphere. Add to your project report.

The greenhouse effect ⟫

The addition of industrial chemicals to the air changes the composition of the atmosphere. Chemicals such as carbon monoxide, sulphur oxides and dioxides create a thick chemical blanket at the top of the Earth's atmosphere, preventing some of the Earth's heat from escaping into space. This produces the greenhouse effect in which the Earth's average temperature is gradually rising.

Project

Research the greenhouse effect. Present your information in a diagram showing how the greenhouse effect works.

Solutions for air pollution ⟫⟫

Some solutions for air pollution are shown in the mind maps.

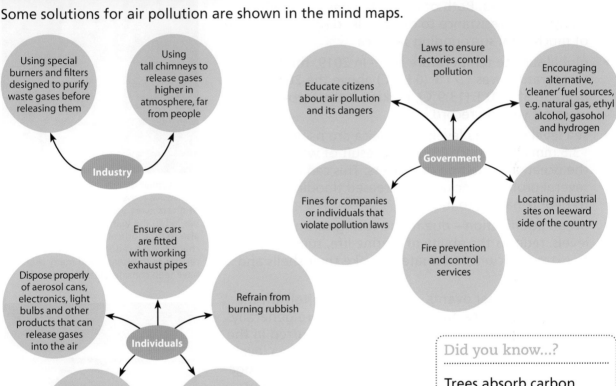

Did you know...?

Trees absorb carbon dioxide so, if forests are destroyed, carbon dioxide and other greenhouse gases are released into the atmosphere. It is estimated that the damaging and clearing of forests is responsible for around 10% of global warming.

Exercise

1. In your own words, explain how human activities contribute to climate change. As the world's population grows, do you think climate change will increase or decrease?

2. Name three ways that agriculture contributes to climate change.

3. Explain how industry contributes to climate change and some possible solutions.

Key vocabulary

deforestation

The effects of climate change

We are learning to:

- predict the consequences of climate change on different environments and different groups of people.

There is much evidence of climate change as we have seen, including:

- warming oceans – climate change has led to the warming of the sea, plus the increasing acidification of the sea, which has a damaging effect on the flora and fauna in the sea. Both of these changes have reduced many coral's resistance to disease, leading to the death of much coral surrounding Jamaica
- global surface temperature rise – In 2019, the average temperature was 1.71°F (0.95°C) above the 20th century average of 57.0°F (13.9°C), making it the second-warmest year on record
- **sea level** rise – Sea levels in Jamaica are rising at ~3.5 mm a year since 1993, as a result of warming of the ocean and melting of glaciers. This can lead to several problems including increased flooding, leading to people having to move
- **ocean acidification** – due to increasing carbon dioxide levels, reduces the ability of marine life, such as coral, to extract calcium carbonate to make their shells and skeletons
- **extreme weather events** – these are definitely on the increase in Jamaica and the Caribbean more generally. A series of devastating hurricanes have occurred in the last twenty years, which, coupled with rising sea levels and other aspects of climate change have caused huge amounts of damage to people and the environment
- **desertification** – is the transformation of fertile land into an arid or semi-arid region as a result of climate change and human activities.

The Cayman Islands are surrounded by impressive reefs which attract thousands of divers every year. Climate change has led to the warming of the sea, and also to its acidification. Both of these changes have reduced many corals' resistance to disease, and many reefs have seen considerable coral die-off.

Flooding in Jamaica is a combined effect of rainfall and topography. Most floods occur in the months of May and September–October when rainfall peaks.

> **Did you know...?**
>
> The five warmest years in the 1880–2019 record have all occurred since 2015, while nine of the 10 warmest years have occurred since 2005.

A house in Harbourview Community which was destroyed by Hurricane Ivan, 2004.

Key vocabulary

sea level

ocean acidification

extreme weather events

desertification

Case study

Deforestation

Deforestation is the clearance of forests so that the land can be used for other purposes – usually agriculture but also urban expansion. Forests are also lost through forest fires that occur accidentally. These are also called wildfires or bushfires and occur most often in forested regions that have a dry season.

Impacts of deforestation

- Flood water carries away unprotected soil
- Without vegetation to soak up water, heavy rain causes floods
- Without humus from rotting leaves, the soil becomes poorer
- Rivers silt up, causing floods and clogging dams
- Burning trees release CO_2 into the atmosphere, adding to 'greenhouse' gases
- Fierce sunshine can dry out the earth, making it useless for crops without irrigation.

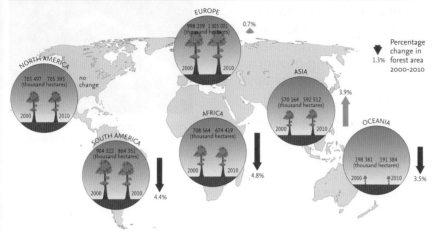

Case study

Tropical storms in the Caribbean

Hurricane Ivan

Hurricane Ivan was a category 5 hurricane that affected the Caribbean in September 2004. It caused a huge amount of damage to the Caribbean and USA as it tore across the Atlantic Ocean.

When the storm hit Grenada, it was only a category 3 hurricane, but it caused widespread damage there. Hurricane Ivan killed 39 people in Grenada and caused serious damage to hospitals, schools, roads and farmland. By the time the hurricane reached Jamaica, it had increased to a category 4 hurricane, and caused widespread flooding.

Hurricane Sandy

Hurricane Sandy was a category 3 hurricane that caused extensive damage to the Caribbean and USA in November 2012.

The storm formed in the Atlantic Ocean and ripped through the Caribbean region, killing 80 people – 60 in Haiti, 11 in Cuba, 2 in the Bahamas, 2 in the Dominican Republic and 1 in Jamaica.

Hurricane Sandy caused millions of dollars' worth of damage in the Caribbean. Roads, schools and hospitals were destroyed, as well as 18 000 homes.

Questions

1. Which country suffered the most from Hurricane Sandy?

2. In your own words, describe the impact that a hurricane of these strengths can have on a country.

The effects of climate change

We are learning to:

- predict the consequences of climate change on different environments and different groups of people.

Coral bleaching

Coral reefs support some of the most biodiverse ecosystems on the planet. Thousands of marine animals depend on coral reefs for survival, including some species of sea turtles, fish, crabs, shrimp, jellyfish, sea birds, starfish, and many more. Coral reefs also provide shelter, spawning grounds, and protection from predators. If reef ecosystems collapse, already at-risk species may face extinction.

When sea temperatures rise, corals will expel the colourful **algae** living in their tissues causing the coral to turn completely white. This is called **coral bleaching**. When a coral bleaches, it is not dead. Corals can survive a bleaching event, but they are under more stress and are at risk of dying. Coral bleaching also happens when there is pollution in the water, extremely low tides or too much sunshine, all of which become more likely with climate change.

Coral bleaching is very serious because once the corals die, reefs rarely come back. With few corals surviving, they struggle to reproduce, and entire reef ecosystems, on which people and wildlife depend, break down.

This is a global issue, not just a problem for Jamaica. According to the National Oceanic and Atmospheric Association, between 2014 and 2017 around 75% of the world's tropical coral reefs experienced heat-stress severe enough to start bleaching. For 30% of the world's reefs, that heat-stress was enough to kill coral.

Coral bleaching also affects peoples' livelihoods, food security, and safety. Coral reefs are natural barriers that absorb the force of waves and storm surges, keeping coastal communities safe. Without them, manmade seawalls need to be made, which are expensive, less effective, and environmentally damaging to construct. Also, reef tourism brings in billions of dollars each year and supports thousands of jobs. Fishing is also likely to be seriously reduced as a result.

Coral bleaching is the effect of any disease causing the coral to die and leave a white patch on its skeleton, as seen by this example from Curaçao. This has seriously affected all the Caribbean reefs and the dive tourist industry.

Key vocabulary

algae

coral bleaching

Case study

Coral bleaching in the Caribbean

2005 was a notable year in climate change – it was the hottest year in the Northern hemisphere since records had begun in 1880. This had the effect of warming large areas of water in the Caribbean and Atlantic oceans. Water temperatures continued to rise through to October of that year.

2005 was also a notable year as there were 26 tropical storms that year, including 13 hurricanes, one of which was hurricane Katrina, which had a devastating effect on New Orleans. Many of the hurricanes caused considerable damage to coral reefs, due the increased action of the waves, as well as drawing in polluted waters into the Caribbean.

2005 became a massive coral bleaching event, as the warmer than normal water temperatures caused large scale bleaching. Corals were affected all over the Caribbean including Colombia, Belize, Mexico, Barbados and the Cayman Islands.

The northern coasts of Jamaica were affected in August, and by September bleaching had begun to make an impact round the south coast of Jamaica (in total 80% of the coral was affected). In addition to this, the southern coral reefs around Jamaica were also affected by hurricanes Dennis, Emily and Wilma which brought heavy rain and windfall. This caused the coral to be turned over in the water, moved or bleached.

What does this mean for the Caribbean?

If global warming continues, it is predicted that events like the 2005 event in the Caribbean, would continue to happen every other year for the next 20–30 years. What was once a very rare event, would become very common. When global warming is combined with human activities in the sea – over-fishing and pollution – it leaves coral reefs, and the fish who live there, at very high risk.

Source: adapted from Coral Reef Information System website

Research

Carry out research into one of the effects of climate change in Jamaica. Create a report on the effects that it is having on human activities and on wildlife and the landscape. Suggest some ways in which people can act to mitigate (or reduce) the effects of climate change for this particular issue. Present your report back to the rest of the class.

The beautiful underwater world of corals and tropical fish.

Exercise

1   Why are coral reefs so important?

2   Explain how coral bleaching occurs.

3   What are the consequences of coral bleaching?

4   Explain why the events of 2005 caused such damage to the coral reefs around Jamaica.

A dead, bleached coral reef.

Organisations which manage and monitor climate change

We are learning to:

- analyse the role of local and international organisations and agreements which manage and monitor climate change.

There are several ways that climate change is being tackled, both in Jamaica and on a global level.

The mission statement from the Jamaican government is:

> 'Jamaica achieves its goals of growth and prosperity for its people while meeting the challenges of climate change as a country with enhanced resilience and capacity to adapt to the impacts and to mitigate the causes in a coordinated, effective and sustainable manner.'

International strategies that Jamaica are part of include:

- Jamaica signed to the **Paris Agreement**, which seeks to guide the treatment of climate change by limiting the rise of the global temperature below 2°C
- Jamaica became a part of the United Nations Framework Convention on Climate Change which seeks to regulate greenhouse gas emissions.

Case study

The Kyoto Protocol

The **Kyoto Protocol** is an international agreement which extends the 1992 United Nations Framework Convention on Climate Change (UNFCCC) that commits countries to reduce greenhouse gas emissions, based on the scientific agreement that global warming is occurring and it is extremely likely that human-made carbon dioxide emissions have predominantly caused it. The Kyoto Protocol was adopted in Kyoto, Japan, on 11 December 1997 and entered into force on 16 February 2005. There are currently 192 parties signed up to the Protocol, including Jamaica, which signed up to the protocol in 1999.

Case study

The Intergovernmental Panel on Climate Change (IPCC)

The IPCC is a part of the United Nations that is dedicated to providing the world with scientific information to help understand the scientific evidence of climate change, including the risks and effects of the process. The IPCC was established in 1988 and was later recognised by the United Nations. One of the IPCC's reports was an important part of the Paris Agreement in 2015.

Activity

Find out when the Paris Agreement was, and which countries signed up to it.

The Intergovernmental Panel on Climate Change (IPCC).

1 Name two international treaties that Jamaica has signed up to, in order to reduce climate change.

2 Explain what is meant by Greenhouse Gas Emissions.

3 What is the Kyoto Protocol and why is it important?

4 What is the role of the IPCC?

Local strategies that Jamaica have taken include:

The Climate Change Division (CCD) was established in 2012, to provide strategic support, coordinate and monitor the transformational change towards a climate resilient society for Jamaica. Its work comes under the Ministry of Water, Land, Environment and Climate Change.

The core strategies of the Climate Change Division are as follows:

1. Coordinate the mainstreaming of climate change adaptation in strategies in policy formulation, development planning and decision-making.

2. Promote the implementation of specific adaptation measures to address key vulnerabilities in Jamaica.

3. Promote actions to reduce GHG emissions through fossil fuel reduction, conservation, and switching to renewable & cleaner energy sources.

4. Promote awareness of climate variability and climate change and corresponding behavioural changes.

The government is also working to ensure:

- better management of water resources
- adopting sustainable farming practices
- planting crops that can withstand erratic weather conditions
- practising proper disposal of garbage.

There are a number of international agreements, where many countries agree to work together to reduce climate change.

Exercise

5 Explain the role the Climate Change Division has in helping to make a better climate for Jamaica.

6 Why do you think the government have introduced a strategy for the proper disposal of garbage?

7 Explain why it is important to make changes at local level, and not just international level, to help reduce the effects of climate change. What role does the individual have?

Project

Imagine you are working for the government and that you are tasked with raising community awareness about climate change.

What would you do? Create a plan to outline the actions you would take.

Research

It's important that agencies tackling climate change are effective. In groups, research one agency undertaking this work and come up with suggestions of how its efforts might be measured. For example, how successful are they in communicating with the public and how do you know?

Key vocabulary

Paris Agreement

Kyoto Protocol

How can you reduce your carbon footprint?

We are learning to:

• propose strategies to mitigate the effects of climate change on Jamaica.

A **carbon footprint** is the amount of carbon dioxide released into the atmosphere as a result of the activities of a particular individual, organisation, or community.

We all have a responsibility to try to reduce climate change, so it is important to become aware of our own individual carbon footprint, so that we can try to reduce the amount of carbon dioxide in the environment.

We all have a responsibility to reduce our carbon footprint.

1. Learn the 5 R's: refuse, reduce, reuse, rot, recycle ❯❯

Going zero waste is a great step towards combating climate change.

You learnt about the 3 Rs in grade 7: Reduce, Reuse and Recycle. But there are two more that are equally important – Refuse and Rot.

• Refuse – Avoid single use plastics and paper products by saying no thank you, opting for reusables.

• Reduce – Downsize what you purchase, opting to be more mindful of what you really need.

• Reuse – Always find a way to keep an item out of the landfill by keeping it in great condition, repairing or recycling it when it breaks.

• Rot – Set up a **compost system** for your food scraps, or find a food scrap drop off centre (like a farmers market, or community garden) near your house.

• Recycle – Properly recycle any plastic, paper, glass or metal you cannot refuse, reduce, or reuse.

Compost is a good way to reuse food waste.

Did you know...?

Trying to follow the 5 Rs means you may become a 'zero waster'.

Activity

Think about the 5 Rs in your school. Organise a campaign to increase people's awareness of the 5 Rs. Design a wall display which explains how people can lower their carbon footprint at school by being better at the 5 Rs.

Key vocabulary

carbon footprint

compost system

toxin

2. Bike more and drive less

- Traditional cars put out a lot of exhaust emissions, which pollute the air. For example, vehicles produce one-third of all air pollution. Motorised transportation uses fossil fuel (oil and gas) and as such, causes more greenhouse gases to be released into the atmosphere.

- The **toxins** (damaging chemicals) emitted by vehicles are also very dangerous for people's health, especially as the tailpipes are at street level where humans can breathe the air directly into their lungs.

- Challenge yourself to use a bike rather than getting a lift in a car. Riding your bike also forces you to utilise your own muscle power.

- If you can't cycle for whatever reason, take public transportation. It puts fewer cars on the road, which reduces the amount of exhaust filling the air.

- Try to avoid flying – aeroplanes produce a lot of carbon dioxide, therefore have a very heavy carbon footprint.

Use a bike instead of a car to reduce your carbon footprint.

3. Conserve water and protect our waterways

Reducing your water usage is really important. When we conserve water it reduces the amount of energy used to treat and pump water that comes to our homes. Reduced energy use means less greenhouse gases are emitted unto the atmosphere.

> **Did you know...?**
>
> 96.5% of the water on Earth is too salty for human consumption.

- Don't leave the tap running while you brush your teeth. Only turn it on when it's time to rinse your mouth out.

- Take shorter showers.

- Don't flush things down the toilet to dispose of them. One flush can waste up to 5 or 7 gallons of water

- Avoid soaps filled with toxins. Conventional dish and body soap contain ingredients that go down the drain and pollute our water supply.

- Choose reusable products, such as water bottles. Lots of disposable items take gallons of water to make. For example, one roll of toilet paper takes 37 gallons of water; a single disposable diaper takes 144 gallons of water. Other products such as paper plates, cups and towels also use gallons of water to make.

Make sure you turn taps off properly to avoid wasting water.

Exercise

1 Explain the idea behind the 5 R's and what they refer to.

2 Why is it recommended that people bike more, but drive less?

3 Explain why it is important that we conserve water.

How can you reduce your carbon footprint?

We are learning to:

- propose strategies to mitigate the effects of climate change on Jamaica.

4. Eat seasonally, locally, and more plants 〉〉

- Try to buy the majority of your food as local produce. Animal products are much more intense as they require more water and resources.
- Imported foods are transported using airplanes or ships, both of which use fossil fuel. Eating locally means we can help reduce the amount fossil fuel used through this means.
- Making the majority of your plate plant-based foods, is healthier and better for the planet.
- Eating seasonal also means eating local, which is great for the environment. When you support local farmers, you don't have to worry about how far your food travelled to get to you.
- Use some reusable produce bags to reduce waste.

Eating local food reduces your carbon footprint.

5. Switch to sustainable, clean energy 〉〉〉

- Fossil fuels are limited, finite resources and the transportation of them causes air pollution. When they are burned, they emit toxins that speed up climate change.
- You can help stop our reliance on fossil fuels by switching to sustainable energy today.
- Solar and wind power are a good source of renewable energy, also water and geothermal power is worth considering.
- Invest in more energy efficient products and make sure to shut off lights when you're not in a room.

Switching to sustainable energy is good for the environment.

Activity

Create a display board with images and ideas about how people in your school can reduce their carbon footprint. Include:

- **a)** transport ideas
- **b)** ideas for food/eating
- **c)** water saving ideas
- **d)** introducing solar powered lights
- **e)** using more energy efficient products at school.

Discuss these ideas with your class and develop a campaign to reduce the carbon footprint of the school.

What can we do as individuals to reduce our carbon footprint?

7.10

Some of the things we can do as individuals to help reduce our own carbon footprint include:

- reduce the amount of meat that people eat – the farming of livestock produces high amounts of carbon dioxide and methane, which adds to the greenhouse effect. By cutting down our meat intake, we can help to reduce this
- reduce the amount of rubbish that you create – lots of house waste goes to landfill, which contributes to climate change. Recycle as much as you can
- go paperless – lots of companies and businesses now offer paperless services, for example you may get a bill electronically, rather than in the post. Cut down on how much you print out, and how much paper you use
- plastic – reduce the amount of plastic that you use and throw out. Reduce the amount of products that you buy which have plastic as part of the product
- compost food waste, rather than just throwing it out
- buy vintage or recycled clothing, so we reduce the amount of new clothes we buy – clothing goes out of fashion very quickly, and when clothing is dumped in landfills it produces methane which contributes to the greenhouse effect
- when you go shopping, buy less stuff – don't impulse buy, take your own re-usable bag, avoid buying goods which have lots of plastic packaging, buy energy efficient lighting products, and always buy from companies who are environmentally responsible
- in your home, do not leave lights on, use low energy light bulbs, have a low flow shower, unplug devices when they are not being used, turn down your water heater, get electricity from clean electricity providers
- transport – use the car less, do not use the car for short journeys, take public transport; when driving avoid unnecessary braking and acceleration, and if you are in a traffic jam, switch off your engine; car share where possible, avoid air travel.

Exercise

1. Write a paragraph explaining what a carbon footprint is, giving examples.

2. Identify three ways you can personally reduce your carbon footprint.

3. Why is riding a bike encouraged as a way to reduce your carbon footprint?

4. How can you encourage others in your school or home to reduce their carbon footprint?

5. Create a poster highlighting ways to save water at home and at school.

Activity

Conduct an online search for a carbon footprint calculator and use it to calculate your carbon footprint.

Questions

See how well you have understood the topics in this unit.

1. _____ is a set of conditions in the atmosphere at a particular time and place.

    a) Climate

    b) Weather

    c) Climate change

    d) Hurricane

2. Explain the difference between weather and climate.

3. Explain two ways that the climate affects human behaviour.

4. Climate graphs show:

    a) the carbon footprint

    b) precipitation

    c) humidity

    d) temperature and rainfall.

5. True or False? Isohyet maps are maps that are used to show rainfall figures

6. Match the examples of some extreme weather phenomena with their definitions.

    1) cyclone

    2) hurricane

    3) tornado

    a) occurs when a tropical cyclone moves faster than 33 m per second

    b) a spinning column of air that forms under thunderclouds

    c) is a tropical storm with a closed, circulating wind pattern

7. Explain what is meant by the greenhouse effect.

8. Write a short definition of the following terms:

    global warming

    carbon dioxide

    greenhouse gas

9. Name three ways that people can reduce their carbon footprint.

10. Which two of these are effects of climate change?

   a) Increasing risk of extreme weather events
   b) Reduced flooding
   c) Rising sea levels

11. Give two examples of international policies to prevent climate change.

12. Explain what a carbon credit is, and how they are used.

13. Give two examples of strategies the Jamaican government have suggested to reduce climate change.

14. Describe two effects of climate change on Coral reefs. Why are they so important?

15. Imagine that you work for an organisation that aims to reduce climate change. Write a paragraph of about 200 words describing your action.

16. Match the climate types with their definitions.

   1) Tropical wet (Equatorial) climate
   2) Tropical moist climate
   3) Tropical climate with seasonal rainfall

   a) Short dry period: Tropical forest dominant
   b) Rain throughout year: Tropical rainforest dominant
   c) Wet and dry seasons: Savannah dominant.

17. Explain the effects of coral bleaching.

18. What is the role of the Climate Change Division (CCD)?

Grade 8 Unit 7 Summary

Weather and climate

In this chapter, you have learned about:

- The difference between weather and climate
- The impact of weather and climate on human activities
- The importance of paying attention to the weather
- The Jamaican climate
- How weather and climate determine clothes, choices, health problems, sporting activities and agriculture
- What is a climate graph is and how to interpret one
- What isohyet maps are and how to interpret them.

Climate change

In this chapter, you have learned about:

- The association between climate change and global warming
- How the use of natural resources contributes to global warming
- What greenhouse gases are and how increased amounts in the atmosphere contribute to global warming and climate change
- The effects of agriculture, deforestation and industry on climate change
- Solutions that individuals, industries and states can implement to reduce air pollution
- The effects of climate change seen in the natural environment
- How coral bleaching in the Caribbean affects the natural environment and people.

Monitoring and reducing climate change

In this chapter, you have learned about:

- The organisations and agreements that manage and monitor climate change
- The Kyoto Protocol
- The Intergovernmental Panel on Climate Change
- What carbon footprint is and how to reduce it
- Implementing strategies that can mitigate the effects of climate change
- What individuals can do to make a positive difference.

Checking your progress

To make good progress in understanding the impact of human activities on climate change, check that you understand these ideas.

Explain and use correctly the term *climate change*.

Describe the greenhouse effect.

Explain the effects of climate change.

Explain and use correctly the terms *carbon footprint* and *carbon credit*.

Name the international treaties on climate change.

Explain the role of the Jamaican government in reducing climate change.

Explain and use correctly the term *carbon dioxide*.

Name three effects of climate change in Jamaica.

Explain why reducing your carbon footprint is important.

Explain and use correctly the term *air pollution*.

Describe the effects of climate change on the weather in Jamaica.

Explain what is meant by a carbon sink.

Unit 8: Hazards and Disasters of the Caribbean

Objectives: You will be able to:

Earthquakes

- define terms and concepts: earthquake, seismic, focus, epicentre, magnitude
- locate on a map major earthquake zones in the Caribbean
- describe the use of seismographs and the Richter scale
- examine the effects of earthquakes on the physical and human environment
- demonstrate an understanding of the mitigation strategies
- create an action plan to assist people affected by earthquakes
- practise responsible behaviour in times of disaster.

Volcanoes

- name and locate on maps, active volcanoes within the Caribbean and other areas of the world
- draw an annotated diagram to show the structure of a volcano
- examine the effects of volcanic eruption on the physical and human environment and appreciate the advantages of volcanoes.

Hurricanes

- classify hurricanes according to Saffir-Simpson scale
- describe the impact of hurricanes in the Caribbean
- describe the weather conditions associated with the passage of a hurricane
- take actions to prepare for and reduce the impact of natural disasters.

Flooding and droughts

- explain the causes and effects of floods and droughts in the region
- compare the impact of natural disasters on various communities.

Institutions and organisations that manage and monitor disaster preparedness

- assess the effectiveness of organisations and institutions which manage and monitor disaster preparedness.

What is a natural disaster and what is a human-induced disaster?

We are learning to:

- distinguish between hazards and disasters, natural and human-induced disasters.

A **hazard** is an agent which has the potential to cause harm to a vulnerable target. Hazards can be both natural and human induced. Sometimes natural hazards such as floods and drought can be caused by human activity.

A **disaster** is a sudden accident or a natural catastrophe that causes great damage or loss of life. So, a disaster is a major event that has happened, whereas a hazard is an event that may happen, or is at risk of happening.

A **natural disaster** is a major adverse event resulting from natural processes of the Earth; examples include **floods,** hurricanes, **tornadoes, volcanic eruptions,** earthquakes, **tsunamis,** and other geologic processes. **Human-induced disasters** are usually the result of things going wrong in our complex technological society.

Usually, a single hazard may result in casualties and damage due to different contributing forces, as in the case of a cyclone where there are strong winds, storm surges, rain and so on. Volcanoes pose problems due to lava streams, fires, ash falling or release of harmful gases, among many others.

On the other hand, a human-induced disaster may be due to human error, negligent behaviour, dysfunction of a human-engineered system or intentional instigation and/or attacks. The impact of a manmade disaster can be just as catastrophic as a natural disaster.

A cyclone is an example of natural disaster.

An oil spill is an example of a human-induced disaster.

NATURAL DISASTER vs HUMAN_INDUCED DISASTER

Natural disasters are caused by natural forces	Human-induced disasters are caused by the activities of humans
Examples: tsunamis, floods, landslides, hurricanes, wildfires, droughts, volcanic eruptions	Examples: hazardous material spills, explosions, chemical, biological attacks
Steps can be taken to minimise the effects	Can be avoided with careful planning and prevention methods

Key vocabulary

hazard

disaster

natural disaster

floods

tornadoes

volcanic eruptions

tsunamis

human-induced disasters

oil spill

Case study

Oil forms underneath the surface of the Earth. In order to extract the oil, people drill into the large reservoirs of oil that are found underground, often under seas and oceans.

Oil is then transported to countries by pipeline or oil tanker. Every so often, it escapes from these pipelines and tankers, which leads to an **oil spill**. This can have damaging effects on the environment.

When oil spills into seas and oceans, coastal vegetation such as mangroves is destroyed, as oil coats the vegetation. This destroys the habitats of coastal wildlife and can lead to loss of life.

Many birds are killed by oil spills as oil coats their feathers, which prevents them from flying.

Marine mammals such as whales and dolphins are killed. Oil clogs their blowholes, stopping them from breathing.

Jamaica suffered its first major oil spill in 1981 when the tanker Erodona spilled 600 tonnes of oil after grounding at Port Kaiser. The majority of the oil moved out to sea and dispersed naturally.

In 2000 the tanker Tradewind Spirit spilled approximately 3 tonnes of heavy fuel oil whilst loading at the Petrojam facilities in the Port of Kingston. This contaminated 3–4 km of mangrove shores to varying degrees. As there were no significant amounts of oil leaching from the contaminated mangroves into other areas, it was decided to allow the vegetation to recover naturally, as any attempt at clean-up would cause damage to individual plants and to the sandy/silty substrate. A programme to monitor the ongoing health of the mangrove was put in place.

There have been a number of other minor bunker spills at the Petrojam terminal. The damage recorded included the following:

- several kilometres of coastline were coated in oil
- coastal vegetation was destroyed by the oil
- many marine animals were killed
- many marine birds were killed.

Exercise

1. Explain the difference between a human-induced and a natural disaster.

2. Give two examples of natural disasters that affect the Caribbean region.

3. Where is oil found? How is extracted?

4. Give two examples of how oil damages the environment.

5. Briefly describe the oil spill disasters in Jamaica in 1981 and 2000.

6. Explain why hazards occur, in your own words, in 250 words.

Ecuadorean President Rafael Correa speaks with people during a visit to Los Sachas, in the Ecuadorean Amazonia, a region affected by oil exploitations on 26 April 2007.

Understanding earthquakes

We are learning to:

- define terms and concepts: earthquake, seismic, focus, epicentre, magnitude
- locate on a map major earthquake zones in the Caribbean
- describe the use of seismographs and the Richter scale in measuring the occurrence and magnitude of earthquakes.

Earthquakes

An **earthquake** is a sudden shaking of the Earth's crust. The shaking happens when tectonic plates move. Earthquakes happen at all plate boundaries.

- At constructive plate margins, the plates are moving away from each other. Magma then rises to the surface. An earthquake can occur as the magma moves through the crust.
- At destructive plate boundaries, two plates are moving towards each other. As they push against each other, the oceanic plate is forced underneath the continental plate. The sudden downward movement of the oceanic plate causes the land to shake violently.
- At conservative plate margins, the plates are sliding past each other. This is not a smooth process and the two plates often jolt and judder suddenly as the move causes the land to shake.
- At continental collision plate boundaries, two plates are moving towards each other. These two plates are made of continental crust, so the land is pushed upwards. Often the upward movement of the crust can cause it to shake.

The term **seismic activity** is used to refer to the movement of tectonic plates and the activity that results, such as earthquakes or volcanic eruptions.

When an earthquake happens, the point at which it happens underground is called the **focus**. The point directly above the focus on the Earth's surface is called the **epicentre**.

Magnitude refers to the size of the earthquake. The **Richter scale** shows the strength of an earthquake.

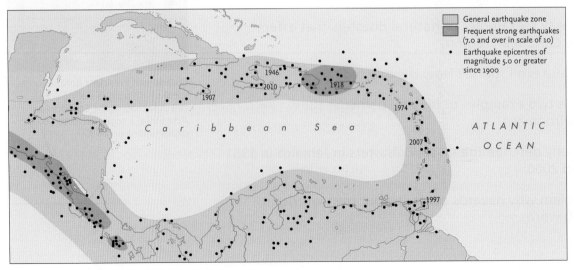

Earthquake zones in the Caribbean.

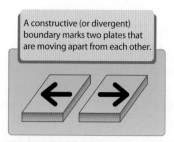

A constructive (or divergent) boundary marks two plates that are moving apart from each other.

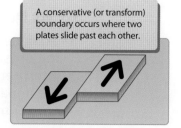

A conservative (or transform) boundary occurs where two plates slide past each other.

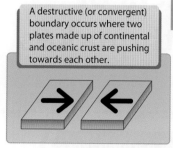

A destructive (or convergent) boundary occurs where two plates made up of continental and oceanic crust are pushing towards each other.

Plate movements.

Recording and measuring an earthquake

When an earthquake happens, **seismic waves** are sent out from the focus and travel through the crust. These waves are then picked up and recorded on instruments called **seismographs**. Some Seismographs are sensitive and are able to detect strong earthquakes anywhere in the world. They can also record the time and location. To pick up smaller magnitudes, local seismographs are used.

Continental plate collision occurs when two continental plates move towards each other.

The size of the earthquake is then shown using the Richter scale. The Richter scale starts at 1.0 but has no upper limit. The most powerful earthquake ever recorded was 9.5 – occurring in Chile, in 1960.

A **Mercalli scale** is a twelve point scale used to measure the **intensity** of earthquakes, in other words the effects, and destruction, that they have. The values in a Mercalli scale range from 1 (not felt, only picked up by seismographs) to 12 (total destruction of all buildings).

Key vocabulary

earthquake

seismic/seismic activity

focus

epicentre

magnitude

Richter scale

seismic waves

seismographs

Mercalli scale

intensity

Usually not felt, but can be recorded by topography	1.0-1.9	Micro
	2.0-2.9	Minor
Vibrations detected	3.0-3.9	
	4.0-4.9	Light
Windows rattle or break, light damage	5.0-5.9	Moderate
Crack in buildings, falling branches	6.0-6.9	Strong
	7.0-7.9	Major
buildings collapse, landslides	8.0-8.9	
		Great
Devastation many deaths	9.0 and greater	

Earthquake magnitude scale.

Exercise

1. Explain how earthquakes occur at constructive and destructive plate boundaries.

2. What is the difference between the focus and the epicentre?

3. What is the difference between magnitude and intensity?

4. What do seismographs pick up?

Effects of earthquakes

We are learning to:

- examine the effects of earthquakes on the physical and human environment
- interpret photographs to analyse the impacts of earthquakes on the environment.

Effects of earthquakes

The damage caused by an earthquake depends on a number of different factors. The strength of the earthquake is one of the most important factors.

Earthquakes with a magnitude of less than 6.0 generally don't cause a lot of damage. However, earthquakes with a magnitude of over 6.0 can be highly destructive. Other factors influencing the amount of damage an earthquake causes include: location (urban vs rural areas), depth of the earthquake (deep earthquakes cause less damage), and geology (rock type).

A road damaged during an earthquake.

Effects of earthquakes on the human environment

Strong earthquakes can have devastating effects on the human environment. The most common effects include:

- buildings and infrastructure (roads and bridges) collapse
- loss of life and property
- injury
- homelessness
- broken gas and water pipes
- fires break out
- contaminated water supplies
- spread of disease.

Research

Using the internet, research photographs and newspaper articles documenting different earthquakes. Analyse the impact of earthquakes on the human and physical environments.

Effects of earthquakes on the physical environment

As with the human environment, there are many effects of earthquakes on the physical environment:

- tsunamis and flooding
- **aftershocks** – small earthquakes following the main one
- **landslides** – sudden movement of rock, earth or debris down a slope
- **mudslides** – wet soil or sand moves suddenly downhill
- farmland and vegetation destroyed by tsunamis, landslides, mudslides and flooding.

Case study

Haiti earthquake

On 12 January 2010, an earthquake measuring 7.0 on the Richter scale affected the countries of Haiti and the Dominican Republic. The epicentre of the earthquake was 16 km west of Haiti's capital of Port-au-Prince. The focus was only 8 km beneath the surface.

Haiti lies on the boundary of the Caribbean and North American Plates. This is a conservative plate boundary – the Caribbean Plate is moving in one direction and the North American Plate goes in the opposite one.

The human effects of the earthquake were devastating. It is estimated that, as a result of the earthquake, approximately 220 000 people were killed and 300 000 were injured. It is believed that 250 000 homes were destroyed and, as a result, 1 million people were made homeless. In total, 3 million people were affected.

Transport and communication links – such as roads and railways – were destroyed or badly damaged. This meant that emergency services couldn't get through to certain areas. More than 50 hospitals are thought to have been badly damaged, as well as 1 300 schools.

Following the earthquake, experts identified that two tsunami waves affected Caribbean regions, with waves approximately 3 m high. The waves affected the coastline along the Bay of Port-au-Prince and the southern coast of the island of Hispaniola. It is believed that the tsunamis killed three people and destroyed several homes.

Following the initial earthquake, there were 52 aftershocks measuring 4.5 or more on the Richter scale, These lasted until 24 January – 12 days after the first earthquake.

Questions

1. Name five effects of earthquakes on the human and physical environment.

2. What caused the earthquake in Haiti in 2010?

3. In total, how many people are thought to have been affected by the earthquake?

4. How many aftershocks followed the initial earthquake?

Did you know...?

The most damaging earthquake recorded in Jamaica was in 1907, in Kingston, an earthquake which shook the capital with a magnitude of 6.5 on the Richter Scale.

Building damage during an earthquake in Türkiye 2011.

Activity

Write three paragraphs, explaining how you felt (or think you would feel) if experienced an earthquake.

Key vocabulary

aftershock

landslide

mudslide

Planning against earthquakes

We are learning to:

- demonstrate an understanding of the mitigation strategies used against earthquakes.

A **mitigation strategy** is a plan to reduce the loss of life and property by lessening the impact of disasters. There are a number of things that people can do to minimise the damage caused by earthquakes.

What can you do? ⟫

When people live in areas that are prone to earthquakes, they are usually well educated in what to do in the event of an earthquake.

- At school, students are taught and regularly practise what to do in the event of an earthquake. Earthquake drills are often used in school in order to prepare the students. These might be rehearsed once a month.
- People stock up on food, water and medical supplies.
- Any business and organisation responsible for many people will also educate their employees on what to do in the event of an earthquake.
- There is a worldwide strategy called 'Drop, Cover and Hold' that people will do during an earthquake.
- Most schools and businesses will also have a tsunami evacuation plan if they are in areas that are vulnerable to natural disasters.

Preparedness kit ⟫

People in areas prone to earthquakes and tsunamis will also be encouraged to have a disaster supply kit in their houses and businesses. This is usually a rucksack or bag filled with belongings that will be useful in the event of a natural disaster. Some of the things that people might put in their disaster supply kit include:

- first-aid kit and medications
- torch and flashlight (with extra batteries)
- water and canned/tinned food
- emergency contact numbers
- cash.

If you are in a building, you should:

DROP to the ground (before the earthquake drops you!),	Take **COVER** by getting under a sturdy desk or table	and **HOLD ON** to it until the shaking stops.

If you are outside, move away from buildings, trees, street lights and power lines, then 'Drop, Cover and Hold' until the shaking stops.

Responding during an earthquake.

Building design ▶▶▶

There are a number of things that countries can do to minimise the damage caused by earthquakes. One of the best things they can do is alter the design and materials used on new buildings and roads.

Traditionally, buildings and roads are made from concrete, which will collapse during an earthquake. Countries such as Japan, which experience a lot of earthquakes, have found that by constructing buildings that gently sway with the movement of the earthquake, they are far more likely to stay standing. Therefore all new buildings and roads are being built in this way.

Insurance ▶▶

People can take out insurance on homes, property and possessions, so that the insurance company will pay out to replace anything that is damaged in an earthquake. This can be great for replacing possessions, but will not make up for sentimental items lost or damaged during an earthquake or tsunami.

Early warning systems ▶▶▶

As earthquakes cannot be predicted, it is only possible to alert people after the earthquake has already happened. Early warning systems send out alerts to people all over the country to say that an earthquake has been detected. Even a few seconds can minimise the damage and loss of life caused by an earthquake, so they are seen as very useful.

When people are alerted of an earthquake, they can prepare for aftershocks and any secondary effects of an earthquake such as a tsunami or an outbreak of fire.

Earthquake-resistant skyscrapers in Tokyo.

Activity

Outline at least three strategies that could be used by individuals or communities to reduce the amount of damage caused during an earthquake.

Exercise

1 What is the 'Drop, Cover and Hold' procedure?

2 Give examples of things that should be included in a disaster supply kit.

3 Describe how building design can help to reduce damage.

4 Why is it beneficial for people to take out earthquake insurance?

Key vocabulary

mitigation strategy

An earthquake action plan

We are learning to:

- create an action plan to assist people affected by earthquakes
- practise responsible behaviour in times of disaster.

Action plan ⟩⟩

In countries where earthquakes are very common, emergency Action Plans will be created so that everybody knows what to do during an earthquake. The following is an example of a school's Action Plan for an earthquake situation. Your school will have one that is very similar.

OBJECTIVES

The main objectives are to:
- ensure the safety of all students, staff and visitors during and after an emergency
- prepare students, staff and visitors for an emergency
- plan a safe and well-designed response to emergencies
- protect the school building and school facilities
- provide the school with a coordinated approach to restoring normal conditions following an emergency.

IDENTIFY TASKS

There are a number of tasks that need to be completed before, during and after an earthquake. These include making sure that:
- every member of staff and student is aware that an emergency is imminent/taking place/has occurred
- all staff/students follow the emergency procedures
- the emergency services are notified
- students are reassured during and after an emergency
- first-aid treatment is given to those that need it
- all staff and students are accounted for following an emergency, and anyone missing is reported immediately
- other members of staff and students are helped
- order is restored.

DELEGATE TASKS

Some members of staff will have more responsibility than others – for example, senior management (headteachers, for example) will be expected to take on more responsibilities before, during and after an emergency. Classroom teachers are expected to follow the emergency procedures thoroughly.

SUCCESS CRITERIA

To measure the success of an emergency situation, the following must be considered:
- the time taken for a drill to be issued and time taken to evacuate the school
- whether all staff and students followed procedures
- the number of casualties
- the time taken for emergency services to respond.

TIME FRAME

The time frame depends on the nature of the emergency. Procedures should be carried out as quickly as possible, ensuring that all staff and students find a safe place or are evacuated from the building as quickly as possible.

RESOURCES NEEDED

It is recommended that the following items are supplied to all classrooms:

- first-aid kit
- blankets
- blank class register
- pens
- whistle
- drinking water
- portable radio
- torch.

EVIDENCE OF COMPLETION

Following an emergency, the headteacher must complete an Emergency Response Form detailing the incident, making specific mention to the success criteria of the emergency.

Project

Imagine that an earthquake situation is about to happen. In groups, write your own Action Plan, using the following headings:

Objectives, Identify tasks, Delegate tasks, Success criteria, Time frame, Resources needed, Evidence of completion.

Use the example Action Plan to help you.

Being responsible ⟫⟫

Above all else, there are things that people should do during an emergency:

- stay calm and try not to panic
- follow instructions that are given to you
- put into practice safety procedures – for example, find a safe place to take cover
- help others where possible, but not at the expense of your own safety
- stay where you are until you are absolutely sure that the disaster is over.

Exercise

1 What are the main objectives of an Action Plan?

2 How is the success of an emergency situation measured?

3 What resources must all classrooms have?

4 Why do you think it is important for schools to have an Action Plan?

5 Why do you think you need to act responsibly during an emergency?

Understanding volcanoes

We are learning to:

- define the term volcano
- name and locate on maps, active volcanoes within the Caribbean and other areas of the world
- draw an annotated diagram to show the structure of a volcano.

Volcanoes

Volcanoes are hills or mountains that allow lava, gas and ash to escape. Volcanoes may be found in one of three different states:

- **active** – could erupt at any time and has erupted in recent history
- **dormant** – has not erupted in recent history but could do again
- **extinct** – has not erupted in the last 10 000 years and will not erupt again.

There are many different types of volcano, depending on where and how they are formed. Two types are:

- **Shield volcanoes** form at constructive plate boundaries. As two plates move away from each other, magma rises to the surface. The lava is very thin and runny, so it spreads out over the land. Eventually the lava hardens to form igneous rock. As more and more eruptions occur, the lava builds up, forming a low-lying, wide hill known as a shield volcano.
- **Composite volcanoes** form at destructive plate boundaries. As the oceanic plate is pushed down into the mantle, magma rises to the surface and explodes over the land. The lava here is very thick, so doesn't flow very fast. The lava and ash build up to form a cone-shaped volcano with alternating layers of lava and ash. As more and more eruptions occur, the volcano becomes higher.

Nevis Peak is a potentially active volcano on Nevis, Saint Kitts and Nevis.

Volcanoes

▲ Currently active   ▲ Dormant   ▲ Extinct

1 Saba, 1640
2 The Quill, St Eustatius, 250 AD ± 150 years
3 Mount Liamuiga, St Kitts and Nevis, 160 AD ± 200 years
4 Nevis Peak, St Kitts and Nevis
5 Soufrière Hills, Montserrat, 1995 – 2011, 2012
6 Bouillante Chain, Guadeloupe
7 La Soufrière, Guadeloupe, 1977
8 Morne Aux Diables, Dominica
9 Morne Diablotins, Dominica
10 Morne Trois Pitons, Dominica, 920 AD ± 50 years
11 Morne Watt, Dominica, 1997
12 Morne Plat Pays, Dominica, 1270 ± 50 years
13 Montagne Pelée, Martinique, 1932
14 Qualibou, St Lucia, 1766
15 Soufrière, St Vincent and the Grenadines, 1979
16 Kick 'em Jenny, Grenada, 2001
17 Mount St Catherine, Grenada

List gives year of last eruption

Volcanoes in the Eastern Caribbean.

Exercise

1 Name the three different states in which a volcano can exist.

2 What are the differences between a shield volcano and a composite volcano?

Structure of a volcano ▶▶▶

All cone volcanoes have a similar structure:

- a magma chamber underneath the Earth's surface
- a cone-shaped hill or mountain built by layers of lava, rocks and ash
- a conduit (pipe) that runs up the centre of the volcano from the magma chamber to the vent, as well as a crater at the top.

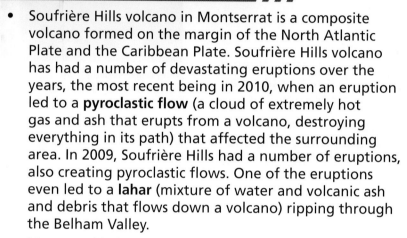

The structure of a volcano.

Active volcanoes in the Caribbean ▶▶▶

- Soufrière Hills volcano in Montserrat is a composite volcano formed on the margin of the North Atlantic Plate and the Caribbean Plate. Soufrière Hills volcano has had a number of devastating eruptions over the years, the most recent being in 2010, when an eruption led to a **pyroclastic flow** (a cloud of extremely hot gas and ash that erupts from a volcano, destroying everything in its path) that affected the surrounding area. In 2009, Soufrière Hills had a number of eruptions, also creating pyroclastic flows. One of the eruptions even led to a **lahar** (mixture of water and volcanic ash and debris that flows down a volcano) ripping through the Belham Valley.

- Mount Pelée is another composite volcano in the Caribbean. It is located in Martinique. One of its most deadly eruptions was in 1902, when the entire city of Saint-Pierre was destroyed by the eruption and pyroclastic flow that occurred on 2 May. There were only a handful of survivors in the whole city. In 1929, the volcano began to erupt again, triggering pyroclastic flows and lahars. However, this was not nearly as deadly as the eruption in 1902, as authorities evacuated the area quickly.

- Morne Watt is a composite volcano found in Dominica. It is a very tall volcano, reaching heights of 1 224 m, which makes it one of the highest peaks in Dominica. There was a major eruption that took place 1300 years ago, as well as a small eruption in 1997.

Project

Using the internet, choose one volcanic eruption that has taken place in the Caribbean and research it fully. Produce a PowerPoint presentation or a poster on the eruption of the volcano.

Exercise

3 Define the terms pyroclastic flow and lahar.

4 Where is the magma chamber in a volcano?

5 What type of materials are composite volcanoes made out of?

6 What type of volcano is Mount Pelée?

7 Draw a diagram or create a model, to show the structure of a volcanic cone.

Key vocabulary

volcano

active

dormant

extinct

shield volcano

composite volcano

pyroclastic flow

lahar

Materials ejected by volcanoes

We are learning to:

- describe the materials ejected by volcanoes.

Materials ejected by volcanoes 》

Not all volcanoes eject the same materials: some volcanoes have gentle eruptions and may release only lava which flows over their sides; some volcanoes erupt violently and will release lava and other materials.

Lava 》》

Lava is the most common type of volcanic material. When it is below ground, it is known as magma. It is not until it has been erupted from a volcano that it becomes known as lava.

Lava is different depending on the type of volcano it is erupting from. Shield volcanoes have thin, runny lava, and are often referred to as having **low viscosity**. **High viscosity lava** is the opposite. This is very thick lava that is ejected from composite volcanoes.

Molten lava coming from Eyjafjallajökull eruption, Iceland, 2010.

Ash 》》》

Volcanic ash is made from the finer material erupted from the volcano. The coarser material can settle around the volcano, but the finer material can drift long distances.

Volcanic ash is very different to ash from burning wood, as it is much harder and coarser. Also, unlike ash from burning wood, it doesn't dissolve in water. It has a sand-/grain-like appearance. Volcanic ash can be very harmful.

Volcanic bombs 》

A volcanic bomb is a large piece of rock that is ejected from a volcano during an eruption. In order to be classed as a volcanic bomb a rock has to be more than 6.4 cm wide, but they can reach sizes of over 5 m.

Exercise

1. What is the difference between high viscosity lava and low viscosity lava?
2. What is volcanic ash made from?
3. What is a volcanic bomb?

Gases

There are a number of gases that are emitted during a volcanic eruption. In fact, some volcanoes only eject gases during an eruption. The most common of these gases are:

- Carbon dioxide – can be deadly. Volcanoes quite often emit carbon dioxide (not just during an eruption). Small amounts of this gas in the air is not harmful to people. However, if the concentration increases, it can lead to headaches, dizziness and even death.

- Sulphur dioxide – more of an irritant than a deadly gas. Emissions of sulphur dioxide can cause irritation to your eyes, nose and throat.

- Hydrogen sulphide – a highly toxic gas. In small concentrations, it can be sensed in the air by our noses, as it has a rotten egg smell. As the amount in the atmosphere increases, its smell disappears. This is a problem, because high concentrations of hydrogen sulphide can very quickly lead to death.

People watching volcanic ash cloud from Eyjafjallajökull eruption, Iceland, 2010.

Pyroclastic materials

A pyroclastic flow is a cloud of extremely hot gas and ash that erupts from a volcano, and then travels down its slopes destroying everything in its path. These are very dangerous events, as they can reach temperatures of up to 1 000 °C and can travel at speeds of 720 km per hour.

The extremely high temperatures, combined with the high speeds, means that pyroclastic flows are one of the deadliest effects of volcanic eruptions. Pyroclastic flows can be life threatening:

- In AD 79, the eruption of Mount Vesuvius and subsequent pyroclastic flow killed everyone in Pompeii (now Naples), in Italy.

- In 1991, over 40 people were killed in Japan when a pyroclastic surge erupted from Mount Unzen.

- In 1997, 19 people were killed on the Caribbean island of Montserrat from a pyroclastic flow down Mosquito Ghaut.

Activity

Your teacher will select documentaries, case studies, DVDs and internet resources of volcanic eruptions for you to review in class.

Exercise

4 Give three examples of volcanic gas.

5 What is a pyroclastic flow?

Project

Your teacher will divide the class into three or four groups. They will give you a worksheet and all the materials to create a model volcano and show how an eruption happens.

Key vocabulary

low viscosity

high viscosity

The negative effects of volcanoes

We are learning to:

- examine the effects of volcanic eruption on the physical and human environment
- interpret photographs to analyse the impact of volcanic eruptions on the environment.

Negative effects of volcanic eruptions

Volcanic eruptions can have devastating effects on an area and can also cause widespread death and destruction.

Damage to buildings

Buildings can be completely destroyed during a volcanic eruption. The eruption itself may not cause too much damage to buildings.

A house is buried by lava on Mount Etna, Sicily, Italy.

However, a pyroclastic flow can be devastating. Pyroclastic flows can completely destroy anything in their path, including buildings and roads.

Lahars can also be devastating, as these are fast-moving flows of water, and volcanic debris and can completely bury buildings and roads. As they travel, lahars also pick up a huge amount of debris that is then able to cause even more damage to structures such as buildings, roads and bridges.

Volcanic ash can be particularly problematic, because when it is mixed with rainwater it becomes very heavy and **dense**. This can cause roofs to collapse.

Destruction of vegetation

As with damage to buildings, volcanic eruptions can also destroy **vegetation** in the area.

Pyroclastic flows will burn or singe plants, trees and other types of vegetation, since they are not able to withstand the very high temperatures. Lahars have the power to uproot trees and transport them as they travel downhill.

Exercise

1. Which causes most damage to buildings – the volcanic eruption or the pyroclastic flow?

2. How do volcanic eruptions cause damage to buildings?

3. How is vegetation destroyed by volcanic eruptions?

Effects on the climate ⟩⟩

Volcanic eruptions can have significant effects on the climate. During a volcanic eruption, large quantities of gases (such as sulphur dioxide) and dust are ejected into the atmosphere. The presence of large amounts of gas and dust in the atmosphere can stop sunlight from getting through and therefore lowers temperatures at the Earth's surface.

Loss of life and property ⟩⟩⟩

Volcanic eruptions are not necessarily the deadliest of natural disasters. However, a number of deadly volcanic eruptions have been recorded. The eruption of Mount Vesuvius in Pompeii (now Naples) is probably one of the deadliest volcanic eruptions, as it killed the entire population of Pompeii.

More recent deadly eruptions include the eruptions of Mount Lamington, which killed 2 942 in 1951; and Mount Pinatubo in 1991, which killed 847. Most people that are killed during a volcanic eruption are killed by pyroclastic flows.

Chances Peak, part of the Soufrière Hills (on the island of Montserrat in the Caribbean) is a volcanic area. In 1995, when it erupted, it had been dormant for almost 300 years. When the volcano began to erupt, it continued to do so for five years. During these years while the eruption continued, the small island population was evacuated. Volcanic eruptions can also destroy property either by destroying them from the initial eruption, or by paths of molten lava.

Eruption of Eyjafjallajökull volcano, Iceland, in 2010.

Research

Using library and internet resources, research the eruption of the Soufrière Hills volcano on Montserrat. Present your findings to your class either in the form of poster or as a PowerPoint presentation.

Travel disruption ⟩⟩⟩⟩

Air traffic can be disrupted during a volcanic eruption, because the volcanic ash is extremely harmful to plane engines. If ash gets into the engines, it can cause them to stall and crash.

In 2010, after the eruption of Eyjafjallajökull in Iceland, the huge ash cloud caused planes to be grounded all over the Europe for almost eight days. This cost airlines an estimated $1.7 billion.

Exercise

4 What is the biggest cause of death during a volcanic eruption?

5 Name some of the deadliest volcanic eruptions in history.

6 What causes flights to be grounded during a volcanic eruption?

Key vocabulary

dense

vegetation

The positive effects of volcanoes

We are learning to:

- appreciate the socio-economic and environmental advantages of volcanoes.

Positive effects of volcanic eruptions 》》

Although the devastation caused by volcanic eruptions can be catastrophic, people continue to live near active volcanoes. This will be considered strange to some, but there are advantages to living close to active volcanoes.

The Blue Lagoon, Iceland, is one of the best known volcanic spas in the world.

Tourism 》》》

Volcanoes attract millions of visitors every year. People have an interest in visiting volcanoes because they have such unique features and landscapes, such as geysers and bubbling mudpools.

The influx of tourists means that new businesses can be set up to cater for these visitors. Cafés, restaurants and shops can also be established in areas where tourist numbers are high. This then benefits the whole community.

Mount Vesuvius is one of the deadliest volcanoes, but it is also one of the most popular tourist attractions in Italy. Mount Etna is another famous volcano in Italy. Iceland is another popular destination, as well as the Kamchatka region in Russia, which has the well-known Mutnovsky volcano. Finally, Hawaii is one of the most popular attractions – in particular the Kilauea volcano.

Spas/mineral springs 》》》》

One of the most well-known volcanic **spas** in the world is the Blue Lagoon in Iceland. This is a human-made pool that is heated by the lava flow to temperatures of 37°C. It is rich in minerals, such as silica, that have medicinal properties.

Exercise

1. Why are tourists attracted to volcanic regions?
2. What are the benefits of tourism in these areas?
3. How is the Blue Lagoon heated?

Geothermal energy

In volcanic regions, there is the opportunity to use the heat from underground to help to generate electricity.

Underground rocks are able to heat water that produces steam. This then drives the turbines and generates electricity.

Geothermal energy is a clean and sustainable renewable energy source. The energy is natural, forming in the Earth, causes no pollution and is completely free to use. Geothermal energy can be used to heat homes, offices and to generate electricity.

Fertile soils

Many farmers choose to live close to volcanoes. This is because the land near volcanoes can be very **fertile**. This means that the soils are very rich in nutrients, so plants grow very well here.

The ash from volcanic eruptions makes the soils very fertile, which means that these areas can be very productive farming areas.

The land beside Mount Vesuvius is particularly fertile, and farmers are able to grow crops there.

New land

There are many countries in the world that would not exist if there had not been volcanic eruptions.

Countries and states such as Iceland, Hawaii and some of those in the Lesser Antilles only exist because of a series of volcanic eruptions. These three volcanic areas all have people living on them. However, there are many more islands that are uninhabited.

A vineyard at the base of Mount Vesuvius, Italy.

The Hellisheidi Geothermal Power Station, Iceland.

Activity

Imagine you live near the Soufrière Hills volcano and your family has been forced to relocate to the north of the island. Write a letter to a friend describing how you feel about the challenges you are facing.

Key vocabulary

spa

geothermal energy

fertile

Exercise

4 What is geothermal energy? What can it be used for?

5 Why is farming so good near volcanoes?

6 Give examples of countries/states formed from volcanic eruptions.

7 Create a photomontage showing at least three negative and three positive effects of volcanic eruptions in the Caribbean.

Understanding hurricanes

We are learning to:

- define the weather system hurricanes
- classify hurricanes according to the Saffir-Simpson scale.

Hurricanes ⟫

A hurricane occurs when a tropical cyclone moves faster than 119 km per hour. The area of a hurricane can measure more than 950 km across, and it can move at speeds of up to 300 km per hour. Hurricanes are also known as cyclones, **typhoons** and **willy-willies**, and are areas of extreme low pressure.

Hurricane Matthew approaching Florida coastline.

Hurricane	North America and the Caribbean
Cyclone	Southeast Asia, such as India and Bangladesh
Typhoon	East Asia, such as Japan
Willy-willy	Australia

They are found in areas between the Tropic of Cancer and the Tropic of Capricorn. Tropical storms need very specific conditions in order to form.

Formation of a hurricane ⟫⟫

- All tropical storms start over warm tropical seas with temperatures over 27°C.
- Warm air rises and water is **evaporated**.
- The warm air and evaporated water rise and cool and **condense** to form thick clouds.
- More air is sucked in to fill the gap caused by the rising air, which is also heated.

- This sucking and rising movement causes the clouds to start spinning.
- The Earth's rotation also helps to spin the storm clouds.
- These storms are now able to move at great speeds across the ocean.

Structure of a hurricane ⟫⟫⟫

- Tropical storms can be over 200 km wide.
- The centre of the storm is called the **eye**.
- The eye is usually 30–50 km across.

- Large, thick rain clouds (cumulonimbi) surround the eye.

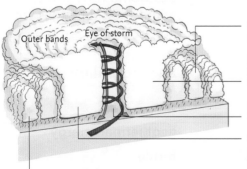

Outer bands   Eye of storm

As the hurricane passes, wind speeds and rainfall decrease and the outer bands bring sunny intervals

After the eye has passed, hurricane-force winds begin immediately from the opposite direction, often accompanied by heavy rain

In the eye of the storm, winds are light and the sky is clear with little rain

Closer to the centre, wind speeds increase to over 100 km/hr, and there may be torrential rain (more than 200 mm/day)

As the hurricane approaches, clouds form and the wind speed increases. The outer bands bring alternate rain showers and sunny intervals

The Saffir-Simpson scale is used to categorise hurricanes. The categories range from 1 to 5, with 5 having the strongest winds.

Saffir-Simpson Hurricane Scale

Category	Wind speed (mph)	Type of damage	
1	74–95	Some damage	• damage mainly to trees • no substantial damage to buildings, some damage to poorly constructed signs.
2	96–110	Extensive damage	• some trees blown down • some damage to windows, doors and roofing, but no major destruction to buildings • coastal roads cut off.
3	111–129	Devastating damage	• large trees blown down • some damage to roofing, windows and doors • some structural damage to small buildings • serious flooding along the coast.
4	130–156	Extreme damage	• shrubs, trees and all signs blown down • extensive damage to roofs, windows and doors • flooding and floating debris cause major damage to houses.
5	157 and above	Catastrophic damage	• considerable damage to roofs of buildings • very severe and extensive damage to windows and doors • complete buildings destroyed • major damage to homes.

Exercise

1 What are the different names by which tropical storms are called?

2 Why are hurricanes only found in tropical regions?

3 What is the centre of a hurricane called?

4 What is the system for measuring hurricanes called?

5 What damage might occur during a category 1 hurricane?

6 What damage might occur during a category 3 hurricane?

7 What damage might occur during a category 5 hurricane?

Key vocabulary

typhoon

willy-willy

evaporated

condenses

eye

Hurricanes in the Caribbean

We are learning to:

- explain the system used to name hurricanes
- describe the impact of hurricanes in the Caribbean.

The system used to name hurricanes 》》

Originally, tropical storms in the Caribbean were named after the saints day on which the hurricane happened – for example, Santa Ana in 1825. In 1953, the United States began to use female names, and in 1979 the practice of using both male and female names began.

Naming tropical storms and hurricanes makes it easier to communicate their details, rather than having to use the longitude and latitude method. It also makes it easier for storms and hurricanes to be identified if there is more than one hurricane at the same time.

Meteorologists start with the letter A and work alphabetically, alternating men and women's names. For example, if the first storm of the season is Adam, the next would be Barbara, and so on. The only letters that are not used are Q, U, X, Y and Z. If a storm has been particularly deadly, costly or devastating, then the name will not be used again. For example, Katrina (2005) will not be reused.

Each storm is given a name once it reaches the level of tropical storm (wind speed of 65 km per hour). If the wind speed increases to 120 km, it is declared a hurricane.

Below is a list of some of the retired names in the Caribbean.

Name	Year	Areas affected
Tomas	2010	Barbados, St Vincent, St Lucia, Haiti, Turks and Caicos
Igor	2010	Newfoundland, Bermuda
Paloma	2008	Cayman Islands, Cuba
Ike	2008	Turks and Caicos, Cuba, Texas (USA)

> **Did you know...?**
>
> In 2019 the named tropical storm (TS) and hurricanes (H) for the atlantic were:
>
> Alex (H)
>
> Bonnie (TS)
>
> Colin (TS)
>
> Danielle (TS)
>
> Earl (H)
>
> Fiona (TS)
>
> Gaston (H)
>
> Hermine (H)
>
> Ian (TS)
>
> Julia (TS)
>
> Karl (TS)
>
> Lisa (TS)
>
> Matthew1 (H)
>
> Nicole2 (H)
>
> Otto (H)

Exercise

1. In your own words, explain why hurricanes are given names.

2. At what wind speed does a tropical storm become a hurricane?

3. For what reason are some hurricane names retired and never used again?

Case study

Tropical storms in the Caribbean

Hurricane Gilbert (1988)

Hurricane Gilbert was a category 5 hurricane that affected the Caribbean in September 1988. Gilbert affected the countries of Jamaica and Mexico in particular. In total, 318 people were killed during the hurricane and approximately $7 billion of damage was created.

Hurricane Sandy (2012)

Hurricane Sandy was a category 3 hurricane that caused extensive damage to the Caribbean and USA in November 2012.

The storm formed in the Atlantic Ocean and ripped through the Caribbean region, killing 80 people – 60 in Haiti, 11 in Cuba, 2 in the Bahamas, 2 in the Dominican Republic and 1 in Jamaica.

Hurricane Sandy caused millions of dollars' worth of damage in the Caribbean. Roads, schools and hospitals were destroyed, as well as 18 000 homes.

Hurricane Ivan (2004)

Hurricane Ivan was a category 5 hurricane that affected the Caribbean in September 2004. It caused a huge amount of damage to the Caribbean and USA as it tore across the Atlantic Ocean.

When the storm hit Grenada, it was only a category 3 hurricane, but it caused widespread damage there. Hurricane Ivan killed 39 people in Grenada and caused much more damage to hospitals, schools, roads and farmland.

By the time the hurricane reached Jamaica, it had increased to a category 4 hurricane, and caused widespread flooding.

Damage caused by Hurricane Sandy in Queens, New York, 2012.

Questions

1. Which of the three hurricanes mentioned has the lowest category?

2. Which country suffered the most from Hurricane Sandy?

3. In your own words, describe the impact that a hurricane of these strengths can have on a country.

Discussion

In groups, discuss the names of hurricanes and the system used to name them.

Activity

Write a two-verse poem about a hurricane that has affected the Caribbean.

Research

Using the internet, go to the National Hurricane Centre website. Research one of the hurricanes (Gilbert, Sandy or Ivan) and write a report detailing its route and the damage it caused. Add any photographs to your report.

Passage of a hurricane

We are learning to:

- describe the weather conditions associated with the passage of a hurricane (before, during and after).

Weather and hurricanes ⟫

Hurricanes are areas of very low pressure. Low pressure tends to bring wind and rain. However, the extreme low pressure that hurricanes experience brings far more severe weather conditions than a normal **depression**.

As a hurricane passes over an area, it will experience different weather conditions depending on what 'stage' of the storm it is in.

Before ⟫⟫

Before a hurricane approaches, the weather starts to change noticeably:

- air pressure starts to fall
- temperatures start to fall
- winds increase
- clouds start to develop
- rain begins.

Satellite photo of a typhoon over the Pacific Ocean.

During ⟫⟫⟫

The eye wall

This is the first wall of thick cloud that approaches. At the eye wall:

- air pressure falls very quickly
- temperatures fall
- winds pick up
- huge storm clouds form
- torrential rain falls.

The eye

This is the centre of the hurricane. In the eye:

- air pressure is very low
- temperatures are higher
- it is calm with very little wind
- it is sunny
- there is no rain.

Hurricane Alex over the Caribbean, 2010.

The second eye wall

This is the second wall of thick cloud that approaches.
At this eye wall:

- air pressure rises
- temperatures fall again
- winds reach their strongest force
- huge, thick clouds forms
- torrential rain falls.

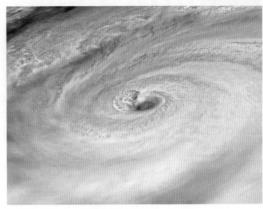

The eye of Hurricane Katrina.

A hurricane makes landfall.

After

After a hurricane passes, all these weather conditions dissipate:

- air pressure continues to rise
- temperatures increase
- winds die down
- the thick cloud breaks up
- rain turns to showers.

Discussion

In groups, discuss what weather to expect during the passage of a hurricane.

Aftermath of a hurricane.

Exercise

1. What is the weather like before a hurricane?

2. Describe the weather conditions in the eye of a hurricane.

3. What is the worst part of a hurricane, and what is the weather like there?

4. What is the weather like after a hurricane passes over?

Key vocabulary

depression

The effects of hurricanes

We are learning to:

* examine the effects of hurricanes.

The effects of hurricanes

Hurricanes are often devastating for a country. Billions of dollars of damage can be caused and many people may get killed. These two pages discuss the most serious effects of hurricanes.

A storm surge is one effect of a hurricane.

Storm surge

Storm surges is one common side effect of a hurricane. A storm surge is a rise in sea level that occurs during hurricanes. They are very dangerous, because they can lead to widespread coastal flooding.

Storm surges occur when strong winds push the surface water towards the coast. They generate large waves that can be very destructive.

Hurricane Katrina, which affected the USA in 2005, produced a 8.5 m storm surge. This was the highest recorded storm surge ever to affect the country.

Flooding

Flooding is a major consequence of hurricanes. Because so much rain falls in such a short space of time during a hurricane, the water can completely cover the land.

Floodwater is very destructive as it can be very powerful; therefore it has the ability to destroy buildings, vegetation and farmland. Flooding can be responsible for the most deaths and most economic damage that a hurricane can cause. Following Hurricane Katrina in 2005, approximately 80% of New Orleans was under water that, in some places, was 6 m deep.

Exercise

1   What is a storm surge and what causes it?

2   Why is floodwater so damaging?

3   Using library and internet resources, research the effects of a hurricane that has affected the Caribbean. Create a presentation and include the following: the name of the hurricane, the island that was affected and at least three effects of the hurricane.

Damage to vegetation »»

Floodwater can drown plants and vegetation and the strong winds can uproot trees. Many acres of farmland can be destroyed during hurricanes, killing all crops.

Following Hurricane Ivan in 2004, Grenada suffered a tremendous amount of damage. In total, it is thought that $900 million worth of damage was made to Grenada – 80% of its buildings were destroyed, 90% of its homes were ruined, 73 of the 75 schools were damaged and 80% of its power was lost. Farmland was also destroyed, and all the year's crops were lost.

Floodwater, following a hurricane, can cause widespread damage to agricultural land, villages, towns and cities, and can cause loss of life.

Loss of life and property »»

Hurricanes can cause widespread loss of life. The winds, rain, floodwater and storm surges can all be deadly for people living in areas affected by hurricanes.

Buildings, roads, houses and bridges can be completely destroyed during a hurricane and people can be killed from the winds, falling trees or buildings, or the floodwater.

The table shows a selection of hurricanes that have affected Caribbean regions over the last 100 years. It is clear from the table that there is no relationship between strength of hurricane and damage and deaths caused.

Name	Category	Cost of damage (millions of $)	Number of deaths
David, 1966	5	$1.5	2 068
Jeanne, 2004	3	$7.6	3 035
Flora, 1963	4	$529	7 193
Galveston, 1900	4	$20	6 000–12 000
Jeremie, 1935	1	$16	2 150

Exercise

4 Look at the table:

   a) Which hurricane caused the most damage?
   b) Which hurricane caused the most deaths?
   c) Following Hurricane Ivan in 2005, what damage was caused to Grenada?

Key vocabulary

storm surge

flooding

Preparing for a hurricane

We are learning to:

- take actions to prepare for and reduce the impact of natural disasters.

How can Caribbean countries, and people who live in those countries, prepare themselves to minimise the impact of a hurricane?

Disaster supply kit

Disaster supply kits are backpacks filled with essential items that people can take to a hurricane shelter. As space is restricted at shelters, people should only take a limited number of items with them – for example, food, such as tinned food, bottles of water, first-aid kits, torch, copies of personal documents and emergency telephone numbers. Clothing and bedding should also be included.

A hurricane shelter on a beach.

Hurricane shelter

Hurricane shelters are safe buildings built specifically to protect the public from the devastating effects of a hurricane.

In the Caribbean, shelters are usually in places such as schools, church halls and community centres etc., that have been designated as a safe area to house people temporarily during and after the hurricane. Other things to do to prepare for a hurricane in the Caribbean include:

- be prepared to evacuate at short notice
- know where it is that you can go and where shelters are if you have to leave your home
- buy any necessary supplies and prepare a supply kit beforehand
- prepare homes – install storm shutters, reinforce door latches and doors, add clips to the roof to make it more storm resistant
- explain to children what could happen
- plan which transport you will use if you have to evacuate.

Research

Using the internet, and working in groups, go to the United Caribbean Trust's website. Research the items they list as necessary in an emergency kit – water, food, clothing and bedding, first aid and toolkit. Then, create your own disaster kit list and share it with the rest of the class.

Exercise

1 What items would you typically include in a disaster supply kit?

2 What are hurricane shelters?

Project

Use materials available to you to make your own hurricane kit. You should include ten items.

Building design ▶▶▶

Although hurricanes occur every year, people continue to live in hurricane-prone areas. However, they do take extra precautions wherever they can. One of the things people do is build their houses to withstand hurricanes. Building design is very important, and some of the building features include:

- deep foundations to make the building stronger
- building houses/buildings on pillars/stilts to raise them above the ground, so floodwater flows underneath the building
- using materials that can get wet
- using shatterproof or plastic windows
- using metal shutters on the windows.

Satellites such as GLONASS (Global Navigation Satellite System) can help to track hurricanes.

Insurance ▶▶

As with earthquakes, insurance can be taken out on homes, property and possessions. This is a policy where the insurance company will pay out to replace anything that is damaged in a hurricane.

This can be great for replacing possessions, but it will not make up for sentimental items lost or damaged during a hurricane.

Early warning and detection ▶▶▶

Nowadays, it is easy to track hurricanes by using satellites, although hurricanes can be quite unpredictable in their movements.

Satellites allow us to take photographs of the hurricane so we can track its speed and direction. From there, warnings can be given out to the public – via radio, television or over the internet. This keeps people informed and ensures that they make arrangements to stay safe during the hurricane.

Activity

In groups, prepare an emergency kit and an emergency contact list of at least three people. When you have finished, share your lists with the rest of the class. Explain why the items in the kit are essential and why you chose the three emergency contacts.

Activity

Design an action plan to assist a neighbouring country that has been affected by a hurricane.

Exercise

3 What design features are important when building houses in hurricane-prone areas?

4 What will insurance not cover?

5 How are people warned about approaching hurricanes?

Key vocabulary

....

hurricane shelter

Understanding flooding and droughts

We are learning to:

- explain the causes and effects of floods and droughts in the region.

The Caribbean region faces significant challenges in terms of flooding and drought.

Flooding refers to an overflow of water that submerges land that is usually dry.

It is a natural event or occurrence where a piece of land (or area) that is usually dry land, gets submerged under water. Some floods can occur suddenly and recede quickly. Others take days or even months to build and discharge.

Flooding can have devastating consequences.

Types of floods

Flash floods usually last a very short time; they may occur within hours or even within minutes. These floods occur suddenly from heavy rainfall or dam breaking. They are the most destructive and can be fatal. There is usually no warning, no preparation and the impact can be very swift and devastating.

Rapid on-set floods take slightly longer to develop and the flood can last for a day or two only. It is also very destructive, but does not usually surprise people like flash floods. With this type of flood, people can quickly put a few things right and escape before it gets critical.

Slow on-set floods occur as a result of water bodies over flooding their banks. These tend to develop slowly and can last for days and weeks. They usually spread over many kilometres and occur more in **flood plains**, which are low-lying areas on either side of a river.

Describing the causes and effects of floods

There are many reasons for floods. A river floods when the water overflows its banks and spreads out onto the surrounding land. This causes major problems for people living close to the river. Natural causes of flooding include:

- heavy rainfall
- long periods of rain
- snowmelt
- steep slopes
- impermeable rock (doesn't allow water through)
- very wet, saturated soils
- compacted or dry soil.

There are also human factors increasing flood risk, which include:

- urban development, because towns and cities have more impermeable surfaces;
- also, improper drainage and poor disposal of wastes causing drains to become blocked;
- deforestation, because removing trees means less absorbtion of water;
- increased run-off into rivers and build up silt in rivers causing overflow;

- Climate change will cause some places around the world to get hotter, which will increase evaporation leading to increased rainfall in other areas. This increased rainfall leads to flooding in some cases.

Drought refers to a long period of abnormally low rainfall, leading to a shortage of water.

Droughts occur when there is abnormally low rainfall for an extended period of time. So, a desert would not be considered in drought unless it had less rainfall than normal, for a long period of time. Droughts can last for varying amounts of time, from weeks to months and even years. Three types of drought exist:

Droughts can last for varying periods of time.

- **meteorological drought** – when the amount of precipitation (rainfall) received in a specific area is less than the average amount

- **hydrological drought** – occurs when reduced precipitation impacts on water supply, for example, where there is decreased streamflow, soil moisture, reservoir and lake levels, and groundwater

- **agricultural drought** – when the two types of drought above impact on agricultural or farming activities, for example, reduced soil moisture or reservoir levels required for irrigation.

Describing the causes of droughts ⟩⟩⟩

- Agriculture – using large amounts of water to irrigate crops removes water from lakes, rivers and groundwater leading to drought. Some crops require more water than others, for example, cotton.

- **Dam building** – large dams can be built across a river to produce electricity and store water in a reservoir. This can reduce river water flowing downstream and cause drought below the dam.

- Deforestation – removing trees can reduce the amount of water stored in the soil as rain tends to fall and wash off the land as surface run-off. This leaves the ground vulnerable to erosion and desertification which may lead to drought.

Key vocabulary

flash floods

rapid on-set flooding

slow on-set flooding

flood plains

drought

meteorological drought

hydrological drought

agricultural drought

dam building

Exercise

1. Explain the different types of floods and the effects that they have.

2. Explain how human activities increase flood risk.

3. Explain the different types of drought and their causes.

4. Which do you think is more serious – a flood or a drought? Explain your reasons.

Understanding flooding and droughts

We are learning to:

- compare the impact of natural disasters on various communities and account for the level of damage suffered.

The effects of droughts

The initial effects of droughts are known as **primary impacts** and include the following:

- animals die of thirst and starvation
- crops may die or fail
- water shortages occur as reservoirs gradually become empty.

The longer term effects are known as **secondary impacts** and include the following:

Drought leads to rivers and creeks drying up.

- water restrictions are enforced, for example, water hosepipe bans
- wildfires occur, which are caused by drought destroyed vegetation and animals' habitats
- creeks and rivers dry up which leads to organisms relying on them dying or migrating
- increased soil erosion can occur, which can destroy vegetation and the creatures which rely on it to survive
- droughts result in the quality of the soil deteriorating, affecting farming for years to come
- some farmers may be forced to sell machinery, land or even move elsewhere and lose their livelihood
- governments end up having to fund drought relief
- with fewer crops and livestock, more food will have to be imported
- this increases the price of food for the whole country
- the tourism industry may be affected.

Strategies to reduce the risk of floods and droughts

There are several strategies in place to reduce or mitigate the risk of floods and droughts.

Drought mitigation strategies

- Water management plans which ensure that water waste is reduced.
- Cultivation of drought-tolerant plant species.
- Irrigation of water to ensure effective use.
- Financial support for farmers.
- Desalination plants (to turn sea water into water that can be used for everyday use).
- More efficient prediction of weather patterns from satellite systems.
- Dams, to ensure that water is stored and used more carefully.
- Domestic water recycling.

Case study

A drought is a period of time, such as a season, a year, or several years, of dry weather and low precipitation (rain) for a region. This results in a shortage of water.

In 2019, cyclone Idai hit Southern Africa. It was one of the worst ever to hit the region and killed over 1 000 people and made up to 4 000 000 people homeless. It brought a huge amount of flooding, but then a drought followed. This combined to create a food and climate crisis. The communities in this region are still struggling to grow food because the land has not had time to recover.

When a drought hits a region it causes famine, death, long term degradation of natural resources, and can displace a huge number of people from their homes. People can be forced to drink dirty water from rivers or streams, which often carry diseases and can make their situation worse.

When floods hit drought stricken regions, you might think that water would solve some problems, but it does not. The ground is so dry it cannot soak up the water, so floods occur. Small streams and rivers break their banks, putting people's homes at risk. So, even heavy rain does not help to solve the problems of drought.

Flooding mitigation strategies

- Building dams can help. Dams are often built along the course of a river in order to control the amount of water flowing. Water is held back by the dam and released in a controlled way, which in turn, controls flooding. Building a dam can be very expensive.
- River management can help reduce the risk of flooding. A river may be widened or deepened, which means that it can carry more water. A river may be straightened so that water can travel faster along the course. The course of the river can also be changed, diverting floodwaters away from settlements.
- Afforestation, or planting of trees where none existed before, near to the river can reduce flooding. This means trees help absorb rainwater and lower river flow. Reforestation is the replanting, or restocking, of forests where they have been cut down previously. This will help the local biodiversity, as well as long term helping to reduce carbon dioxide levels.
- Managed flooding can be arranged, which means that the river is allowed to flood naturally in places, to prevent flooding in other areas – for example, near settlements.
- Planning decisions can help reduce flooding. For example, policies to control urban development close to or on the floodplain (where there is a known risk of flooding).

Exercise

1 Explain two reasons that floods and doughts occur.

2 Why does climate change mean that there will be an increase in droughts and floods in the Caribbean?

3 In your opinion, which are the most effective flood and drought mitigation strategies?

4 Explain why when countries or regions fall into a drought-flood cycle it causes problems.

Key vocabulary

primary impacts

secondary impacts

Institutions and organisations that manage and monitor disaster preparedness

We are learning to:

- assess the effectiveness of organisations and institutions which manage and monitor disaster preparedness.

Caribbean Disaster Emergency Management Agency 》

The Caribbean Disaster Emergency Management Agency (CDEMA) is a supportive network of independent emergency units throughout the Caribbean. It was established on September 1, 2005 as the Caribbean Disaster Emergency Response Agency (CDERA), before its name was changed to CDEMA in September 2009.

CDEMA's aims have been to provide disaster assistance to member countries. For example, in Grenada and Jamaica when, in early September, 2004 Hurricane Ivan caused considerable damage.

During the mid-1990s, other events such as the surprise eruption by the Soufriere Hills Volcano in Monserrat meant CDEMA was called into action, to provide additional support to the people on the island. CDEMA not only responds to disasters, it also regularly monitors potential hazards, such as the Soufriere Hills volcanoes well as monitoring the active undersea volcano named Kick 'Em Jenny to the north of Grenada.

Emergency management organisations help people when there is a natural disaster.

Office of Disaster Preparedness and Emergency Relief Coordination 》》

In June 1979, the western part of Jamaica was hit by a serious flood. Because of this, the government recognised the need to establish a disaster preparedness organisation, which would be coordinate responses to disasters such as floods, hurricanes, earthquakes and human-induced hazards such as chemical spills. The Office of Disaster Preparedness and Emergency Relief Coordination (ODIPERC) was set up in 1980, and in 1993 it was changed to the Office of Disaster Preparedness and Emergency Management (ODPEM). Today, they provide all disaster related management in Jamaica, which includes maintaining national preparedness, identifying how to reduce risk, providing awareness of disaster scenarios and training, and establishing how agencies can work together at a time of disaster.

National Emergency Management Office 》》》

The National Emergency Management Office (NEMO) in St Vincent was set up in 2002 to coordinate all local resources in to prepare for, respond to and deal with the aftermath of disasters. The disaster management programme has four phases – preparedness, response, recovery, mitigation.

World Health Organization

The World Health Organization (WHO) has had an Emergency Preparedness and Disaster Relief program for over three decades. Their aim is to:

- mobilise (put into motion, or prepare to initiate) the Regional Health Disaster Response Team
- strengthen health information for governments to help them with decision making
- prepare to deliver humanitarian support, such as promoting communication, and generating up-to-the-minute reports
- ensure that the United Nations can access the area to offer support
- maintain health standards and ensure access to health services in complex emergencies
- coordinate international assistance and ensure that humanitarian supplies and donations reach the people who need them.

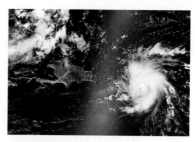

World Health Organization

How effective are disaster preparedness organisations and strategies?

Hurricane Dorian hit Bahamas' Grand Bahama and Abaco Islands in 2019 with devastating effect. They also revealed a serious problem for the Caribbean region: small countries are often hardest hit natural disasters, and they may be least equipped to deal with them.

Hurricane Dorian was the second strongest hurricane ever recorded in the Atlantic, with sustained winds of more than 180 miles per hour. The storm stayed over the Bahamas for almost 48 hours, causing 61 fatalities, destroying entire communities and causing damage totalling $7 billion. Research shows that storms like this will become more damaging as climate change continues.

Disaster preparation organisations in the Caribbean are improving their effectiveness in every country in the region. But Hurricane Dorian shows that adapting to climate change also requires a regional, coordinated response from beyond the Caribbean community, since preparation, relief, recovery and rebuilding efforts are huge.

Hurricane Dorian.

Discussion

Discuss the effects of Hurricane Dorian. What problems did it reveal about preparation for natural disasters? How can the Caribbean region be more prepared for natural disasters in the future?

It is now agreed that investing in preparing for a disaster before it occurs is much better than relying heavily on post-disaster recovery. Protection and preparation can save lives. Post-disaster response to help countries recover is still very important and can take many years.

Exercise

1. Explain the term disaster preparedness.

2. What is the role of Office of Disaster Preparedness and Emergency Relief Coordination in Jamaica?

3. Explain why international and local organisations should work together in disaster preparedness.

Questions

See how well you have understood the topics in this unit.

1. A natural disaster is:

    a) created by humans

    b) created by technology

    c) caused by natural events.

2. A _____ studies earthquakes.

    a) meteorologist

    b) seismologist

    c) volcanologist

    d) astronaut.

3. Mitigation means:

    a) to increase the severity of something

    b) to reduce the severity of something

    c) to keep the effects of something the same.

4. Jamaica's most damaging Earthquake was in:

    a) 1907

    b) 2001

    c) 1962

    d) 1945.

5. True or False? Hurricanes are measured by the Richter scale.

6. Correct this statement: The Saffir-Simpson scale is used to categorise hurricanes. The categories range from 1 to 5, with 1 having the strongest winds.

7. Explain three ways you should respond to an earthquake.

8. Name three natural disasters that have occurred in recent years in the Caribbean.

9. Write a paragraph explaining what mitigation strategies are, giving examples.

10. In your own words, define the terms earthquake, seismic, focus, epicentre and magnitude.

11. Explain why early warning systems are helpful in minimising damage.

12. How do volcanic eruptions cause temperatures to decrease?

13. Draw a mind map to show the effects of an earthquake on the human and physical environment.

14. Explain the difference between an active, dormant and extinct volcano.

15. Name the materials that are ejected by volcano during an eruption.

16. Write 250 words on the positive and negative effects of volcanoes.

17. Label the diagram of the structure of a volcano with terms from the word box below.

crater	layers of lava and ash	ash	rock
conduit	magma chamber	lava flow	

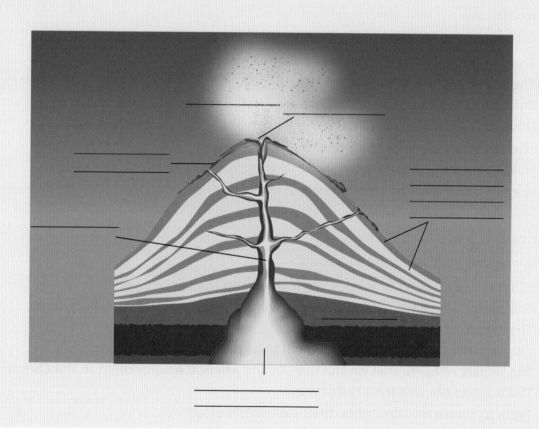

Grade 8 Unit 8 Summary

Earthquakes

In this chapter, you have learned about:

- How a natural disaster is different from a human-induced disaster
- What an earthquake is and how it is caused
- How earthquakes are recorded and measured
- The effects of earthquakes on the human and physical environments
- Planning for earthquakes and earthquake mitigation strategies.

Volcanoes

In this chapter, you have learned about:

- The states and types of volcanoes and their structures
- The active volcanoes in the Caribbean
- The different types of material that are ejected from volcanoes.
- How volcanic eruptions damage the human and physical environments
- The economic benefits of volcanoes
- How the natural environment benefits from volcanoes.

Hurricanes, floods and droughts

In this chapter, you have learned about:

- What hurricanes are, how they are formed and their structure
- The categories of the Saffir-Simpson scale that is used to measure hurricanes
- The system of naming hurricanes
- The weather conditions associated with the passage of a hurricane
- The impact of hurricanes on the human and physical environment in the Caribbean
- The ways to prepare for a hurricane
- Types of floods and droughts, their causes and effects
- Mitigation strategies for floods and droughts
- The national and regional institutions and organisations that manage and monitor disaster preparation.

Checking your progress

To make good progress in understanding different aspects of hazards and disasters of the Caribbean, check to make sure you understand these ideas.

Understand the difference between manmade and natural disasters.

Discuss the natural disasters that have been experienced in Jamaica.

Explain what is meant by mitigation.

Examine the effects of earthquakes on the physical and human environment.

Outline strategies to reduce the amount of damage caused during an earthquake.

Create an action plan for an earthquake.

Examine the effects of volcanoes on the physical and human environment.

Examine the positive and negative effects of volcanoes.

Create a photo montage showing at least three positive and three negative effects of volcanic eruptions in the Caribbean.

Describe the way that hurricanes are measured.

Explain the way that hurricanes are named.

Examine the effects of hurricanes and precautions used to minimise the effects of hurricanes.

Unit 9: Environmental Problems and Solutions

Objectives: You will be able to: ▶▶▶

Our physical and natural heritage

- define relevant terms and concepts: physical/natural heritage, indigenous, biodiversity, ecology, ecological sites and ecological heritage
- examine the features of Jamaica's physical/natural heritage.

Ecotourism and sustainability

- assess the measures which have been implemented to reduce the impact of environmental problems.

Flora and fauna

- examine the features of Jamaica's physical/natural heritage
- describe the biodiversity of Jamaica's indigenous flora and fauna: plants and flowers; birds, mammals, reptiles, and insects.

Our wetlands and rainforests coastal areas and waterfalls

- examine the features of Jamaica's physical/natural heritage
- value the significance of our physical/natural heritage.

Threats to our natural heritage/ecosystems

- gather, analyse and synthesise information from multiple sources on consequences of unsustainable use of natural resources on the economy and human health.

Preservation and conservation of the environment

- differentiate between preservation and conservation of the environment
- justify the need for the sustainable use of physical resources
- analyse the functions and the level of success of the institutions and government agencies that are responsible for managing environmental issues.

Key concepts and components of an ecosystem

We are learning to:

- define and use key concepts
- identify components of an ecosystem.

An **ecosystem** refers to a natural environment that includes the flora (plants) and fauna (animals) that live and interact within that environment. Flora, fauna and bacteria are the **biotic** or living components of the ecosystem. Ecosystems are dependent on the following **abiotic** or non-living components:

- the climate – this refers to the temperature and amount of rainfall. These are very important in determining which species can survive in the ecosystem
- soil – the particular soil type is important as this supplies the nutrients that will support different plants
- **water** – the amount of water available in an ecosystem will determine what plants and animals can survive.

The relationship between the biotic and the abiotic parts of an ecosystem are complex. If there is change in one part, it will affect the other.

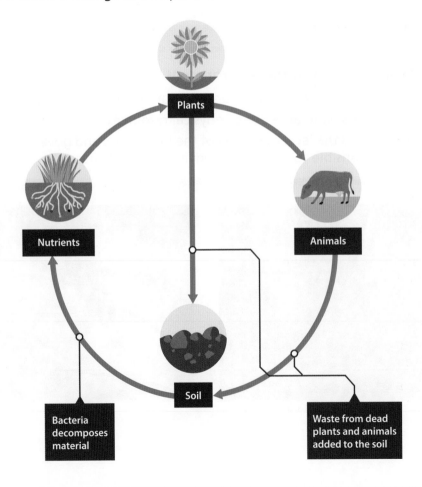

Types of ecosystems:

- Terrestrial system – this is a land based ecosystem, which is made up of the organisms that live within a given area. Examples of a terrestial ecosystem include tundra, tropical rainforests, grasslands, polar and deserts.
- Aquatic ecosystem – this ecosystem is made up of a body of water and the animals that live in that water, and how they interact with each other. There can be fresh water (rivers, streams, wetlands, ponds, springs) and marine ecosystems (lagoons, mangroves, coral reefs and even the sea floor).

What happens when there are changes to ecosystems?

Ecosystems are very sensitive to change. The living and non-living components of the ecosystem can be altered by either natural factors or human management.

Some examples of changes to the ecosystem caused by humans include:

- introducing more or different types of fish (fish stocking)
- altering the drainage of the land which may influence the amount of water
- changing the acidity level of the water
- using fertilisers, altering the nutrient levels of the water.

Changes to an ecosystem that are caused by natural factors include drought, flood, fire and disease.

Any of these changes can have a negative impact on the ecosystem and could lead to a collapse of an ecosystem.

A coral reef is an example of an aquatic and marine ecosystem.

How can an ecosystem be improved?

There are a number of ways that an ecosystem can be improved including:

- using renewable forms of energy and environmentally sound technology
- recycling more and reducing the over-exploitation of our resources
- conservation and preservation of the environment and reducing environmental problems.

Activity

Think about your local ecosystem. What could you do to help improve it? Produce a poster with a 5-point action plan for your school, explaining what can be done to help.

Exercise

1. Explain the difference between the biotic and abiotic parts of an ecosystem.

2. In your own words, explain the relationship between the biotic and abiotic parts of an ecosystem.

3. Write a short essay explaining factors which affect ecosystems.

Key vocabulary

ecosystem

biotic

abiotic

water

Our physical and natural heritage

We are learning to:

- define relevant terms and concepts: physical/natural heritage, indigenous, biodiversity, ecology, ecological sites and ecological heritage
- examine the features of Jamaica's physical/natural heritage.

The features of Jamaica's physical heritage

Our **physical heritage** is the part of our environment that is inherited from previous generations, is maintained in the present and will be passed on to future generations. Examples include the Black River Lower Morass and the Portland Bright Wetlands.

Our physical heritage is also part of the ecosystem of Jamaica. An ecosystem is a group of living organisms that live in and interact with each other in a specific environment. Plants and trees have their own natural habitats, which means they grow easily in certain types of environment. Some plants are **indigenous**, meaning they are native to, or originate in, a particular region or country. **Indigenous flora** refers to all natural vegetation in a particular area, such as trees and flowers, while **indigenous fauna** refers to all animal life in a particular area. A plant that is indigenous to the Caribbean is the Lignum Vitae, the National Flower of Jamaica.

The **biodiversity** of Jamaica is considered one of the largest among all the Caribbean islands. Biodiversity is short for **biological diversity**, meaning a great variety of different forms of life. We can study biodiversity on many levels:

- **ecological diversity** – diversity of ecosystems, natural communities and habitats on planet Earth
- **species diversity** – variety of different species; for example, the mangroves have a great biodiversity of birds and fish
- **genetic diversity** – the variation in genetic material within a particular species or group; for example, trees.

There is a wide diversity of species in Jamaica:

- 3 003 species of flowering plants
- more than twenty species of **endemic** birds
- 27 endemic reptile species
- 21 endemic amphibian species
- more than 500 endemic species of Jamaican land snails
- 3 endemic types of bats
- At least 134 species of butterflies and moths

Exercise

1 In your own words, define biodiversity, physical heritage and indigenous.

2 Explain what is meant by indigenous flora and fauna.

Ecology is the study of the relationships between plants, animals, people and their environment. Our **ecological heritage** (the same as **natural heritage**) includes all elements of biodiversity, including plants and animals and natural features. However, ecological heritage is not just a collection of pretty things to look at. We rely on our ecological heritage for water, food and fresh air. We need natural resources such as water, wood and minerals in our everyday lives. In Jamaica thousands of people work in the tourism industry. Without our natural heritage, many tourists would not visit the island.

Wildlife reserves and nature reserves protect our natural heritage from human activities. They are also **ecological sites**. Some famous national parks and protected areas in Jamaica include:

- Blue and John Crow Mountains National Park
- Montego Bay Marine Park
- Negril Marine Park
- Black River Lower Morass
- Portland Bright Wetland and Cays
- Cockpit Country, is also an area of outstanding natural beauty.

Case study

Jamaica's unspoilt rainforest

The Blue and John Crow Mountains contain a forested mountainous region in the eastern section of Jamaica, which provided a safe space for the indigenous Tainos fleeing enslavement and then for Maroons. They developed strong spiritual connections with the mountains, still manifest through the intangible cultural legacy of, religious rites, traditional medicine and dances. The site is a biodiversity hotspot for the Caribbean Islands with a high proportion of endemic plant species.

This area is protected by a range of laws such as the Natural Resources (National Park) Act (1993), the Forestry Act (1996). The real atmosphere of this rainforest is found in the hundreds of paths that connect villages in the region. The area was designated a UNESCO World Heritage Site in 2017 as an area of outstanding universal value.

Key vocabulary

physical heritage

endemic

indigenous

indigenous flora

indigenous fauna

biodiversity

biological diversity

ecological diversity

species diversity

genetic diversity

ecology

ecological heritage/ natural heritage

ecological site

Exercise

3 What is ecology? Explain, using your own words.

4 Why are ecological sites important?

5 Explain why the Blue and John Crow Mountains are significant to Jamaica's history.

Ecotourism and sustainability

We are learning to:

- assess the measures which have been implemented to reduce the impact of environmental problems.

Sustainability

Sustainable activities do not damage the resources that make them possible. For example, if tourists visited a river and polluted or littered the environment, or removed fish, then they could destroy the natural environment for future generations. This type of tourism is unsustainable.

Ecotourism is a type of tourism that focuses on protecting the environment and local culture. Ecotourism means:

- travelling to undisturbed or unspoilt natural areas
- enjoying, studying or experiencing the natural environment without damaging it
- treating the environment responsibly and carefully
- benefiting local communities
- supporting conservation projects
- providing education to travellers and local communities.

In Jamaica, there are specialist tourist operators that run holidays and tours for visitors who wish to see the natural heritage without damaging it. **Eco-friendly** accommodation tends to be smaller than big hotels and resorts. They are often lodges that can accommodate small groups, and usually have activities organised that help to support local sustainable initiatives. For example:

- Hotel Mocking Bird Hill in Port Antonio. Set in excellent birdwatching and hiking country, with good locally produced good food, and comfortable accommodation.

- Strawberry Fields Together, in St Mary Parish, set on 18 acres of a tropical nature reserve and sanctuary. This is surrounded by thousands of acres of undeveloped coast to explore. This property is situated in one of the last unspoiled stretches along Jamaica's north coast.

- Zion Country Eco Beach Cabins, in Portland. These cabins, set on an acre of fertile land with a private beach, between Manchioneal and Long Road in the east of Jamaica.

Unspoilt beach, Jamaica.

Project

Design an eco-friendly hotel. Suggest ways to make your hotel eco-friendly in terms of its size, materials, style of design, and the activities that it may offer.

Discussion

What do you know about the Rocklands Bird Sanctuary? Discuss in groups and then with the whole class.

Research

Copy or trace a map of Jamaica. Find out the locations of at least three different ecotourism resorts. Add these on your map.

- Turtle-watching and bird-watching – two popular ecotourism activities in Jamaica include observing the nesting leatherback turtles in spring and early summer, and watching the many species of birds.

- There are community-run ecotourism projects, such as bamboo rafting on the Blue Lagoon, and hiking trips to the Blue Mountains to reduce the environmental footprint created by tourism.

Green sea turtles in a turtle farm, Caribbean Sea.

Case study

Jamaica's award-winning ecotourism

The island has many attractions for ectourists: the biodiversity of plants and animals, and natural habitats such as beaches, reefs, rainforest and mountains. Without initiatives to protect these resources, the ecotourism industry will lose the very features that allow it to exist. For this reason, the government sees sustainable tourism as the key to the island's economy.

Questions

1. Suggest three geographical features that make Jamaica an ideal island for ecotourism.

2. Why is sustainable tourism important for the economy of Jamaica?

3. Explain why each activity on this page could be described as an ecotourism project.

4. Name two geographic features and three animals that have provided opportunities for ecotourism.

Activity

Choose an ecotourism project in Jamaica and do a case study on it. Find out where it is, the history of the project, the kinds of activities it offers, and which aspects of the environment it focuses on. Write up your case study in a booklet, providing pictures and information.

Did you know...?

Did you know that there are approximately 21 endemic species of frogs in Jamaica.

Key vocabulary

sustainable

ecotourism

eco-friendly

Exercise

1. In your own words, define sustainability and ecotourism.

2. Do you think ecotourism is good for Jamaica? Explain why/why not.

Flora: plants and flowers

We are learning to:

- examine the features of Jamaica's physical/natural heritage
- describe the biodiversity of Jamaica's indigenous flora: plants and flowers.

Flora and **fauna** are the plants and animals that live in a particular place. The tropical climate of Jamaica and its rich rainforests and wetlands are home to some of the most diverse plants and animals in the Caribbean. Fauna means animals. It includes all animals: mammals, birds, amphibians, reptiles and fish.

Flora is a scientific word meaning plants. It includes all plant life – from tiny single-celled algae that live in water, to the enormous ferns, bamboos and trees of our rainforests.

Some of the plants of the rainforest are so brightly coloured that they look like birds or insects. This heliconia looks like it has bright wings.

Our diverse plant life

Jamaica has a high diversity of plant life. There are several reasons for this.

- Islands are surrounded by water on all sides. This makes them isolated environments where plants may evolve in ways not found in other places.
- The high rainfall produces tall trees such as the blue mahoe – also called Cuba bark (*hibiscus elatus*), lignum vitae (*guiacum officinale*), and the bull thatch palm (*sabal martima*).
- The warm, wet tropical climate of the Caribbean is an ideal place for many different kinds of plants.
- The trees of the rainforest provide an environment that supports other types of vegetation, such as rare, exotic shrubs that live in the shade of the tall trees.
- The seasonal flooding and dry periods in the savannah areas provide a home for plants that only need water for part of the year.

Research

In a scrapbook, collect pictures of the different types of flora that are endemic to Jamaica. Use magazines, the internet, newspapers or brochures. For each species, write down its name, anything interesting about its appearance, where it can be found, whether it is a flower or a plant, and any special facts about it.

Exercise

1. Explain the terms flora and fauna and give some examples of each that you see every day.

2. Explain in your own words three reasons why Jamaica has such a high diversity of plant life.

3. How many different types of plants do you think you see every day? Try counting them one day.

Plants in their natural habitat ▶▶▶

We have seen that certain types of plants and trees have their own natural habitats, which means they grow easily in certain types of environment. Indigenous plants are well suited to provide food for indigenous animals, as they have evolved together in their environment.

Plants that grow naturally in an area are usually well adapted to the conditions of that area. For example:

- plants that grow in a desert are adapted to surviving dry, hot conditions
- plants that live in wetlands are adapted to survive in lots of water and high salinity (salt levels).

The table below shows the vegetation of some of the habitats in Jamaica.

Habitat	Vegetation
Savannah	Grasses, low shrubs
Rainforests	Tall trees, shrubs, creepers
Swamp	Dense mangrove trees and shrubs
Beach	Tall palm trees, grasses, short shrubs that do not require much water

Brightly coloured bromeliads and orchids are some of the special flowering plants that live in the understory, on branches and trunks of trees.

Some plants and flowers can be endemic – this means that they are native to a particular country or region. There are 830 flowering plants and 82 ferns that are only found in Jamaica. There also are 28 species of birds, 27 reptiles, 21 amphibians, and 500 land snails only found in Jamaica.

Project

Choose three species of flora found in Jamaica to research. Create a poster showing the three species, detailing their names, habitat, size, appearance and any other interesting details.

Exercise

4. Why do you think a plant from the wetlands would not survive very long in the desert?

5. How many of these plants and flowers listed below have you seen before? Which one is a plant and which one is a flower?

ackee	breadfruit	dasheen
aloo (potato)	Desert Rose	Blue Mahoe
Lignum vitae	chaconia	jackfruit

6. Which of the flowers listed above is our national emblem?

Key vocabulary

flora

fauna

Fauna: birds, mammals, reptiles and insects

We are learning to:

- examine the features of Jamaica's physical/natural heritage
- describe the biodiversity of Jamaica's indigenous fauna: birds, mammals, reptiles and insects.

Birds 》

Fauna are all the animals that live in a particular place.

Jamaica is home to more than 326 **species** of birds. Of these, 28 are endemic, 20 have been introduced by humans, and 156 are rare. The varied vegetation of the islands – rainforests, wetlands, scrubland, marshes and mangroves – offer many important habitats for birds. Because of Jamaica's location, many birds come here when they migrate during the cold winter months.

- When it is winter in the northern hemisphere (October to March), birds migrate here from North America.
- Between May and September, many birds migrate from South America, especially Argentina. This makes the country very attractive to bird-watchers.

The savannah habitat area has rich birdlife. Some of the common savannah and grassland bird species include the Jamaican blackbird, the black and white warbler, the white crowned pigeon and the Jamaican Oriole.

Bird sanctuaries are special reserves that protect habitats that are rich in birdlife. They may offer tours, viewing points and educational tours.

There are many bird sanctuaries in Jamaica, such as the Rocklands Bird Sanctuary in Wiltshire St James. However, there are also many unspoilt sites that are popular for bird-watching.

The Swallow-Tail Hummingbird, or 'Doctor Bird' is the national bird of Jamaica.

Some birds that bird-watchers look for in Jamaica:

- Jamaican Euphonia
- Jamaican Spindalis
- Orangequit
- White-chinned Thrush
- Jamaican Crow
- Blue Mountain Vireo
- Jamaican Elaenia
- Sad Flycatcher.

Exercise

1. Suggest two reasons why Jamaica has such a rich variety of bird species.

2. How does a bird sanctuary differ from any other bird-watching site?

3. Research what birds live in your area. Are there any endangered species in the area where you live?

Mammals >>>

A **mammal** is any animal where the female feeds her young on milk from her own body. Examples of mammals include humans, dogs, lions, bats and whales (the largest mammal on Earth). Worldwide, there are over 5 000 species of mammals.

Jamaica has more than 36 species of mammal, including rodents, bats and manatees.

There is only one land mammal native to Jamaica, the coney, a large, brown rodent which looks similar to a guinea pig. Conies are hunted by a ferocious predator: the mongoose. The mongoose is a small but fierce mammal with a long bushy tail.

Some mammals live in water, such as the West Indian manatee which lives in the canals and rivers. Due to their habitat preferences, **manatees** are most common on the south-west coast of Jamaica where rivers feed into wetlands but are occasionally seen on the north coast too.

Manatees are a highly endangered species. The manatee is often found in warm, shallow waters. They used to be hunted, but they are now a protected species. Even though they are protected, they face danger from collisions with boats, getting tangled in fishing nets and loss of food due to water pollution. The biggest threat is the loss of the warm waters that provide their natural habitat.

Activity

Research the birds and mammals of Jamaica. Collect pictures of as many of these different types of fauna as you can from the internet, magazines, newspapers or brochures. Write down their names, anything interesting about their appearance, where they can be found and how they contribute to the heritage of Jamaica.

A West Indian manatee.

Exercise

4 In your own words, explain what a mammal is.

5 How many different types of mammal are there in the world, and how many are there in Jamaica?

6 How many different types of fauna do you think you see every day? Try counting them one day.

Key vocabulary

species

mammal

manatees

Fauna: birds, mammals, reptiles and insects

We are learning to:

- examine the features of Jamaica's physical/natural heritage
- describe the biodiversity of Jamaica's indigenous fauna: birds, mammals, reptiles and insects.

Reptiles ▶▶

Reptiles include snakes, lizards, crocodiles, turtles and tortoises. They are **cold-blooded** animals that lay eggs, and have dry, scaly skin. Amphibians – like frogs, toads and newts – are also cold-blooded animals that have a stage in their life when they can breathe underwater using gills.

The habitats of Jamaica are home to many other animals besides birds. Many species of snakes, frogs and other reptiles and amphibians live in our wetlands, forests and scrublands.

The Jamaican boa or yellow snake, can reach lengths of up to 6 and a half feet.

The Jamaican iguana, endemic to the island, was thought to be extinct, until 1948, when a farmer, Edwin Duffus, discovered them in Hellshire Hills in 1990. The endangered species was then the focus of concentrated conservation efforts, which have, to some extent, been successful.

There are 21 native species of frogs on Jamaica: all of these are endemic – their natural range is restricted entirely to Jamaica. These endemic frogs are divided into two families: true treefrogs and rainfrogs.

The Jamaican boa, or yellow snake.

The Jamaican treefrog.

Insects ▶▶▶

An **insect** is a small animal that has six legs and a three-part body. Most insects have wings. Examples include ants, flies, butterflies and beetles. The tropical environment of Jamaica provides a home for many types insects, including:

- batismamselle dragonfly
- atydid
- jumping spider
- longhorn beetle
- katydid
- firefly
- cricket.

Adult sea turtles can live for up to 80 years.

Exercise

1 Where have you seen the following types of animals?
   a) snakes   **b)** frogs   **c)** lizards.

2 Why do you think the climate of Jamaica is so well suited to amphibians such as tree frogs?

3 Write a list of the 10 most endangered species in Jamaica.

Case study

Insect hunter

Hi, I'm Adrian Hoskins: **entomologist** and natural history tour leader. My passion for butterflies and nature has taken me on many travels.

A Heliconiinae butterfly.

I am from Britain, but have always dreamed about visiting a tropical rainforest.

My wish to explore tropical places took me to Jamaica, where I was awestruck by the wonders of the rainforest.

I saw my first Papilionidae, Heliconiinae – species that I had dreamed about since childhood.

The hummingbirds and oropendolas, the haunting sound of cicadas, the high-pitched chirping of thousands of tiny frogs, and, best of all, my 'discovery' of the incredible moth *Siculodes aurorula* will stay in my mind until I die.

For the last 20 years I have been lucky enough to study and photograph the stunning butterflies of the rainforests, cloudforests and grasslands around the world.

I organise and lead butterfly-watching tours to many fascinating places.

Source: adapted from Learn About Butterflies website

Questions

1. An entomologist studies insects. What type of insect is Adrian Hoskins' special interest?

2. Why do you think he dreamed of visiting a tropical rainforest?

3. What was the name of the moth that Adrian found?

4. Which three types of habitat does he now visit in his work?

5. In a scrapbook, collect pictures of as many different types of fauna indigenous to Jamaica as you can find. Use magazines, the internet, newspapers or brochures. Include details about their habitats, what they eat, threats to their survival and any efforts to help protect them.

Project

Choose three species of reptiles that are found in Jamaica to research. Create a poster showing the three species, detailing their names, habitat, size, what they eat, and any other interesting details.

Key vocabulary

cold-blooded (of an animal)

insect

entomologist

Our wetlands

We are learning to:

- examine the features of Jamaica's physical/natural heritage
- value the significance of our physical/ natural heritage: wetlands.

Wetlands ⟩⟩

A wetland is an area of land that is regularly soaked with water. Wetlands link bodies of water (such as seas and rivers) to the land. Coastal wetlands connect the land to the ocean. Inland wetlands fill with fresh water from rivers. Wetlands such as the Carbarita Swamp in Westmoreland, the Hauge Swamp in Trelawny, and the Negril Swamp in Westmoreland and Hanover, form part of our rich physical heritage.

Like sponges, wetlands become soaked or filled with water during part of the year or all year round. This helps keep river levels **stable**. Some wetlands have a mix of salty and fresh water, depending on the tides. Wetlands have some important functions, including:

- collecting floodwater so it doesn't flood the land
- cleaning and storing water
- wetland trees such as mangroves prevent erosion
- creating a protective **buffer** against hurricanes, storms and high tides
- providing habitats for birds and other animals
- acting as nurseries for many species of fish
- providing livelihoods for people who depend on wetland resources
- recreation, pleasure and tourism.

The roots of a mangrove.

Discussion

In groups, discuss whether tourism harms or helps the wetlands. How can tourism help to protect our natural heritage?

Mangroves ⟩⟩⟩

Mangroves are specially adapted to live in wetlands. They can survive very wet soil with low oxygen and high salt levels. Their dense, tangled roots are called 'prop roots', because they keep the trees standing as the tide moves in and out around them. Most mangroves get flooded with sea or river water at least twice a day.

Mangroves are an important part of Jamaica's economy. The many organisms that live and reproduce here help to support the populations of birds and fish that form part of our environment and economy. Without the mangroves, the island would be at risk of regular damage from flooding and storm damage.

Activity

Prepare a presentation or leaflet entitled 'Appreciating our wetlands, our gift from nature'.

The tourist industry relies on the mangroves. Tourists like to visit this special habitat. The mangroves also protect the coastline, which is a major tourist attraction. The farming industry relies on mangroves to help to ensure the balance of nutrients in the water and soil because they act as filters.

Threats to mangrove forests and wetlands

At least half of the world's mangroves have been destroyed, and human development continues to threaten wetlands and mangroves. Some of the threats are:

- land draining and reclaiming of land to build hotels and housing developments
- aquaculture – farming of fish, especially shrimp
- pollution and chemical run-offs – these are chemicals such as herbicides and pesticides used in farming
- changes in the tides or river flow caused by human development such as dams
- rise of sea levels as a result of climate change.

☐ Wetland

The wetlands of Jamaica.

Exercise

1. Why are there very few wetlands in the middle of the island of Jamaica?

2. Along which areas of coastline are there the most wetlands?

3. Identify the parishes that have inland wetlands.

4. List four ways that wetlands benefit humans.

5. Why are wetlands part of our physical heritage?

6. Why are wetlands important to our economy?

Key vocabulary

stable

buffer

mangrove

Our forests

We are learning to:

- examine the features of Jamaica's physical/natural heritage
- value the significance of our physical/natural heritage: forests.

Forests of Jamaica ➤➤

Forests have an extremely high level of biodiversity, with thousands of species of plants and insects, and hundreds of different animals, all living together.

There are two types of forest in Jamaica: Evergreen forests, or deciduous/mixed forest in the northwest and moist lowland forests in the southeast. Rainforests have rain all year round, whereas dry forests have some dry seasons. In 2018, it was found that forests cover 67% of the land in Jamaica.

The slopes of the Blue and John Crow mountains are covered with forests, with enormous trees such as juniper, cedar, blue mahoe and soapwood trees. They support creepers and vines, and tower over the canopy-level trees such as mahogany, balata, palms, poui and immortelle. The trees of the forest keep the air cool and damp throughout the day.

Activity

Look at the map showing the locations of the forests in Jamaica. Trace and copy the map, and add labels to your map to show major cities and towns, and where you live. Use the internet to research the names of the forests and label your drawing.

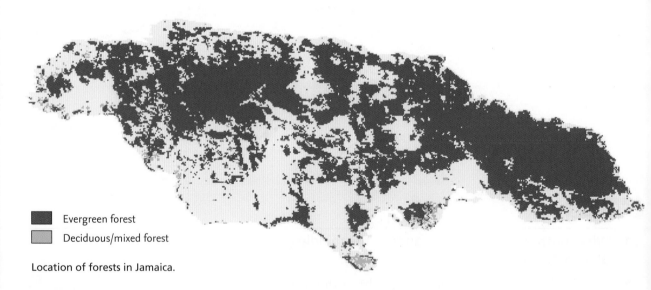

■ Evergreen forest
☐ Deciduous/mixed forest

Location of forests in Jamaica.

Deforestation ➤➤➤

Deforestation is the intentional removal of trees or forests. There are number of reasons why this process occurs, including for land, wood and for mining.

Afforestation refers to the growth of new forest or trees.

The forests in Jamaica perform a number of important functions:

- *Prevent soil erosion* – the trees break the fall of the raindrops on their way to the ground, meaning their force does not break up the earth and soil. The root systems of trees act as filtration systems. Trees take up some pollutants through their roots. Some trees can actually break down pollutants such as solvents and pesticides.
- *Flooding* – the roots soak up water that would otherwise flood the area.
- *Oxygen* – trees give out oxygen, so the proportion of fresh oxygen in the atmosphere is greater in forested areas.
- *Air quality* – trees absorb pollution from the atmosphere, such as nitrogen oxide, carbon monoxide, ozone and other chemicals. They also reduce air temperature. Some pollutants, such as ozone, only form at high temperatures, so the lower air temperatures reduce the formation of these pollutants.
- *Habitat* – many animals use trees for nesting, roosting and breeding. Trees next to watersheds provide protection for some water species. Tree debris such as leaf matter and chunks of broken wood get used by fish and other aquatic animals. Branches, leaves, fruit and flowers form part of the food webs of many ecosystems.
- *Temperature* – trees provide shade along the banks of rivers and dams, and release water in the form of water vapour through transpiration. This has a cooling effect on the temperature.

Activity

Research plants and animals of the Jamaican forests. Collect pictures – these may be drawings, photographs, tracings or photocopies. Create a poster entitled 'Plants and animals of the Jamaican forests' to put up in your classroom.

Exercise

1 What two types of forest are found in Jamaica?

2 Which of the following describes the climate of a tropical rainforest:

   a) rainy and cool
   b) warm and wet
   c) warm and dry.

3 What functions do the rainforests in Jamaica perform? What do you think would happen if there were no rainforests?

4 Write a letter to a newspaper about the importance of preserving the rainforests.

Discussion

In groups, discuss what Jamaica would be like if there were no forests.

Key vocabulary

afforestation

Coastal areas and waterfalls

We are learning to:

- examine the features of Jamaica's physical/natural heritage
- value the significance of our physical/natural heritage: coral reefs, coastal areas, beaches, waterfalls.

Coral reefs

Coral reefs are the sea's most diverse ecosystems. They support so much plant and animal life that they are known as the rainforests of the sea.

Coral reefs are highly valuable to life on Earth. They perform many important functions including providing food and tourism, protecting shorelines, and producing some medicines.

Coral reefs are endangered by global warming and pollution.

Coastal areas and beaches

In Jamaica, some of our greatest natural resources are our beaches. Beaches, such as Seven Mile Beach, Doctors Cave Beach, Cornwall Beach and Rose Hall Beach, are some of the main attractions to tourists. Our beaches, seas, rivers and coral reefs are all resources that need to be protected.

Fishing beds

Like many islands and coastal cities around the world, Jamaica has a long history of fishing. The waters around Jamaica are home to tuna, snapper, flying fish, kingfish, carite, croakers, bechine and shrimp.

However, fish populations all over the world are under threat because of trawling, overfishing and pollution.

Waterfalls

The physical environment of Jamaica includes other fascinating features such as waterfalls. **Waterfalls** are places where river flows over a steep edge of a cliff or mountain. The sound and spectacle of falling water is a natural wonder for people all over the world. There are many waterfalls in Jamaica, including the Dunn's River Falls, which is an impressive 55 metres tall and Reggae Falls, which is 21 metres.

Fish feeding at a coral reef.

Did you know...?

One quarter of all species of sea animals depend on coral reefs for shelter and food, yet coral reefs cover less than 1% of the Earth's surface.

Project

Research some of the different types of coral found around Jamaica. You may use books or the internet. Print or draw pictures of at least five different types of coral.

Case study

Reach Falls is situated in the Montane Forest on the John Crow Mountain Range. Reach Falls was first discovered by runaway enslaved people from plantations from the neighbouring parish of St Thomas.

Reach Falls has a waterfall which runs down a rock face into an emerald river pool. It is a spectacular tourist destination which has a picnic area, an underwater cave and has a guided tour.

The YS Falls is another favourite tourist destination. It is situated in the parish of St Elizabeth near Negril. The YS Falls are on a working ranch farm – people are transported up to the Falls by tractor. YS was originally a cane farm, with a factory and it also supplied logwood for export to Europe.

It has a total of seven waterfalls, which fall into natural pools, and is surrounded by gardens and high trees. There are designated swimming areas and people can also have a go on a zip wire which runs across the Falls.

Both the Reach Falls and YS Falls are said to be the best waterfalls to visit in Jamaica.

One of the highest waterfalls in the Caribbean are Dunn's River Falls, which over a distance of 180 metres, falls 55 metres. The waterfalls are like huge, natural stairs, and have people climb them from the bottom to the top, sometimes with guides, sometimes not. A path runs alongside the waterfall for people not wanting to go in the actual waterfall.

Questions

1. Why do you think these waterfalls are popular with tourists?

2. Of the activities mentioned at the waterfalls, which one would you choose to do? Why?

The Reach Falls in Jamaica.

The Upper waterfall at YS Falls, Jamaica.

Exercise

1. In your own words, describe why it is important to protect coral reefs.

2. What threatens the coral reefs?

3. What threats are there to the fishing beds in Jamaica?

4. Research a beach near you. Find out:

   a) the size of the beach and who mainly uses it

   b) facilities available to visitors

   c) whether any environmental problems are facing the beach.

   Prepare a written report about this beach. Draw a map of your island and locate the beach on it.

Discussion

Are our beaches part of our heritage? If so, how should we protect them?

Key vocabulary

coral reef

waterfall

269

Threats to our natural heritage/ ecosystems

We are learning to:

- gather, analyse and synthesise information from multiple sources on consequences of unsustainable use of natural resources on the economy and human health.

Endangered habitats

Human activities easily damage and destroy natural habitats. An **endangered** natural habitat is one that is in danger of becoming destroyed or extinct, by human activities or other changes. When a particular type of habitat is destroyed, the plants and animals that live there lose their natural homes. These plants and animals may also become endangered or extinct. This is a great threat to the biodiversity of the planet.

Some threats to natural habitats include:

- land clearing and cattle grazing
- logging and deforestation
- global warming and climate change
- drilling for oil and gas
- overfishing.

The environment can be harmed by pollution.

The forest of Cockpit Country.

Case study

Jamaica's Cockpit Country has been under threat from bauxite mining for many years. Cockpit Country is the largest natural forest left in Jamaica. It stores and releases fresh water by almost 40 rivers and supplies about 40% of Western Jamaica's water needs. There are many animals and plants that are only found in these forests in Jamaica.

However, a large portion of the forest has been identified as an area for bauxite mining. The bauxite would be mined and then exported. The mining though would cause huge environmental issues, such as water run-off, erosion, sedimentation of the natural drainage system and the potential of flooding. The sinkholes and caves, that are a famous part of Cockpit Country, could also be threatened. In addition, dust caused by the mining and moving of the bauxite could get into the freshwater system.

In 2017, the Jamaican Prime Minister the Rt. Hon. Andrew Holness announced the designated Cockpit Country Protected Area (CCPA) boundary in Parliament. This is an area closed to mining. However, it is still feared that mining would take place outside of the CCPA and until the whole area is designated as protected, there is concern about its future.

Questions

1. What threat does the bauxite mining pose to Cockpit Country?
2. In your own words, write an essay of about 200 words, putting forward your case why Cockpit Country should be designated a protected area.

Human activities cause many changes to the environment. We clear land in order to develop cities, roads, factories and other built environments.

What happens to animals and plants that used to live in a particular habitat when we clear it? Some species can migrate to other areas. Many others simply can no longer survive. When a whole species ceases to exist, we say it has become extinct.

A species is endangered if it is in danger of becoming extinct in the near future. Endangered species meet one of these criteria:

- Their habitat is about to be changed or destroyed.
- The species has been overused – for example, overfished or overhunted.
- Diseases or predators are causing the population to drop faster than the species can breed to replace it.
- Natural or human-induced factors are affecting the species.
- The population is declining and scientists do not have enough information to know how many individuals are left.

Jamaica has 28 species on the endangered list, including five mammals, eight reptiles and seven birds. For example, the Giant Swallowtail Butterfly, the Hawksbill Turtle and the Jamaican Iguana.

Research

In a scrapbook, collect as many pictures of the different ecological sites in Jamaica as you can. Use magazines, the internet, newspapers or brochures. Write down its name, anything interesting about it, where it can be found and any special facts about it.

The Jamaican Iguana.

Research

Research the 'Pear Tree Bottom' case and look into the issues involved and the arguments on both sides. Write a short report.

Exercise

1. Name five threats to natural habitats.

2. Give three reasons why some species are in danger of becoming extinct.

3. Why do you think some habitats and species have become endangered?

4. Suggest three ways we can prevent more species from becoming endangered.

5. List five human activities that endanger habitats and species.

Key vocabulary

endangered

Preservation and conservation of the environment

We are learning to:

- differentiate between preservation and conservation of the environment
- justify the need for the sustainable use of physical resources to protect the environment.

We often refer to **preservation**, **conservation** and **sustainability** when we talk about the environment. The natural environment needs to be protected so that future generations can enjoy its benefits as much as we do today.

Coral reefs are in need of preservation.

Preservation

Preservation of the environment means protecting areas at risk with strict laws and regulations that prevent them from being damaged. Countries might do this by declaring areas, national parks or nature reserves where any activity that will damage the environment is prohibited. Areas in Jamaica that are heavily protected by legislation include the Montego Bay Marine Park and Ocho Rios Marine Park.

Conservation

Conservation is concerned with managing the use of natural resources. Conservation regulations state that people can use these natural resources as long as some of them are left for future generations.

A good example of this would be fossil fuels such as oil and gas. These are a non-renewable resource, which means that once they are used up they cannot be replaced. In Jamaica there are several conservation strategies designed around the use of the tropical forests.

Did you know...?

Environmental stewardship refers to responsible use and protection of the natural environment through conservation and sustainable practices.

Sustainability

Sustainability is concerned with the use of natural resources in such a way that their quantities are maintained. If sustainability is practised, the resource will be available for future generations.

It is often possible to replace renewable resources, such as trees, as they are used. For example, if a forest is deforested, more trees can be planted in its place.

Activity

In groups, discuss the difference between preservation, conservation and sustainability. Give examples of each one and share your ideas with the other groups.

Using and protecting our natural resources

Our planet has many resources that humans have enjoyed for thousands of years. There are amazing landscapes that should be protected, wildlife and plant species that need to be protected and natural resources that must be maintained.

You are going to choose an area in Jamaica and examine the positive and negative effects of the way the land is used. You will decide whether the land is being used well, and give recommendations on what else could be done. Then you will share your ideas in a presentation to the class.

Planting new trees help combat the effects of deforestation.

Follow these steps:

1. Choose a place in Jamaica that is rich in natural resources.
2. Decide whether the resources are renewable (they can be replaced) or non-renewable (they can never be replaced).
3. Do some research to find out how the land is being used. For example:
   - Are the resources being used? If so, what for?
   - Are the resources being preserved by the government? If so, how? What laws exist to protect the area?
   - Are there any conversation strategies in the area? If so, what are they?
   - If the resources in the area are renewable, are they being used with sustainability in mind?
4. Conduct field observations, interviews and surveys to help with your project.
5. Decide whether or not you think the use of the land you have chosen is acceptable. Why?
6. Create a PowerPoint presentation to share information on your chosen place.

Your presentation must include the following:
- location of study
- the way in which the land is used
- positive and negative effects of land use
- evidence of primary and secondary sources of information – for example, library and internet sources, articles from newspapers, magazines, journals
- proper citation of sources.

Key vocabulary

conservation/conserve

preservation/preserve

sustainable/sustainability

The role of the Jamaican government in managing the environment

We are learning to:

- analyse the functions and the level of success of the institutions and government agencies that are responsible for managing environmental issues.

The Jamaican government plays an important role in managing the environment and ensuring that others do the same. In fact, there is a whole agency which focusses on ensuring there are laws and policies in place to ensure that the environment is protected.

The National Environment and Planning Agency

The **National Environment and Planning Agency (NEPA)** was established in April 2001. Its mission is to: "to promote sustainable development by ensuring protection of the environment and orderly development in Jamaica through highly motivated staff performing at the highest standard".

The main role of NEPA is to ensure the conservation and protection of natural resources in Jamaica.

- *Environmental management* – making sure that the environment is managed and protected
- *Planning* – to make sure that plans for building carefully consider the protection of natural environment
- *Compliance and enforcement* – making sure that individuals and businesses are punished if they do not follow environmental protection guidelines
- *Public education* – making sure that the public is aware of the need to protect the environment, and explain how it is being done
- *Policy and research* – to produce new laws and policies, to carry out research into the effectiveness of these policies.

National Environment and Planning Agency

The Forestry Department

Jamaica's Forestry Department is a government agency which leads in the protection and preservation of the island's forest resources, including those on public land. They oversee about 40% of Jamaica that is covered with forest. The Forestry

Department has existed in one form or another since 1937 when the Forest Act created a Forest Branch within the (then) Lands Department. Their role includes:

- supporting the management and conservation of the forests
- implementing the National Forest Management and Conservation Plan
- ensuring reforestation of suitable lands
- running education programmes to improve understanding of how forests contribute to national well-being and development.

Water Resources Authority

The Water Resources Authority (WRA) was formed by the Water Resources Act 1995. Its role is to regulate, allocate, conserve and manage the water resources of Jamaica. Their role includes:

- collecting data about the water resources of Jamaica
- managing Jamaica's Water Resources Master Plan
- managing Water Quality Control Plans
- advising departments or agencies of Government, in respect of any projects related to water resources.

There are a number of laws that have been passed by the Jamaican government to help address environmental issues:

- Natural Resources Conservation Authority Act, 1991
- Clean Air Act, 1964
- Wild Life Protection Act, 1945, amended 1991
- Endangered Species Act, 2000
- Beach Control Act, 2020
- Cockpit Country Protected Area (CCPA), 2017.

Exercise

1. Identify three areas that are protected in Jamaica.

2. What does it mean when an area is protected?

3. What are the potential dangers to protected areas?

4. Carry out research into a protected area and explain the reasons it is protected, naming the endangered flora and fauna that live there.

5. Explain the roles of the The Forestry Department and the Water Resources Authority in managing environmental issues in Jamaica.

Activity

Find out why the Cockpit Country has become a Protected Area. What is meant by a ground truthing map? Draw a map of the Cockpit Country and write a list of the flora and fauna there.

The Cockpit Country became a protected area in 2017.

Research

Research two of the Governments Act's opposite and write a short report of the aims of those Acts with regard to the environment.

Key vocabulary

National Environment and Planning Agency (NEPA)

The value of conservation and preservation

We are learning to:

- examine multiple sources and formulate questions about biodiversity, conservation and preservation.

Conservation refers to the process of reducing the use of natural resources, towards using natural resources more efficiently; especially, non-renewable resources. Preservation, on the other hand, means to protect or save natural resources now for the purpose of using them in the future.

During the environmental movement of the early 21st century, two opposing groups have emerged: conservationists and preservationists. Conservationists attempt to regulate human use of natural resources while preservationists seek to eliminate human impact altogether.

Conservation and preservation are both important for the following reasons:

- to ensure that finite natural resources are protected for Jamaica and beyond
- to ensure that the habitat of flora and fauna are not destroyed
- to make sure that our environment continues to be enjoyed
- to avoid waste, or to reduce it
- to ensure that we can enjoy clean air, land and water.

We have seen that unsustainable activities will make our heritage unavailable to future generations. But we have also seen that the economy of a country can develop, by using sustainable activities. This is sustainable economic growth.

What are the benefits of preservation and conservation?

The tourism industry in Jamaica is important as a way to preserve and conserve our physical resources (forests, beaches, savannah, sea, and so on). Tourists like to visit places that have interesting local culture and unspoilt natural environments.

Research

Look up the terms co-exist, preservation and conservation in a dictionary or on the internet to broaden your understanding of these terms. Then write a short paragraph to explain what each means.

Discussion

Imagine your class is in charge of deciding how to reduce the impact of climate change on Jamaica.

What will you do and why?

In turn, visitors to Jamaica help to create jobs (employment).

This helps to:

- improve standards of living
- increase economic activity in the community
- create more jobs, and retain them for the future
- reduce the poverty rate
- improve the people's economic wellbeing.

The Blue Mountains are a conservation site.

Case study

Save Jamaica's Sea Turtles

The Jamaica Environment Trust (JET) has worked with communities in Portland, St Elizabeth and Westmoreland to monitor sea turtle nesting. Community members and other organisations have been trained in sea turtle biology and monitoring, and received equipment such as headlamps, handheld GPS units, and disposable cameras. The data gathered by the communities is given to the National Environment and Planning Agency (NEPA). This ensures that numbers are being monitored to ensure that the sea turtle population are protected.

A hawksbill turtle.

Case study

Save the Jamaican iguana

The Jamaica Environment Trust (JET) and its partner the International Iguana Foundation (IIF) are raising awareness about and helping and protecting the Jamaican iguana.

The Jamaican iguana (*Cyclura collei*) is endemic to Jamaica and can be found only in specific regions of Jamaica, the Hellshire Hills of St Catherine. This lizard's diet consists mostly of plants. It can grow very large, with a body size of up to 150 cm, making it the island's largest native land animal. The Jamaican iguana is listed as critically endangered. In the 1940s, the iguana's population declined dramatically and the species was believed to be extinct for several decades. Then, in the 1990s, a small population was found in the Hellshire Hills. Since its rediscovery, conservation efforts have successfully increased the population of the Jamaican iguana to over 300 lizards.

Exercise

1. In your own words, explain what is meant by preservation and conservation.

2. Explain why there might be disagreement between a preservationist and a conservationist.

3. Visit a local nature conservation centre and explain the work that is being done to conserve natural resources, flora and fauna.

Questions

See how well you have understood the topics in this unit.

1. Match the key vocabulary word with its definition.

   i) human-made (built) heritage
   ii) human-made
   iii) built environment
   iv) heritage
   v) heritage site

   a) a place that has special historic, cultural or social value, usually protected by law in order to preserve it
   b) something that has been built or made by people
   c) features that belong to the culture of a society that were created in the past and have an historical importance to that society
   d) buildings created by people which form an important part of our cultural history
   e) surroundings formed by structures made by people

2. What is the name of the only UNESCO World Heritage Site in Jamaica?

3. Name three species that are endangered in Jamaica.

4. What is the difference between flora and fauna?

5. What type of vegetation would you expect to see in these environments?

   a) Savannah
   b) Rainforests
   c) Swamp
   d) Beach

6. True or false? Reptiles are warm-blooded and have dry, hairy skin.

7. Give three functions of the wetlands.

8. Why are mangroves important to Jamaica?

9. Explain in 100 words the important functions that the rainforests in Jamaica perform.

10. Why are fishing beds being threatened in Jamaica?

11. Explain in no more than 50 words why, as a nation, we need to conserve our resources.

12. Indicate if these species are flora or fauna.

ackee
anteater
armadillo
breadfruit
caimite
chaconia
grass mouse
monkey apple
ocelot
possum
sapodilla

13. On the map, label the names of wetlands and swamps in Jamaica.

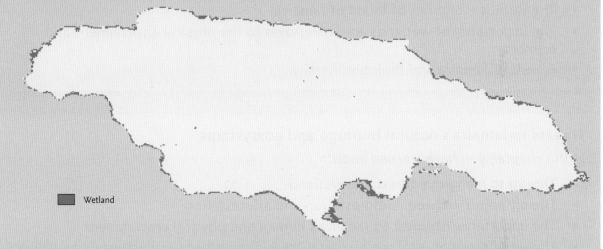

Wetland

14. Explain two reasons why the environment in the Caribbean needs preservation and conservation.

15. Describe a conservation project in Jamaica, giving examples of the work that it does in conserving natural resources.

16. Explain the role of the Jamaican government in managing the environment, giving examples of the agencies involved and their role.

Grade 8 Unit 9 Summary

Jamaica's physical and natural heritage

In this chapter, you have learned about:

- What an ecosystem is and its biotic and abiotic components
- How sensitive ecosystems are and the effect of changes on them
- Ways to improve an ecosystem
- The features of Jamaica's physical heritage
- Jamaica's ecological heritage and some protected ecological sites
- What sustainable activities include
- The meaning of ecotourism and ecotourism projects in Jamaica
- The diverse flora of Jamaica
- The various categories of fauna of Jamaica
- The importance of wetlands and mangroves to the physical environment and economy
- Forests of Jamaica and their biodiversity.

Threats to Jamaica's natural heritage and ecosystems

In this chapter, you have learned about:

- Threats to mangrove forest and wetlands
- The difference between deforestation and afforestation
- The importance of forest to Jamaica's human and physical environment
- The significance of coral reefs, coastal areas, fishing beds and waterfalls to Jamaica
- The factors and elements that endanger Jamaica's habitats and species.

Preservation and conservation

In this chapter, you have learned about:

- What the benefits of preservation and conservation are
- Preservation, conservation and sustainable use of the natural environment
- The role of government agencies in managing and monitoring the environment
- The importance of the preservation and conservation efforts on Jamaica and the wider global community.

Checking your progress

To make good progress in understanding different aspects of environmental problems and solutions, check to make sure you understand these ideas.

Define *biodiversity* and *habitat*.

Examine natural heritage sites in Jamaica.

Explain the significance of natural heritage.

Define *conservation* and *preservation*.

Explain what is meant by deforestation and afforestation.

Explain why sustainable tourism is important for the economy of Jamaica.

Name species of flora that are endemic to Jamaica.

Name species of animals and plants that are endangered in Jamaica.

Explain the role of the Jamaican government in protecting natural heritage sites.

Name features of Jamaica's physical heritage.

Name World Heritage Sites in the Caribbean.

Explain why we need to conserve our resources.

End-of-term questions

Questions 1–6 〉〉

See how well you have understood the ideas in Unit 7.

1. What is the difference between the weather and climate?

2. Match the following terms with the correct definitions below:
   a) temperature
   b) precipitation
   c) humidity
   d) air pressure

   i) usually refers to rainfall
   ii) the measure of heat energy in the atmosphere around the Earth
   iii) the weight of the Earth's atmosphere on its surface
   iv) the measure of how much water vapour is in the air at a given time

3. Briefly describe an isohyet map

4. Describe the climate in Jamaica.

5. Explain the effects of oil spills.

6. Explain what the Greenhouse effect is.

Questions 7–11 〉〉

See how well you have understood the ideas in Unit 8.

7. Explain the difference between human-induced and natural disasters.

8. Provide two examples of natural disasters that may occur in Jamaica.

9. Give two examples of strategies that reduce the amount of damage caused during an earthquake.

10. Explain the positive effects of volcanoes

11. What is the role of a seismologist?

Questions 12–16 ⟫

See how well you have understood the ideas in Unit 9.

12. Explain the difference between a habitat and an ecosystem.

13. Why is it important to ensure development is sustainable? Write a short paragraph to explain.

14. Write a short essay of six paragraphs in which you explain how the environment is protected in Jamaica.

15. Explain why you think some species are becoming endangered in Jamaica. Give at least three examples in your answer.

16. Create a spidergram showing endemic flora and fauna of Jamaica.

Glossary

abiotic of non-living substances or environmental factors.

acetate a type of clear plastic.

active (volcano) could erupt at any time.

advertising the promotion of goods or services for sale through impersonal media, such as radio or television.

afforestation the process of planting large numbers of trees on land which has few or no trees on it.

aftershock a smaller earthquake that follows the main one.

agricultural drought when the two types of drought above impact on agricultural or farming activities, for example, reduced soil moisture or reservoir levels required for irrigation.

algae a type of plant with no stems or leaves that grows in water or on damp surfaces.

amenities things such as shopping centres or sports facilities that are provided for people's convenience, enjoyment, or comfort.

ancestor the people from whom you are descended.

animal hide animal skin.

anonymous without giving one's name, keeping one's identity secret.

arable farming the growing of crops.

bay an area where the coast curves inland.

beach an area of sand or stones that have been deposited along the coastline.

biodiversity (biological diversity) the great variety of life forms on Earth.

biotic of or relating to living organisms.

bird's-eye view a view from directly above the ground.

bitcoin a digital currency used as a means of payment on the internet.

budget the amount of money that is available to spend.

buffer a barrier to prevent damage.

cape/headland a narrow piece of land that extends into the sea.

capital city the urban area where the government is based.

carbon dioxide a gas produced by breathing out, and by chemical reactions.

carbon emission see **carbon footprint**

carbon footprint a measure of the amount of carbon dioxide released into the atmosphere by a single endeavour or by a company, household, or individual through day-to-day activities over a given period.

cardinal points the four main points of the compass, north, south, east, and west.

Caribbean identity the idea of what it means to belong to the Caribbean region.

cartographer a person whose job is drawing maps.

cartography the study of maps and drawing maps.

cementation crystals help to glue all the sediment together forming a rock.

census a way of collecting information about the population of a country by asking questions about each household.

certify to endorse or guarantee.

chatroom a place on the internet where people swap messages.

choropleth map a map that shows the population density of a country or area.

citizen someone who is a member of a country and who has certain rights in that country, but also has duties towards that country.

citizenship someone who is a member of a country and who has certain rights in that country, but also has duties towards that country.

city a large town, with a large population.

climate the average weather conditions over a period of time.

climate change the change of the Earth's temperature and weather patterns as a result of increased carbon dioxide in the air.

climate graphs give us information about the temperature and rainfall in one place over a particular period of time.

coast/coastline an area of land beside the sea.

cold-blooded (of an animal) having its temperature rise and fall depending on the temperature of its environment; unable to produce its own body heat.

committed supporting; in favour of.

communicable diseases a disease that is passed from one person to another, for example hepatitis, influenza and HIV/AIDS.

communication the transfer of information between a sender and receiver.

communication technology the transfer of information between a sender and receiver using technology.

communications transport facilities, such as roads, railways, ports and airports.

compaction the weight of sediment squeezes down on the previous layer and squeezes out the water.

compass instrument used for identifying direction.

competition when two or more people try to achieve the same thing.

composite volcano a cone-shaped volcano made up of alternating bands of lava and ash.

compost system a system for turning food and garden waste into compost.

condense the process where water vapour cools and turns back to a liquid.

conservation/conserve protecting, restoring and preserving something.

consumer a person who uses goods and services.

consumer society when consumers buy more new goods than they really need, due to having more disposable income.

consumerism the excessive buying of goods and services.

contribution something someone can do to make a product or make it successful.

convention the usual way of doing something.

coral bleaching occurs when coral polyps expel algae that live inside their tissues; caused by rising sea temperatures.

coral reef a long, mass of coral which lies just below the surface of the sea.

creolised when a language has developed from other languages to become the main language of a particular place.

cultural relating to a particular society and its ideas, customs, and art.

cultural background the beliefs and traditions that a group of people share.

cultural heritage the cultural traditions that we have inherited from past generations.

cultural icon a symbol, logo, picture, name, face, person, building, or other image of great cultural significance.

cultural identity the identity of belonging to a particular group of people who all share the same characteristics of that society, for example their ethnicity, history, geography and customs.

culture the customs, arts, shared language, history and ideas of a group.

cyber abuse abuse via computer applications, usually over the internet.

cyberbullying bullying that takes place through internet chat rooms or social media.

cybercrime crime committed by means of computers or the internet.

cyclone a violent tropical storm or wind where the air moves very fast in a circular pattern.

dam-building process of building dams.

dance a particular series of graceful movements of your body and feet, which you usually do in time to music.

decision making the process of reaching decisions, especially in a large organisation or in government.

deforestation the removal of trees and vegetation to create open spaces for human activities.

demand the amount of goods and services consumers are willing to purchase at a particular price and point in time.

dense something that is dense contains a lot of things or people in a small area.

deposited laid down.

depression an area of low pressure with cloudy, wet and windy weather.

desertification the process by which a piece of land becomes dry, empty, and unsuitable for growing trees or crops on.

disaster a very bad accident such as an earthquake or a plane crash, especially one in which a lot of people are killed.

dormant (volcano) has not erupted in 10,000 years but could do again.

dot map a map that shows population distribution and population density.

drought an extreme water shortage caused by low rainfall or no rainfall for a long period.

earthquake a sudden shaking of the Earth's crust.

eastings horizontal lines, drawn from east to west on a map.

ebook electronic book.

eco-friendly not damaging to the environment; sustainable.

ecological diversity the variety of different habitats, ecosystems and life forms on Earth.

ecological heritage/natural heritage all elements of biodiversity, including plants and animals and their natural features.

ecological site a place where the natural heritage is preserved.

ecology is the study of the relationships between plants, animals, people and their environment.

economic institutions institutions that relate to how goods and money is distributed in society.

economy the system of how industry, trade and finance is organised in a country, region or worldwide to manage wealth.

ecosystem a system formed by an environment and the living and non-living things within it.

ecotourism tourism that does not damage or destroy the natural environment or local culture.

email electronic message sent from one computer to another computer.

endangered in danger of extinction.

endemic native to a particular country or region.

entomologist someone who studies insects [entomology is the study of insects).

epicentre the point directly above the focus on the Earth's surface.

erosion the process of wearing away the land.

ethnicity features that belong to the culture of a society that were created in the past and have an historical importance to that society.

evaporation the process where water surfaces are heated (usually by the sun) and the water turns to water vapour.

expenditure the amount of money spent on something.

extinct (or extinction) the process where an animal or plant species disappears forever.

extreme weather events weather events which cause damage or destruction, for example cyclones, floods, hurricanes and tornadoes.

extrusive rock forms above the surface.

eye (hurricane) the centre of a hurricane.

fact an event or thing known to have happened or existed; a truth verifiable from experience or observation.

fauna animals and wildlife that are found in a country or region.

feedback information in response to an inquiry, experiment, etc.

femininity the qualities that are considered to be typical of women.

fertile soils that are rich in nutrients.

financial stability the prudent use of financial resources to meet future goals over an extended period without becoming indebted.

flash flood a sudden rush of water over dry land, usually caused by a lot of rain.

flood a large amount of water covers an area which is usually dry, for example when a river flows over its banks or a pipe bursts.

flood plain a flat area on the edge of a river, where the ground consists of soil, sand, and rock left by the river when it floods.

flooding festivals that promote cultural activities like dance and story-telling.

floor plan a view of a building's layout from directly above.

flora plants that grow in a particular region.

focus the point, underground, at which an earthquake happens.

formal savings where savings are out into commercial banks and other commercial organisations.

Four Ps of Marketing product, price, place and promotion.

frostbite when skin is exposed to very cold temperatures and freezes.

genetic diversity the variety within a particular species.

geothermal energy energy stored in the form of heat beneath the Earth's surface.

GIS (Global Information Systems) a system of information which combines cartography and geography.

global worldwide or relating to the whole world.

global village the way people all over the world have become connected through technology.

global warming an increase in global temperatures.

globalisation a process of making the world more connected, with goods and services being traded globally and people moving around freely.

governance the way in which an organisation, or a country, is run.

GPS (Global Positioning System) a navigation system that provides data about time and location.

greenhouse effect the problem caused by increased quantities of gases such as carbon dioxide in the air. These gases trap the heat from the sun, and cause a gradual rise in the temperature of the Earth's atmosphere.

greenhouse gas a naturally forming gas in the atmosphere.

grid lines vertical and horizontal lines over a map.

grid reference a pair of letters and numbers that show the position of a place on a grid.

hamlet a very small village with a few houses.

hazard something which could be dangerous to you, your health or safety, or your plans or reputation.

heritage features that belong to the culture of a society that were created in the past and have an historical importance to that society.

high viscosity thick, gloopy and slow flowing lava.

human environment the area where humans live and work.

human-induced disasters disasters caused by human activity.

humid moist; damp.

hurricane an extremely violent wind or storm.

hurricane shelter a purpose-built shelter to protect people from hurricanes.

hydrological drought occurs when reduced precipitation impacts on water supply, for example, where there is decreased streamflow, soil moisture, reservoir and lake levels, and groundwater.

ideal thought of as perfect or as a perfect model; exactly as one would wish; of a perfect kind.

identity the way you think about yourself, the way the world sees you and the characteristics that define you.

igneous rocks rocks formed from the cooling of hardening of magma.

immigrant a person who has come to live in a country from some other country.

income the amount of money a person (or business) earns.

indigenous native to, or originate in, a particular region or country.

indigenous fauna indigenous animals.

indigenous flora indigenous flowers or plants.

informal savings where savings are put into non-commercial organisations.

information overload the experience of receiving too much information and being unable to process all of it.

insect a small animal that has six legs, a three-part body and often has wings.

instant messaging (IM) a typed message sent and received via the internet through messaging software.

intensity the state or quality of being intense.

internet café where people can go and pay to access the internet.

intimidate to make another person feel powerless and afraid.

intrusive rock forms inside the Earth.

isohyet maps maps that are used to show rainfall figures.

karst denoting the characteristic scenery of a limestone region, including underground streams, gorges, etc.

karstic hazards problems that exist due to karst landscapes, for example seasonal drought and flooding.

Kyoto Protocol an amendment to the United Nations international treaty on global warming in which participating nations commit to reducing their emissions of carbon dioxide, negotiated in Kyoto, Japan, in 1997.

lahar mixture of water and volcanic ash and debris that flows down a volcano.

land degradation the reduction in quality of the land either by extreme weather or by human processes.

landslide the sudden movement of rock, earth or debris down a slope.

legend/key a list of what each symbol represents on a diagram or chart.

limestone is a whitish-coloured rock which is used for building and for making cement.

linear scale a scale expressed showing a line distance and what that distance represents in real life.

linear settlement houses and other buildings built in lines, often along a road or river.

livestock farming the rearing of animals.

lobby to attempt to influence (legislators, etc) in the formulation of policy.

location a site or position.

low viscosity thin, runny and fast flowing lava.

magnetic north the direction in which a compass needle points, which moves slightly over time because of the position of the Earth's axis.

magnitude the size of the earthquake.

malware a type of computer program that is designed to damage or disrupt a computer.

mammal any animal where the female feeds her young on milk from her own body.

manatee a mammal which lives in the sea and looks like a small whale with a broad, flat tail.

mangrove a tree whose roots are above the ground and grow along coasts or on the banks of large rivers.

map a picture that shows an area of the Earth as seen from above, showing either physical or political features.

map scale the relationship between distances on a map and the corresponding distances in real life.

market any structure that allows people to buy and sell goods and services.

marketing the process through which demand for a product is created, such as advertising.

masculinity a way of describing the qualities traditionally associated with being a man.

mass media media that could reach thousands of people at the same time.

media the means of communication that reach large numbers of people, such as television, newspapers, and radio.

media literacy the extent to which people have the skills to use the various forms of media to communicate.

medium a way or means of expressing your ideas or of communicating with people.

Mercalli scale a 12-point scale for expressing the intensity of an earthquake, ranging from 1 (not felt, except by few under favourable circumstances) to 12 (total destruction).

metamorphic rocks rocks that are formed under extreme pressure of heat.

meteorological drought when the amount of precipitation (rainfall) received in a specific area is less than the average amount.

migration the temporary or permanent movement of people from one place to another; reasons can include 'pull factors' such as for work, education and change of location.

mitigation strategy a plan to reduce the loss of life and property by lessening the impact of disasters.

mixed economic system a mixture of businesses and organisations, some of which are owed privately and others are owned and operated by the government.

money the coins and notes that you use to buy things, get paid by your employer or have in your band.

mountains high points of land which are higher than hills (above 600m) and are steeper; mountains are the result of tectonic activity.

mouth the place where a river meets the sea.

mudslide when wet soil or sand moves suddenly downhill.

multicultural consisting of many cultures.

nation an individual country considered together with its social and political structures.

national development the growth and development of a nation.

National Environment and Planning Agency (NEPA) national organisation for promotion of sustainable development.

national identity a sense of who you are and that you are part of a country.

nationalism the desire for political independence of people who feel they are historically or culturally a separate group within a country.

natural disaster a natural event which causes a lot of damage and kills a lot of people.

need something that you need to survive or for your well-being.

needs planning identifies our future needs and the source of future income to pay for these needs when they arise.

non-verbal consists of things such as the expression on your face, your arm movements, or your tone of voice, which show how you feel about something without using words.

northings vertical lines, drawn from north to south on a map.

nucleated settlement houses and other buildings grouped together around a central point, such as a church.

observation careful looking.

ocean acidification decrease in pH in the oceans, caused by the increase of carbon dioxide in the atmosphere.

oil spill when oil escapes from a pipeline or tanker.

online gaming sites a place on the internet which allows people to play online games with each other.

online shopping buying goods over the internet.

opinion judgment or belief not founded on certainty or proof.

Order of National Hero the highest decoration awarded by the government of Jamaica. It may be given only to Jamaican citizens for "services of the most distinguished nature" to the nation.

pace a long step, usually about a metre in distance.

Paris Agreement legally binding international treaty on climate change, signed by 196 parties in Paris, 2015.

patois a form of language spoken in a particular region that has developed from a mixture of other languages.

patriotism showing a deep love for, and devotion to, your country.

physical heritage the part of our physical environment that is inherited from previous generations, such as oceans, mountains, forests and wetlands, and is maintained in the present and will be passed on to future generations.

plains large areas of flat land.

political institutions institutions that help ensure that a country is governed and runs smoothly.

population the total number of people living in a specific geographic area at a particular point in time.

population density the average number of people living in one squared kilometre.

population distribution how the population is spread out.

precautionary need money needed for unexpected events.

Glossary

preservation/preserve maintaining an original state.

primary impacts initial effects, impacts.

primary industry an industry that harvests raw materials OR involved in the extracting and developing of raw materials.

private economic institution privately owned institutions which seek to make a profit.

propaganda information, often inaccurate information, which a political organisation publishes or broadcasts in order to influence people.

protection the act of protecting or the condition of being protected.

public economic institution financial institutions which are run and monitored by the government and are not run to make a profit.

pyroclastic flow a cloud of extremely hot gas and ash that erupts from a volcano destroying everything in its path.

qualities the characteristics that someone or something has.

range the difference between the maximum temperature and the minimum temperature.

rapid on-set flooding floods that take slightly longer than flash floods to develop, and can last for a day or two.

ratio scale a scale expressed as a number ratio or fraction, e.g. 1:100 means 1 cm on the map represents 100 cm or 1 m in real life.

receiver a person who receives something; recipient.

recreational facilities services that offer opportunities for people to enjoy themselves.

regulate to bring into conformity with a rule, principle, or usage.

relief the height and shape of the land.

Richter scale the scale used to show the strength of an earthquake.

river a long stretch of freshwater that flows towards the sea.

road map a map showing the roads of a particular region, usually in a folded form that is easy to carry in a car.

rock any aggregate of minerals that makes up part of the Earth's crust. It may be unconsolidated, such as a sand, clay, or mud, or consolidated, such as granite, limestone, or coal.

rugged having an uneven or jagged surface.

rural areas villages and hamlets with not many services.

sanitation having a clean supply of water and good sewage system.

savings money that has been put aside OR money that has been saved up.

savings the money that one has saved, esp in a bank or a building society.

scale a drawing or object that has been reduced or enlarged from its original size.

scale statement scale expressed in a statement; for example, 1 cm = 1 000 km.

scattered/ dispersed houses and other buildings are spread far apart over a large area.

sea level the average level of the sea with respect to the land. The height of mountains or other areas is calculated in relation to sea level.

seasonal drought Seasonal drought occurs in climates that have well-defined annual rainy and dry seasons.

seasonal flooding Seasonal flooding occurs in climates that have well-defined annual rainy and dry seasons.

secondary impacts longer term effects, impacts.

secondary industry an industry mostly involved in processing and manufacturing OR manufacturing industries which make products from raw materials.

sedentary not active, mostly sitting down.

sedimentary rocks rocks that are formed under seas and oceans.

seismic waves shock waves that are sent out from the focus and travel through the crust.

seismic/seismic activity the movement of tectonic plates and the resultant activity such as earthquakes or volcanic eruptions.

seismographs an instrument used to measure ground movement.

sender a person or thing that sends.

services public utilities and facilities that are provided for settlements where people live.

settlement a place where people settle down and live.

settlement pattern the shape of the settlement.

shield volcano a wide, low-lying volcano found at constructive plate boundaries.

slow on-set flooding occur as a result of water bodies over flooding their banks; tend to develop slowly and can last for days and weeks.

smartphone a mobile phone that can run applications like a small computer; it can send and receive email, browse the internet and take photos.

social institutions institutions that relate to areas of life that govern our relationships with other people.

social media websites and applications that allow people to post and share content in order to connect with others.

social networking site a place on the internet which allows people to interact with each other.

soil the substance on the surface of the Earth in which plants grow.

solidified when a liquid solidifies or is solidified, it changes into a solid.

source the place where a river starts.

sovereign a king, queen, or other royal ruler of a country.

sovereignty the power that a country has to govern itself or another country or state.

spa a place where water with minerals in it comes out of the ground.

species a type of animal or plant.

species diversity varieties of species.

speculative need money held in a different form, for example a house, which can later be converted into money.

stable not likely to change or come to an end suddenly.

standardisation the process of changing things so that they all have the same features.

standard of living the level of comfort and wealth that a person or family may have.

state the structure, form, or constitution of something.

stereotype having a one-sided thought or belief about how another person, or group of people, acts or behaves.

storm surge a rise in sea level that occurs during hurricanes.

survey to view or consider in a comprehensive or general way.

sustainable/sustainability something that can be continued without destroying the resources that make it possible OR able to continue at the same level without destroying the resources it relies on.

tablet an electronic device the size of a book, larger than a phone and smaller than a computer, with applications similar to a laptop or smartphone.

technology devices and systems which have been created for practical purposes.

template an outline or grid.

tertiary industries an industry that provides services OR service industries which sell manufactured goods OR involves providing services and making goods available to customers, like banking for example.

timeline a visual representation of a sequence of events, especially historical events.

to scale uniformly reduced or enlarged; showing the relationships in proportion to real life.

topography the study and description of the physical features of an area, for example its hills, valleys, or rivers, or the representation of these features on maps.

tornado see **typhoon**

town urban area of up to 100,000 people, smaller than a city.

toxin any poisonous substance produced by bacteria, animals, or plants.

trade the activity of buying, selling, or exchanging goods or services between people, firms, or countries.

trafficking the act of conducting trade or business, esp of an illicit kind.

transaction need money to make everyday purchases.

transnational company an organisation that has business interests in more than one country.

transported carried.

tsunami a giant wave that moves very fast across the surface of the sea.

typhoon one of the four names give to tropical storms around the world.

universal suffrage the right of all adults (with minor exceptions) to vote in elections.

unregulated not regulated; uncontrolled.

urban areas towns and cities with many services.

utility a public service, such as the bus system; public utility.

valley a low stretch of land between hills, especially one that has a river flowing through it.

value what we believe is important in life.

vegetation plant life as a whole, especially the plant life of a particular region.

verbal of, relating to, or using words, esp as opposed to ideas, etc.

village a settlement of between a few hundred and a few thousand people OR a small community in a country area.

volcanic eruption when volcanoes explode.

volcano a mountain from which hot melted rock, gas, steam, and ash from inside the Earth sometimes burst.

voluntary performed, undertaken, or brought about by free choice, willingly, or without being asked.

want something that you would like to have, but is not essential.

water a clear thin liquid that has no colour or taste when it is pure. It falls from clouds as rain and enters rivers and seas. All animals and people need water in order to live.

waterfall where water falls over the edge of a steep cliff.

weather conditions of the atmosphere, such as temperature, wind, air pressure and rainfall.

willy-willy see **typhoon**

World Heritage Site a natural or manmade area or structure which is recognised as being of international importance and therefore deserving special protection.

Index

Acknowledgements

The publishers wish to thank the following for permission to reproduce photographs. Every effort has been made to trace copyright holders and to obtain their permission for the use of copyright materials. The publishers will gladly receive any information enabling them to rectify any error or omission at the first opportunity.

p6: Ozphotoguy/SS; p6: Gustavo Frazao/SS; p6: Photo Spirit/SS; p7: Greg Meland/SS; p7: Non-library; p7: orenthomasphotography/SS; p8: Muhammad Aamir Sumsum/SS; p8: pockygallery/SS; p9: Elzloy/SS; p9: Sakchai.K/SS; p10: Felix Kunze/Getty; p11: Kevin Schafer / Alamy Stock Photo; p11: David Carillet /SS; p14: Non-library; p15: Xinhua / Alamy Stock Photo; p16: Photo Spirit /SS; p17: Phonlamai Photo /SS; p17: r.classen /SS; p18: Real Window Collective /SS; p18: Debbie Ann Powell/SS; p18: Debbie Ann Powell /SS; p19: Debbie Ann Powell /SS; p19: Naleen Graphics /SS; p22: Niyazz/SS; p23: Kononova Nina /SS; p28: Andrey_Popov/SS; p28: Per Bengtsson/SS; p28: Allexxandar/SS; p29: Viktollio/SS; p29: michaeljung /SS; p30: GaudiLab/Getty; p31: Sakchai.K/SS; p32: 3Dsculptor/SS; p32: fizkes/SS; p35: Jeffrey Blackler / Alamy Stock Photo; p37: John Frost Newspapers / Alamy Stock Photo; p37: Tomas Griger / Alamy Stock Photo; p38: astudio/SS; p39: Leszek Glasner/SS; p39: Shawshots/Alamy ; p40: Purestock / Alamy Stock Photo; p41: Mario Tama/Getty; p42: Rohane Hamilton/SS; p42: 13_Phunkod /SS; p43: Sasha Ka/SS; p44: Primakov/SS; p46: siridhata/SS; p47: vystekimages /SS; p52: Debbie Ann Powell/SS; p52: Ozphotoguy/SS; p52: Debbie Ann Powell/SS; p53: Debbie Ann Powell/SS; p53: Anthony Pidgeon/Alamy; p54: Andrew Park/SS; p58: Mihai-Bogdan Lazar /SS; p59: Debbie Ann Powell/SS; p60: Petr Toman/SS; p61: Janusz Pie⊠kowski / Alamy Stock Photo; p62: PHATCHARADA DUEANDAO/SS; p63: Michael DeFreitas Caribbean / Alamy Stock Photo; p66: Georgios Kollidas / Alamy Stock Photo; p66: Ron Case / Stringer/Getty; p66: Universal History Archive/Getty; p66: Janusz Pienkowski /SS; p67: Keystone Press / Alamy Stock Photo; p67: Prachaya Roekdeethaweesab /SS; p67: Reuters/Alamy; p67: Prachaya Roekdeethaweesab /SS; p67: Ted Small/Alamy; p68: Pictorial Press Ltd / Alamy Stock Photo; p68: Everett Collection Inc / Alamy Stock Photo; p69: GARY DOAK / Alamy Stock Photo; p69: Sabena Jane Blackbird / Alamy Stock Photo; p70: imageBROKER / Alamy Stock Photo; p71: Bob Olsen/Getty Images; p71: LeonMorris/Getty Images; p72: Aflo Co. Ltd / Alamy Stock Photo; p73: Science History Images / Alamy Stock Photo; p73: Vince Talotta/Getty Images; p74: David Redfern/Getty; p82: LBSimms Photography/SS; p82: Marc Stephan/SS; p82: Words As Photos/SS; p83: Debbie Ann Powell/SS; p83: Paul Wishart/SS; p83: Ievgenii Bakhvalov/SS; p84: Debbie Ann Powell /SS; p84: vvoe/SS; p85: Styve Reineck/SS; p85: Tyler Boyes/SS; p86: eric laudonien/SS; p86: Nicola Pulham/SS; p86: Emily Eriksson/SS; p86: Pawel Kazmierczak/SS; p86: Karl Eichinger/SS; p87: Cyrustr /SS; p88: Poliorketes/SS; p88: Geza Kurka /SS; p88: Jesus Keller /SS; p89: LBSimms Photography /SS; p89: rafapress/SS; p90: Craig F Scott/SS; p97: KishoreJ/SS; p102: NAPA/SS; p102: Matyas Rehak/SS; p104: Sevenstock Studio/SS; p105: Lano Lan/SS; p109: Chris Hellier / Alamy Stock Photo; p111: delaflow/SS; p111: Lost Mountain Studio/SS; p126: PST Vector/SS; p132: Craig F Scott/SS; p132: Debbie Ann Powell/SS; p132: Janusz Pienkowski/SS; p133: Debbie Ann Powell/SS; p133: Ground Picture/SS; p135: Lisa Strachan/SS; p135: Rosemarie Mosteller/SS; p135: Craig F Scott /SS; p138: larry1235/SS; p140: Debbie Ann Powell/SS; p142: Jarretera /SS; p143: Thamyris Salgueiro/SS; p145: AS photostudio/SS; p147: byvalet /SS; p149: Valery Brozhinsky/SS; p149: j-mel / Alamy Stock Photo; p150: WAYHOME studio/SS; p152: istock/ Getty; p153: Sunshine Seeds/SS; p158: ronstik/Alamy; p158: byvalet/SS; p158: byvalet/Alamy; p159: Rawpixel/SS; p159: Ralf Liebhold/SS; p160: Kenneth Man/SS; p161: Lena Ivanova/SS; p165: Daniel M Ernst/SS; p166: Lightspring/SS; p166: New good ideas/SS; p167: Rawpixel.com; p168: Debbie Ann Powell /SS; p169: Consumer Affairs Commission Jamaica; p170: oksana2010 /SS; p172: Rawpixel.com/SS; p173: JAY DIRECTO / Stringer/Getty; p174: ValeStock/SS; p176: fizkes/SS; p184: lavizzara/SS; p184: Marlon Trottmann/Alamy; p184: Debbie Ann Powell/SS; p185: Katrevich Valeriy /SS; p185: Sevenstock Studio/SS; p185: Jason Benz Bennee/SS; p186: Mike Hill / Alamy Stock Photo; p188: kasakphoto/SS; p189: Brian A Jackson/SS; p189: biletskiyevgeniy.com/SS; p193: m.malinika/SS; p196: Broadbelt/SS; p196: ZUMA Press, Inc. / Alamy Stock Photo; p196: Debbie Ann Powell /SS; p199: V_E/SS; p199: Richard Whitcombe/SS; p200: OJPHOTOS / Alamy Stock Photo; p202: Johan Swanepoel /SS; p202: Imagesine /SS; p203: Ozphotoguy/SS; p203: bakhistudio /SS; p204: Debbie Ann Powell /SS; p204: Cleon Green /SS; p210: US Marines Photo/Alamy; p210: vouvraysan/SS; p211: Debbie Ann Powell/SS; p211: SKT Studio/SS; p211: Debbie Ann Powell/SS; p212: NASA Images /SS; p212: Signature Message /SS; p213: JOSE ALMEIDA/Getty; p215: tuksaporn rattanamuk / Alamy Stock Vector; p216: NigelSpiers/SS; p217: Prometheus72/SS; p219: Barry Lewis / Alamy Stock Photo; p222: Sean Pavone/SS; p223: Designua/SS; p224: Moodboard Stock Photography / Alamy Stock Photo; p225: ARCTIC IMAGES / Alamy Stock Photo; p226: Stuart Hunter / Alamy Stock Photo; p227: Johann Helgason/SS; p228: Suranga Weeratuna / Alamy Stock Photo; p229: Jef Wodniack/SS; p229: Johann Helgason/SS; p230: Harvepino/SS; p233: FashionStock.com/SS; p234: Stocktrek Images, Inc. / Alamy Stock Photo; p234: Artsiom P/SS; p235: Dennis Hallinan / Alamy Stock Photo; p235: Everett Collection/SS; p235: Multiverse/SS; p237: Mark Pearson / Alamy Stock Photo; p239: Mechanik/SS; p240: 2M Media /SS; p241: Todd Aaron Sanchez/SS; p242: Piyaset/SS; p244: CDEMA; p244: Gillian Holliday/SS; p245: S_E /SS; p245: Zenobillis /SS; p250: Amaraklei/SS; p250: Debbie Ann Powell/SS; p251: Eric Laudonien/ SS; p251: Marcin Sylwia Ciesielski/SS; p251: Tetra Images/Alamy; p253: silvae/SS; p256: Kkulikov/SS; p257: Wolfi Poelzer / Alamy Stock Photo; p258: Art Directors & TRIP / Alamy Stock Photo; p259: Florapix / Alamy Stock Photo; p260: FourOaks/Getty; p261: ullstein bild/ Getty; p262: Vladislav T. Jirousek/SS; p262: Johann Schumacher / Alamy Stock Photo; p262: blue-sea.cz/SS; p263: John A. Anderson/SS; p264: Jacques Jangoux / Alamy Stock Photo; p268: Mark Conlin / Alamy Stock Photo; p269: mr.innis/SS; p269: Sherry Talbot/SS; p270: Eye Ubiquitous / Alamy Stock Photo; p270: Universal Images Group North America LLC / DeAgostini / Alamy Stock Photo; p271: National Geographic Image Collection / Alamy Stock Photo; p272: Damocean/SS; p273: Meryll/SS; p274: NEPA; p275: Marcin Sylwia Ciesielski/SS; p277: ANNI Orlova/SS; p277: blue-sea.cz/SS